GRE®

Verbal GRAIL

Copyright, Legal Notice and Disclaimer:

Aristotle Prep GRE Verbal Grail

10-digit International Standard Book Number: 9350872889

13-digit International Standard Book Number: 978-9350872888

Publisher: Aristotle Prep

Contents

Introduction to the GRE

The GRE is one of the most widely accepted graduate admissions test across the globe. Earlier it used to be popular only amongst students looking for non-management courses but now the Revised GRE General Test is accepted by several business schools as well, such as Harvard Business School and The Wharton School, for their MBA programs.

The Revised GRE General Test comprises the following three sections:

1) Analytical Writing

2) Quantitative Reasoning

3) Verbal Reasoning

The scope of this book will be limited only to the Verbal Reasoning section of the GRE Revised General test.

To provide students with a comprehensive resource that meets all their GRE verbal needs, we have come up with this book – the GRE Verbal Grail. This book covers every question type tested on the GRE verbal section in detail, providing both strategies and sufficient practice questions to perfect these strategies on.

This book will first take you through the Text Completion section followed by the Sentence Equivalence section. Each of these sections will cover strategies relevant to that section along with a 100-question practice set for each.

This book will then take you through the Reading Comprehension section, covering each question type tested in this section in detail. There is a special sub-section dedicated to Critical Reasoning type questions that are increasingly being tested on the GRE.

Vocabulary has always played an important role in preparing for the GRE and, while the stress on vocabulary has gone down in the GRE revised General Test, you still need to cover around a 1000 words before you can confidently tackle the actual test. The last section of this book contains a 1000 word High frequency word list along with a separate list of frequently confused deceptive words.

We hope that you will find this book useful in your quest to achieve a high GRE score. Please send us your thoughts on this book at feedback@aristotleprep.com.

Good luck!

SECTION 1

Introduction to the GRE Verbal Section

GRE Verbal Reasoning

The GRE Revised General test will comprise exactly two verbal sections (barring any unscored section) of 30 minutes duration each, with 20 questions in each section. The questions will be divided into three question types – Text Completion, Sentence Equivalence, and Reading Comprehension.

The following is the break-up of these question types within each verbal reasoning section:

1) Text Completion – 6 questions in each section

2) Sentence Equivalence - 4 questions in each section

3) Reading Comprehension - 10 questions in each section from approx 5 passages

Essentially, the GRE Verbal Reasoning section will test students on the following two areas - Vocabulary and Comprehension. The Text Completion and Sentence Equivalence questions will primarily test students on their vocabulary skills while the Reading Comprehension questions will test a students' understanding of unfamiliar textual matter.

Before we look at each question type in detail, it is important to point out the importance of vocabulary on the GRE Revised General Test. There seems to be a general belief among students that the Revised GRE lays much less stress on vocabulary compared to the older GRE test. However, if you look at the break-up of the verbal reasoning section, you will notice that 50% of the test still comprises questions that are primarily a test of vocabulary. So a lot of effort will still have to be put in to improve vocabulary, especially by those students who are non-native speakers of English. The only good thing now is that the vocabulary will not be tested out of context, as in the Analogies and Antonyms sections of the older GRE test.

SECTION 2

Text Completion

How to approach any Fill in the Blank Question

Text Completion and Sentence Equivalence questions are both, in essence, fill in the blank questions, wherein the correct word needs to be inserted in the blank(s). Thus, the basic fundamentals for both these question types are the same. The word that should go in the blank (s) cannot be a figment of your imagination; rather it has to make sense with the meaning being conveyed by the rest of the sentence. To understand the meaning of the sentence you always try to look for two kinds of clues:

1) The Keywords

2) The Connectors

Keywords are words that tell you the meaning of the word that should go in the blank.

For example consider this sentence:

Known for their valour, horses are used as symbols of ________ in several cultures

(A) *arrogance*

(B) *courage*

(C) *fidelity*

(D) *speed*

(E) *stamina*

As most of you might have guessed, the correct answer should be (B), courage. But why can't the answer be (C), fidelity? Because the sentence talks about horses being known for their 'valour' i.e. courage, so 'valour' becomes your Keyword in this sentence. Hence, even though horses are also known for fidelity, speed, and stamina, the answer still has to be *courage* because it is connected to the keyword in the sentence.

Remember that the Keyword does not necessarily have to be a word; it can also be a phrase or a clause.

If valour were to be replaced with 'devotion' in the original sentence, then what should be the answer?

Known for their devotion, horses are used as symbols of ________ in several cultures

The answer will then change to 'fidelity' i.e. loyalty, because the Keyword now becomes 'devotion'. This is how Keywords can help you decide which word to go with in the blank, so you must consciously look for the keyword in every sentence that you see.

However, sometimes the Keyword, on its own, may not always be enough to convey the entire meaning of the sentence. For example, consider a variation of the above sentence:

Although horses are known for their devotion, in some cultures they are used as symbols of ________

(A) *arrogance*

(B) *courage*

(C) *fidelity*

(D) *speed*

(E) *treachery*

The Keyword is still 'devotion' but the meaning of the sentence has reversed because of the use of 'Although'. We calls such words *Connectors* because they help you determine the connection between two parts of a sentence – whether they are connected in the same manner or in a contrasting manner.

In the above example the word that goes into the blank has to contrast with the Keyword 'devotion', so the answer should actually be 'treachery'.

Here is a list of some common 'contrasting' and some 'same-direction' Connectors:

Same Direction Connectors

— Because

— Since

— And

— Hence

— As a result of

— Also

— Due to

— Thus

— Likewise

— Moreover

— Consequently

— Additionally

— ; (yes, the semi colon is also a same direction connector)

Contrasting Connectors

— Despite

— Yet

— But

— However

— Nonetheless

— Nevertheless

— Paradoxically

— While

— Although

— Ironically

— Rather

— Contrastingly

Note that every sentence may not necessarily have a Connector. In such sentences the thought, obviously, always goes in the same direction.

EXCEPTION – *Sometimes the Connector itself may have to be put in the blank. If you see some typical Connectors in the list of options, then check whether the sentence is actually implying a contrast or going in the same direction.*

Thus, to summarize, in every 'Fill in the blank' type question you always look for two kinds of clues – the Keyword, which has to be present in every sentence, and the Connector, which may or may not be present in every sentence.

There are two types of Fill in the Bank questions that will be tested on the GRE – Text Completion and Sentence Equivalence.

Text Completion

In a text completion question you will have a sentence given to you with one, two, or three blanks. For each blank, separate tables of options will also be provided. For a one-blank question, the table will always have five options and for a two or three blank question the table will always have three options for each blank. You need to select the correct word for each of the given blanks. Remember that no partial credit will be given; you will be marked correct only if you get all the blanks correct in a sentence.

Use your knowledge of Keywords and Connectors to make a prediction for each of the blanks and go with whichever option best matches your prediction.

You will get 6 Text Completion questions in each verbal section on the GRE (i.e. 12 questions in the entire test)

Tips to keep in mind when attempting Text Completion Questions

- **Have an answer in mind before you look at the options** – It is always a good idea to have an answer in mind before you look at the options. At least you should be able to predict whether the word will be a positive or a negative one or whether there should be some kind of a relation between the words in a multiple blank sentence.

  This strategy will also help you assess whether you are able to understand the meaning of the sentences correctly. If your predictions are correct but your actual answer is wrong, then you need to work on your vocabulary but if your prediction itself is incorrect then, even if you know all the words, you will not get the answer right. In this case you will need to start working on your comprehension skills.

- **Start with whichever blank looks easier** – In a multiple blank sentence, it is not necessary that you always start predicting for the first blank. Actually, in most cases, the second or third blank will be easier to predict an answer for, so start with these instead.

- **Avoid Synonyms** – If you see a pair of synonyms or similar words in a table, these will most likely not be the answer so go with one of the other options instead. For example, if the three options given to you are joy, happiness, and salubrious, then you should go with *salubrious* (even if you don't know its meaning) because joy and happiness almost mean the same whereas there can be only one correct answer for the blank.

Text Completion Practice Set

One-Blank Questions

1. Even though human beings _________ in certain aspects, fundamentally they are similar.

A. coexist
B. differ
C. quarrel
D. agree
E. astound

2. Learning to read men and women is a more ____________ process than learning to read books, for every person you see is a true story, more romantic and absorbing than any story bound in covers.

A. trite
B. unenjoyable
C. delightful
D. beautiful
E. alleviating

3. Our actions follow our thoughts. Every thought, however __________, causes muscular action, which leaves its trace in that part of the physical organism which is most closely allied to it.

A. transitory
B. important
C. pertinent
D. amenable
E. loquacious

4. Our ancestors developed massive jaws as a result of constant combat. As civilization decreased the necessity for combat, nature ____________ the size of the average human jaw.

A. magnified
B. modified
C. reduced
D. ruminated
E. parodied

5. Sceptical as Montaigne shows himself in his books, yet during his sojourn at Rome he ___________ a great regard for religion.

A. ridiculed
B. galvanized
C. obviated
D. jeopardized
E. manifested

6. The scientists did not employ ___________ methods; they only used information and methods that were available freely from scientific literature.

A. old
B. hackneyed
C. novel
D. vitriolic
E. interesting

7. It is ___________ that some people and even some countries will be advantaged by the effects of global warming, even if the overall global impact is vastly detrimental.

A. inevitable
B. unlikely
C. unthinkable
D. viable
E. humane

8. The rich, like most voters, have ___________ views, often supporting liberal and conservative positions simultaneously.

A. ambidextrous
B. positive
C. eclectic
D. narrow
E. finicky

9. Britain has long been ___________ society, and in recent years the gap between the rich and the poor has grown ever wider.

A. an impartial
B. an egalitarian
C. a deficient
D. a perspicacious
E. an unequal

10. The party's instinct, born out of all those years of success, is to tighten its grip, so dissidents are ________ .

A. revered
B. extolled
C. harassed
D. exonerated
E. congealed

11. He has been off the radar for a while but now it seems that the actor is ___________ his comeback story.

A. ignoring
B. vacillating
C. fortifying
D. crafting
E. condoning

12. Even the most omnivorous collectors of friends ___________ that sometimes it is necessary to cross out some names from their little black book.

A. forswear
B. acquiesce
C. repudiate
D. ordain
E. imprecate

13. The President has declared his commitment to arms control, but there is no ___________ of that in the budget plan.

A. reflection
B. speculation
C. animadversion
D. incineration
E. felicity

14. The immigrants have managed to sustain links with the country of their origin against tremendous __________ .

A. assistance
B. odds
C. advantage
D. prestige
E. fidelity

15. The tone of the author's new book is ___________, free of stylistic tricks or evasiveness.

A. circuitous
B. tortuous
C. forthright
D. deceitful
E. foppish

16. The Presidents' description of his ministers was truly ___________, devoid of any emotion or personal prejudice.

A. dispassionate
B. jaded
C. spurious
D. emotional
E. involved

17. ___________ all their talk about ecology, major companies have actually spent very little to fight pollution.

A. Due to
B. For
C. As a result of
D. Lacking
E. Venerating

18. Many critics consider modern remakes of classic movies ___________ and a waste of time and money.

A. disrespectful
B. venal
C. sanguine
D. reprobate
E. verbose

19. One requirement of a good book is that it deepen and extend our knowledge, not that it merely ________ what we already know.

A. enhance
B. confirm
C. modify
D. reduce
E. vilify

20. The judges for the cooking show were true ___________, noting subtle differences between dishes that most people would not detect.

A. dilettantes
B. iconoclasts
C. neophytes
D. gourmands
E. dissidents

21. Some people might believe that measuring sleepiness is a fairly ___________ task but it is of paramount importance to a sleep researcher.

A. easy
B. trivial
C. straightforward
D. arduous
E. noisome

22. The sound produced by the newly formed band was so ___________ that even its least experienced members were abashed.

A. sonorous
B. caustic
C. mellifluous
D. indigent
E. strident

23. To avoid being ___________, the author always makes it a point to put in an element of surprise in his books.

A. ignored
B. criticized
C. predictable
D. improbable
E. unforeseeable

24. The CEO was known for his ___________ behaviour: he became irritated even if a minor issue was not taken care of .

A. volatile
B. euphoria
C. fastidious
D. vexing
E. capricious

25. Because the plants had already been weakened by disease, a harsh summer would have had __________ consequences for them.

A. ameliorating
B. deleterious
C. placating
D. neutralizing
E. inebriating

26. Predictably, meticulous employees are ___________ at keeping track of the myriad particulars of a situation.

A. adept
B. inept
C. indolent
D. maladroit
E. ingenuous

27. ___________ about our human need to wake by day and sleep by night, we come to associate night dwellers with people who are up to no good and who are defying nature.

A. Unsure
B. Ambivalent
C. Chauvinistic
D. Infelicitous
E. Esoteric

28. Even though only parts of clay vessels may be recovered, these pottery shards are ___________ to the archaeologist.

A. incontrovertible
B. pristine
C. worthless
D. invaluable
E. redoubtable

29. Though Jerry eagerly sought out his father's ___________, he eventually did not heed that advice.

A. counsel
B. admonition
C. procrastination
D. fulmination
E. temerity

30. The beauty of the mountain peak is difficult to see because clouds ___________ the summit on most days.

A. magnify
B. obscure
C. mitigate
D. inordinate
E. rarefy

31. The company launched its new product just as demand was reaching its peak; this _______ marketing made the company more successful than its peers.

A. blithe
B. recalcitrant
C. insolent
D. grandiloquent
E. opportune

32. The large number of awards given this year to biochemists ___________ the significant gains that have been made in the field of biochemistry.

A. masks
B. accentuates
C. understates
D. blandishes
E. lampoons

33. The existence of corruption in sports is no longer a point of ___________ ; government, public, and even sportspersons agree that this is a serious problem.

A. ridicule
B. vendetta
C. honour
D. dispute
E. transgression

34. By portraying a wide range of characters in his one-man show, the actor provides a ___________ to the theatre's tendency to offer a limited range of roles to actors.

A. proof
B. quirk
C. corrective
D. kernel
E. stimulation

35. Julie mentioned Tom's habitual boasting about his wealth as an example of his ___________ manner.

A. modest
B. braggart
C. unassuming
D. gregarious
E. compassionate

Two-Blank Sentences

36. Modern science has proved that the ___________ traits of every individual are ___________ stamped in the shape of his body, head, face and hands—an X-ray by which you can read the characteristics of any person on sight.

Blank (i)
A. nugatory
B. fundamental
C. piddling

Blank (ii)
D. superficially
E. indelibly
F. equivocally

37. __________ his essays and lectures, Emerson left behind some poetry in which are __________ those thoughts which were to him too deep for prose expression.

Blank (i)
A. Besides
B. For
C. As a result of

Blank (ii)
D. missing
E. embodied
F. precluded

38. I read the other day some verses written by an eminent painter which were __________ and not __________.

Blank (i)
A. prosaic
B. iconoclastic
C. verbose

Blank (ii)
D. blasphemous
E. conventional
F. stolid

39. There are many things to be said against American newspapers, but much of the __________ is __________ when one considers that every now and then they develop a great writer like Don Marquis.

Blank (i)
A. blandishment
B. somnolence
C. indictment

Blank (ii)
D. quashed
E. underscored
F. kindled

40. Occasionally one hears today the statement that we have come to realize that we know __________ about evolution. This point of view is a healthy reaction to the over-confident belief that we know __________ about evolution.

Blank (i)
A. plentiful
B. nothing
C. heaps

Blank (ii)
D. everything
E. iota
F. temerity

41. Successful government programs have helped ___________ poverty and inequality in the last couple of decades, but compared with rich countries, Latin American countries ___________ fall short.

Blank (i)
A. abate
B. erase
C. invigorate

Blank (ii)
D. no longer
E. understandably
F. still

42. With 'paid news' and other ills making the media ___________ to state and corporate control, social networking sites are acting as a ___________ force for ordinary citizens.

Blank (i)
A. abominable
B. vulnerable
C. corruptible

Blank (ii)
D. deleterious
E. countervailing
F. munificent

43. ___________ of a free internet have mounted a determined bid to ___________ new legislation that can chill free speech.

Blank (i)
A. Advocates
B. Opponents
C. Antagonists

Blank (ii)
D. stall
E. absolve
F. occult

44. In many countries, the hope is that export growth can ___________ for ___________ domestic demand.

Blank (i)
A. compensate
B. renege
C. jostle

Blank (ii)
D. sluggish
E. spirited
F. unstinting

45. __________ proving the impossibility of airborne transmission, the mutant strain has also ______ three other important assumptions about the virus wrong.

Blank (i)
A. Apart from
B. Despite
C. Because of

Blank (ii)
D. abetted
E. proven
F. extrapolated

46. Like many struggling businesses, book publishers are __________ costs and __________ work forces.

Blank (i)
A. aggravating
B. mutilating
C. paring

Blank (ii)
D. aggrandizing
E. trimming
F. hedging

47. Although Thoreau was sometimes __________ about the mechanization that he saw around him, at other times he was very __________, as in his response to the railroad.

Blank (i)
A. ambivalent
B. euphoric
C. xerothermic

Blank (ii)
D. enthusiastic
E. polemical
F. kindred

48. __________ castles were made obsolete by the invention of the cannon in the fourteenth century, many __________ to the present day as fascinating relics of a bygone era.

Blank (i)
A. Since
B. Besides
C. Though

Blank (ii)
D. dilapidate
E. survive
F. flourish

49. Even though the hypothesis that dinosaurs became extinct as part of one single event has gained ________ in recent years, the supporting evidence is still ____________ .

Blank (i)
A. notoriety
B. credence
C. disbelief

Blank (ii)
D. self evident
E. inconclusive
F. incontrovertible

50. The novel's story was ____________ ; you could ____________ the fate of the villain halfway through the book.

Blank (i)
A. engrossing
B. prosaic
C. tedious

Blank (ii)
D. foresee
E. forestall
F. foreswear

51. Although easily ____________ by the students' mischievous behaviour, the teacher could be ___________ by their expression of remorse.

Blank (i)
A. assuaged
B. vexed
C. admonished

Blank (ii)
D. placated
E. exacerbated
F. reneged

52. The themes of the great classical novels are ____________ , so we should not let them become ______

Blank (i)
A. trite
B. jaded
C. enduring

Blank (ii)
D. modern
E. fossils
F. antediluvian

53. The President's speech was both ___________ and ___________ : though brief, it was instructive.

Blank (i)

A. succinct
B. prolix
C. ambivalent

Blank (ii)

D. enlightening
E. hackneyed
F. curt

54. A social movement is a ___________ rather than ___________ enterprise.

Blank (i)

A. dogmatic
B. collaborative
C. germane

Blank (ii)

D. a harmonizing
E. a participative
F. an individualistic

55. One of the main characteristics of slang is the continual ___________ of its vocabulary; in order for slang to feel slangy, it has to have a feeling of ___________ .

Blank (i)

A. rejuvenation
B. jingoism
C. cynicism

Blank (ii)

D. felicity
E. novelty
F. affinity

56. Venus is almost the same size as earth, and its gravitational field is only slightly weaker than the earth's, so logically it might seem that Venus and Earth have ___________ atmospheres but _______ this is not so.

Blank (i)

A. antithetical
B. torrid
C. similar

Blank (ii)

D. practically
E. rarely
F. ideally

57. Although its reputation is not as ___________ as it once was, the university is still ___________ of its productive, intelligent graduates, many of whom have gone on to earn national recognition.

Blank (i)
A. sterling
B. detestable
C. importunate

Blank (ii)
D. abashed
E. proud
F. modest

58. ___________ spending several hours scrutinizing the text, the researcher was ___________ to decipher it because the writing was too faint.

Blank (i)
A. Because of
B. Despite
C. Continuously

Blank (ii)
D. unable
E. craven
F. gullible

59. The Prime Minister did not give either oral or spoken permission to go ahead with the tax cuts; his ___________ was, however, ___________ by his approving smile.

Blank (i)
A. disapproval
B. consent
C. objurgation

Blank (ii)
D. abnegated
E. desecrated
F. implied

60. The Second World War was a ___________ event for all Americans. It brought the Great Depression to an end and marked the ___________ of significant socioeconomic and political changes for women and racial minorities.

Blank (i)
A. seminal
B. nugatory
C. deferential

Blank (ii)
D. culmination
E. beginning
F. exodus

61. __________, the very people who proclaim liberating philosophies sometimes also engage in __________ practices.

Blank (i)
A. Consequently
B. Paradoxically
C. Magnanimously

Blank (ii)
D. dominant
E. emancipating
F. repressive

62. John is a __________, so he always tends to __________ discussions rather than take action.

Blank (i)
A. procrastinator
B. charlatan
C. neophyte

Blank (ii)
D. eschew
E. prolong
F. abbreviate

63. That French novelist Honore de Balzac could be financially __________ in his fiction while losing all his money in life was __________ duplicated in his other matters as well.

Blank (i)
A. maladroit
B. astute
C. disaffected

Blank (ii)
D. a malediction
E. an irony
F. an extrapolation

64. The __________ policy led to a sustained uprising that could not be __________ by the administration's impassioned pleas.

Blank (i)
A. amenable
B. complaisant
C. contentious

Blank (ii)
D. quelled
E. fostered
F. galvanized

65. It is a myth that scientists are so absorbed with ___________ that they have no ___________ interests.

Blank (i)
A. experiments
B. abstractions
C. apprehensions

Blank (ii)
D. utopian
E. practical
F. gargantuan

66. For a long time it was ___________ that soaking in large amounts of sunlight was relatively harmless; now, however, it has been realized that excessive exposure to sun's rays can be _________

Blank (i)
A. contradicted
B. disputed
C. believed

Blank (ii)
D. salubrious
E. deleterious
F. frivolous

67. The issue of whether nuclear energy is a ___________ or a ___________ is often debated.

Blank (i)
A. benediction
B. paradox
C. larceny

Blank (ii)
D. bane
E. misnomer
F. paragon

68. Even though John has made ___________ remarks about almost all his friends, nobody _________ his company because he is a very witty man.

Blank (i)
A. vitriolic
B. commendable
C. laudatory

Blank (ii)
D. balks at
E. recants
F. squanders

69. __________ they can be replaced by a faster and more __________ means of transportation, trucks will continue to carry most of the freight within a country.

Blank (i)
A. Since
B. Until
C. For

Blank (ii)
D. lethargic
E. indolent
F. efficacious

70. Plato's writing is considered __________ by most readers who find it almost impossible to make sense of the __________ text.

Blank (i)
A. arcane
B. archaic
C. verbose

Blank (ii)
D. lucid
E. baffling
F. spurious

Three-Blank Sentences

71. To some people, life is hard, cruel and __________ . These set of people see life as __________ and therefore __________ themselves to fate, believing all is finished.

Blank (i)
A. salutary
B. sanguine
C. unsparing

Blank (ii)
D. a punishment
E. an exoneration
F. an aberration

Blank (iii)
G. resign
H. sacrilege
I. torpor

72. When a terrier comes into the room you instinctively draw away __________ you want to be jumped at and greeted __________ . But you make no such movement to protect yourself from a St. Bernard because you read, on sight, the __________ natures of these two from their external appearance.

Blank (i)
A. because
B. nevertheless
C. unless

Blank (ii)
D. effusively
E. stoically
F. tractably

Blank (iii)
G. coherent
H. incomprehensible
I. disparate

73. ___________ birds who fly away to ___________ for grain and bring it home in the beak, without tasting it themselves, to feed their young, our ___________ go picking knowledge here and there, out of books, and hold it at the tongue's end, only to spit it out and distribute it away.

Blank (i)	Blank (ii)	Blank (iii)
A. Contrary to	D. forage	G. pedants
B. Like	E. simper	H. virtuosos
C. Because of	F. undulate	I. wastrels

74. Changes to the world economy have had ___________ effect on the nationalities of private-jet buyers. A market that as recently as 15 years ago was ___________ by American clients now ______ the rise of smaller nations.

Blank (i)	Blank (ii)	Blank (iii)
A. a telling	D. dominated	G. foretells
B. an obviating	E. yielded	H. reflects
C. a deleterious	F. eschewed	I. abnegates

75. Houghton's pilot program in Riverside was ___________ the first attempt to use e-books in education. Indeed, digital textbooks have been ___________ for more than a decade, but have made ___________ impact on education so far.

Blank (i)	Blank (ii)	Blank (iii)
A. possibly	D. around	G. seminal
B. not	E. redundant	H. little
C. supposedly	F. defunct	I. consequential

76. A brave and highly decorated officer, the army General is ___________ as a brilliant strategist and a reform-minded leader who is ___________ corruption, as reflected in the hard line he adopted against ___________ officers in the recent Housing scam.

Blank (i)	Blank (ii)	Blank (iii)
A. revered	D. unexceptional on	G. erring
B. reviled	E. unforgiving of	H. scrupulous
C. propounded	F. equivocal about	I. artless

77. During the recent wave of revolutions across the Arab world, rap music has played a ___________ role in ___________ citizen ___________ over poverty, rising food prices, blackouts, unemployment, police repression and political corruption.

Blank (i)	Blank (ii)	Blank (iii)
A. inconsequential	D. articulating	G. complacence
B. trivial	E. belying	H. euphoria
C. pivotal	F. exculpating	I. ire

78. Attention-deficit drugs increase ___________ in the short term, which is why they work so well for college students ___________ for exams at the last minute. But when given to children over long periods of time, they neither ___________ school achievement nor reduce behaviour problems.

Blank (i)	Blank (ii)	Blank (iii)
A. concentration	D. simulating	G. diminish
B. aesthetics	E. cramming	H. augment
C. reparation	F. reverberating	I. wane

79. ___________ the bus driver has become a super successful tycoon now, his ___________ has not been without ___________ .

Blank (i)
A. Since
B. Because
C. Though

Blank (ii)
D. ascent
E. assent
F. capitulation

Blank (iii)
G. ecstasy
H. controversy
I. euphemism

80. The ___________ costs of rare musical instruments mean that many players must rely on loans from ___________ patrons, a situation that can ___________ an artist's dignity and cause disruptions in his life.

Blank (i)
A. catastrophic
B. stratospheric
C. acerbic

Blank (ii)
D. affluent
E. braggart
F. grandiloquent

Blank (iii)
G. sap
H. bolster
I. knack

81. Half a century ago, any economist could have told you that austerity in the face of depression was a very bad idea. ___________ policy makers, pundits and many economists decided, largely for political reasons, to ___________ what they used to know, and millions of workers are paying the price for their wilful ___________ .

Blank (i)
A. however
B. so
C. enigmatically

Blank (ii)
D. forget
E. apply
F. bereft

Blank (iii)
G. misdemeanour
H. insomnia
I. amnesia

82. The newly married couple had characters that would not __________ – he was __________ and she was spirited; he was worldly, and she, perhaps, __________ .

Blank (i)
A. discord
B. harmonize
C. abate

Blank (ii)
D. irascible
E. jaunty
F. astute

Blank (iii)
G. rational
H. quixotic
I. insolent

83. Conditions for journalism have never been better: __________ media profits, __________ legal protections, and __________ technology.

Blank (i)
A. prosaic
B. flagging
C. robust

Blank (ii)
D. lack of
E. strong
F. iota of

Blank (iii)
G. sophistry
H. sophisticated
I. lackadaisical

84. The talk-show host was both __________ and __________ : he was blatantly proud and __________ bold.

Blank (i)
A. modest
B. imperial
C. cantankerous

Blank (ii)
D. timorous
E. curt
F. impudent

Blank (iii)
G. offensively
H. entreatingly
I. abashedly

85. Book titles can often be __________ – a book that sounds __________ on the shelf could actually turn out to be __________ and boring once you get it home and vice versa.

Blank (i)
A. spurious
B. misleading
C. caustic

Blank (ii)
D. great
E. hackneyed
F. irksome

Blank (iii)
G. engaging
H. benign
I. trite

86. Lincoln was from boyhood very good at ___________ any unpleasant ___________ ; one of his modes of getting rid of troublesome friends, as well as troublesome enemies, was by telling a story. He began these tactics early in life, and grew to be wonderfully ___________ in them.

Blank (i)	Blank (ii)	Blank (iii)
A. eschewing	D. solution	G. adept
B. advancing	E. predicament	H. adapt
C. coalescing	F. epiphany	I. absolve

87. So profoundly ___________ of the nature of slavery are many persons, that they are stubbornly _________ whenever they read or listen to any recital of the cruelties which are daily _________ on its victims.

Blank (i)	Blank (ii)	Blank (iii)
A. querulous	D. supercilious	G. inflicted
B. cognizant	E. incredulous	H. imparted
C. ignorant	F. mesmerized	I. imbibed

88. The Englishmen at the time of Queen Elizabeth almost ___________ their queen. Even though at times she could be hard, cruel, and ___________ , she was the most ___________ of all English monarchs.

Blank (i)	Blank (ii)	Blank (iii)
A. venerated	D. vindictive	G. loathed
B. jeered	E. altruistic	H. loved
C. conscripted	F. benevolent	I. baneful

89. Great men, even during their lifetime, are usually known to the public only through a __________ personality. Whether they themselves believe in their public character, or whether they merely permit the __________ to stage-manage it, there are at least two __________ selves, the public and regal self, the private and human.

Blank (i)	Blank (ii)	Blank (iii)
A. fictitious	D. chamberlain	G. distinct
B. disingenuous	E. bastion	H. overlapping
C. complacent	F. sycophant	I. specious

90. Few elected officials would ever dare say that voters making public policy decisions through ballot-box referendums are __________ capable or wise than legislators deliberating under a capitol dome. But now a federal lawsuit __________ the state's 20-year-old taxpayer-controlled budgeting process, is speaking truth to power, and __________ the assumption that voters always know best.

Blank (i)	Blank (ii)	Blank (iii)
A. equally	D. challenging	G. validating
B. more	E. supporting	H. questioning
C. less	F. extenuating	I. asseverating

91. __________ budget cuts and financial difficulties, museums across the world have done well to attract more visitors in the year that has just ended,__________ no one can predict whether this trend will be __________ in the coming year.

Blank (i)	Blank (ii)	Blank (iii)
A. Despite	D. and	G. contradicted
B. Due to	E. consequently	H. objurgated
C. Similar to	F. but	I. replicated

92. ___________ flaws in present laws that do not cover foreign owned and operated sites, ________ of the new anti-piracy bill say it protects the intellectual property market and is necessary to ___________ enforcement of copyright laws, especially against foreign websites.

Blank (i)
A. Despite
B. Citing
C. In defence of

Blank (ii)
D. proponents
E. opponents
F. epicures

Blank (iii)
G. undermine
H. bolster
I. hinder

93. According to ___________ of the big-bang theory, the equations used in big-bang calculations are treated by the science elite as the ultimate reality of the universe. They say that even after these equations are shown to ___________ with observational facts, they are retained by big bangers because of an irrational ___________ that the theory must be correct regardless of the facts.

Blank (i)
A. critics
B. plaudits
C. advocates

Blank (ii)
D. be discordant
E. harmonize
F. adhere

Blank (iii)
G. prejudice
H. tolerance
I. acrimony

94. In what is a classic case of ___________, people ___________ deny the possibility of gods outside of their own belief system, yet become very ___________ when someone reciprocates that point of view.

Blank (i)
A. abnegation
B. contradiction
C. extrapolation

Blank (ii)
D. covertly
E. candidly
F. malevolently

Blank (iii)
G. defensive
H. euphoric
I. iconoclastic

95. Historical ___________ are the subject of a growing number of legal and political claims to repair the harm they caused. In some instances, the consequences of such acts persist into the present. As a consequence, states and societies throughout the world are being asked to ___________ for historic abuses and provide ___________ to victims or their descendants.

Blank (i)	Blank (ii)	Blank (iii)
A. injustices	D. arbitrate	G. vendetta
B. maledictions	E. account	H. proclivity
C. equities	F. chronicle	I. redress

96. Although the women's liberation movement began among students and professional women, the demands it raised, ___________ with the growing contradictions within the capitalist system, began to ___________ much broader layers of people. It began to ___________ the consciousness, expectations, and actions of significant sections of the working class, male and female.

Blank (i)	Blank (ii)	Blank (iii)
A. recompensed	D. assuage	G. affect
B. combined	E. mobilize	H. effect
C. prevaricated	F. exacerbate	I. denigrate

97. Along with the rise and fall of the Soviet Union, the rise of fascism in Germany is another major event of the twentieth century that has not been ___________ . Countless historical articles, papers and books have been written on the theme, and most aspects of the Third Reich have been ___________ in detail. But as far as the historical lessons of these events are concerned, there is an enormous amount of ___________ .

Blank (i)	Blank (ii)	Blank (iii)
D. comprehended	A. delved	G. orientation
E. misconstrued	B. invigorated	H. confusion
F. obviated	C. repudiated	I. dejection

98. The eighteenth-century botanist Carolus Linnaeus' ___________ and essential contribution to natural history was to ___________ a system of classification whereby any plant or animal could be identified and ___________ into an overall plan.

Blank (i)
A. marginal
B. enormous
C. capricious

Blank (ii)
D. devise
E. diagnose
F. divulge

Blank (iii)
G. severed
H. slotted
I. inflicted

99. For better or worse, listening to audio books almost always feels like a ___________ experience. I feel myself not merely a ___________ audience but engaged in a kind of ___________ . Readers are not reading to me; we are reading together.

Blank (i)
A. cognizant
B. ethereal
C. shared

Blank (ii)
D. passive
E. recondite
F. ebullient

Blank (iii)
G. benediction
H. vitriol
I. exchange

100. Much of science in science fiction is ___________ ; some of it is totally wrong. But beneath all the surface trickery of science fiction, there is a general ___________ for science and some appreciation of its methodology, which is probably more ___________ than the facts that can be found in a textbook.

Blank (i)
A. esoteric
B. aggravated
C. exaggerated

Blank (ii)
D. respect
E. slumber
F. abhorrence

Blank (iii)
G. pertinent
H. pejorative
I. seminal

Text Completion - Answers & Explanations

Q No.	Answer	Q No.	Answer	Q No.	Answer	Q No.	Answer
1	B	26	A	51	B, D	76	A, D, G
2	C	27	C	52	C, E	77	C, D, I
3	A	28	D	53	A, D	78	A, E, H
4	C	29	A	54	B, F	79	C, E, H
5	E	30	B	55	A, E	80	B, D, G
6	C	31	E	56	C, D	81	A, D, I
7	A	32	B	57	A, E	82	B, D, H
8	C	33	D	58	B, D	83	C, E, H
9	E	34	C	59	B, F	84	B, F, G
10	C	35	B	60	A, E	85	B, D, I
11	D	36	B, E	61	B, F	86	A, E, G
12	B	37	A, E	62	A, E	87	C, E, G
13	A	38	B, E	63	B, E	88	A, D, H
14	B	39	C, D	64	C, D	89	A, D, G
15	C	40	B, D	65	B, E	90	C, D, H
16	A	41	A, F	66	C, E	91	A, F, I
17	B	42	B, E	67	A, D	92	B, D, H
18	A	43	A, D	68	A, D	93	A, D, G
19	B	44	A, D	69	B, F	94	B, E, G
20	D	45	A, E	70	A, E	95	A, E, I
21	B	46	C, E	71	C, D, G	96	B, E, G
22	E	47	A, D	72	C, D, I	97	A, D, H
23	C	48	C, E	73	B, D, G	98	B, D, H
24	C	49	B, E	74	A, D, H	99	C, D, I
25	B	50	B, D	75	B, D, H	100	C, D, G

1) **Keyword** - fundamentally they are similar

Connector – Even though (contrast)

The Connector implies a contrast so we need to go with a word that contrasts with the keyword

Prediction – differ, contrasts, opposite to

Differ exactly matches our prediction and should be the correct answer

2) **Keyword** - every person you see is a true story, more romantic and absorbing

Connector – For (same direction)

The Keyword tells us that the word has to be a positive word. Hence eliminate trite and unenjoyable straight away

Prediction – interesting

Delightful comes closest to our prediction and should be the correct answer

3) **Keyword** - Our actions follow our thoughts

Connector – However (contrast)

The Keyword tells us that actions always follow thoughts. The contrasting 'however' is being used to suggest that even if the thought is extremely fleeting, it would lead to some action

Prediction – short, fleeting, unimportant

Transitory comes closest to our prediction and should be the correct answer

4) **Keyword** - Our ancestors developed massive jaws as a result of constant combat.

Connector – As (same direction)

The Keyword tells us that there is a direct correlation between the size of jaws and the need for constant combat. So the more the need for combat the bigger the jaws and vice versa as in the second part of the sentence

Prediction – decreased, reduced

Reduced exactly matches our prediction and should be the correct answer

5) **Keyword** - Sceptical as Montaigne shows himself in his books

Connector – yet (contrast)

A sceptical person will ideally doubt everything but the use of 'yet' suggests that Montaigne will have a great regard for religion

Prediction – showed, demonstrated

Manifested comes closest to our prediction and should be the correct answer

6) **Keyword** - they only used information and methods that were available freely

Connector – ; (same direction)

The semi colon implies that the thought in the first part of the sentence will continue into the second part.

Prediction – new, original, innovative

Novel comes closest to our prediction and should be the correct answer

7) **Keyword** - the overall global impact is vastly detrimental

Connector – even if (contrast)

The Keyword suggests that the overall impact of global warming is detrimental but the contrasting connector suggests that some entities will actually be advantaged by the same.

Prediction – unavoidable

Inevitable comes closest to our prediction and should be the correct answer

8) **Keyword** - often supporting liberal and conservative positions simultaneously.

Connector – None (same direction)

Prediction – unclear, ambiguous, broad

Eclectic comes closest to our prediction and should be the correct answer

9) **Keyword** - the gap between the rich and the poor has grown ever wider

Connector – and (same direction)

Prediction – unequal, biased

Unequal matches our prediction and should be the correct answer

10) **Keyword** - to tighten its grip

Connector – so (same direction)

If the party is tightening its grip, then the word obviously has to be a negative

Prediction – expelled, punished

Harassed comes closest to our prediction and should be the correct answer

11) **Keyword** - He has been off the radar for a while

Connector – but (contrast)

The use of the contrasting 'but' suggests that the actor is now trying to make a comeback

Prediction – working on, creating

Crafting comes closest to our prediction and should be the correct answer

12) **Keyword** - sometimes it is necessary to cross out some names

Connector – None (same direction)

This is a straightforward sentence suggesting that almost everybody will *agree* to a particular action

Prediction – agree, accept

Acquiesce comes closest to our prediction and should be the correct answer

13) **Keyword** - declared his commitment

Connector – but (contrast)

The contrast implies that the President's commitment is not visible in the budget plan

Prediction – sign, mention

Reflection comes closest to our prediction and should be the correct answer

14) **Keyword** - managed to sustain links

Connector – against (contrast)

The contrast implies that the immigrants have sustained their links despite tremendous problems

Prediction – problems, opposition

Odds comes closest to our prediction and should be the correct answer

15) **Keyword** - free of stylistic tricks or evasiveness

Connector – None (same direction)

The word that goes in the blank should basically mean something that is not tricky or evasive

Prediction – straightforward, clear

Forthright comes closest to our prediction and should be the correct answer

16) **Keyword** - devoid of any emotion or personal prejudice

Connector – None (same direction)

The word that goes in the blank should basically mean 'not prejudiced'

Prediction – impartial, unbiased

Dispassionate comes closest to our prediction and should be the correct answer

17) **Keyword** - companies have actually spent very little

Connector – The sentence doesn't have a flag post but the options contain some common Connectors such as *due to* and *for*. This should provide a hint to students to check the sentence again for meaning.

In this case the sentence is clearly trying to suggest that even though major companies talk a lot about ecology, they have actually done very little to control this problem. Thus the sentence needs a contrasting Connector

Prediction – any contrasting Connector

The use of *For* along with the use of 'actually' in the latter part of the sentence suggests a contrast; hence 'for' should be the correct answer

18) **Keyword** - a waste of time and money

Connector – and (same direction)

The word that goes in the blank should also be a negative word to match the negatives used after 'and'

Prediction – improper, bad

Disrespectful comes closest to our prediction and should be the correct answer

19) **Keyword** - deepen and extend our knowledge

Connector – not (contrast)

The word that goes in the blank has to contrast with the keyword'

Prediction – reiterate, restate

Confirm comes closest to our prediction and should be the correct answer

20) **Keyword** - noting subtle differences between dishes

Connector – None (same direction)

The sentences suggests that the judges were basically very good in their field

Prediction – experts, masters

Gourmands comes closest to our prediction and should be the correct answer

21) **Keyword** - it is of paramount importance

Connector – but (contrast)

The blank needs a negative word to contrast with paramount importance

Prediction – useless, unimportant

Trivial comes closest to our prediction and should be the correct answer

22) **Keyword** - members were abashed

Connector – so…..that (same direction)

The blank needs a negative word because the members were abashed or ashamed at the sound

Prediction – noisy, unpleasant

Strident comes closest to our prediction and should be the correct answer

23) **Keyword** - an element of surprise

Connector – avoid (contrast)

The blank needs a negative word to contrast with 'surprise'

Prediction – hackneyed, boring

Predictable comes closest to our prediction and should be the correct answer

24) **Keyword** - became irritated even if a minor issue was not taken care of

Connector – ; (same direction)

Prediction – perfectionist, meticulous

Fastidious comes closest to our prediction and should be the correct answer

25) **Keyword** - plants had already been weakened

Connector – because (same direction)

The blank needs a negative word to follow the negative thought in the first part of the sentence

Prediction – disastrous, harmful

Deleterious comes closest to our prediction and should be the correct answer

26) **Keyword** - meticulous employees

Connector – Predictably (same direction)

The blank needs a word that agrees with or describes meticulous'

Prediction – good, skilled

Adept comes closest to our prediction and should be the correct answer

27) **Keyword** - human need to wake by day and sleep by night, we come to associate night dwellers with people who are up to no good

Connector – None (same direction)

Prediction – Biased by, Because of

Chauvinistic comes closest to our prediction and should be the correct answer

28) **Keyword** - only parts of clay vessels may be recovered

Connector – even though (contrast)

The sentence suggests that even though only pieces of pottery are recovered, these pottery shards are also very valuable to archaeologists

Prediction – precious, useful

Invaluable comes closest to our prediction and should be the correct answer

29) **Keyword** - did not heed that advice

Connector – None (same direction)

The sentence suggests that even though Jerry asked for his father's advice, he did not actually pay any importance to it

Prediction – suggestion, advice

Counsel comes closest to our prediction and should be the correct answer

30) **Keyword** - beauty of the mountain peak is difficult to see

Connector – because (same direction)

The sentence suggests that the beauty of the mountain peak cannot be seen because the clouds cover the peak

Prediction – hide, cover

Obscure comes closest to our prediction and should be the correct answer

31) **Keyword** - launched its new product just as demand was reaching its peak

Connector – ; (same direction)

The blank needs a positive word to suggest well-timed

Prediction – appropriate, fortunate

Opportune comes closest to our prediction and should be the correct answer

32) **Keyword** - significant gains

Connector – None (same direction)

The sentence suggests that the large number of awards highlights an aspect of the field of biochemistry

Prediction – highlights, showcases

Accentuates comes closest to our prediction and should be the correct answer

33) **Keyword** - this is a serious problem

Connector – ; (same direction)

The sentence suggests that there is total consensus that corruption is present in sports

Prediction – dispute, disagreement

Dispute matches our prediction and should be the correct answer

34) **Keyword** - By portraying a wide range of characters in his one-man show

Connector – None (same direction)

The sentence suggests two things – that the actor portrayed a wide range of roles and that there is a belief that theatre only offers actors a limited range of roles. Clearly there is a contrast between the two parts that needs to be highlighted

Prediction – counter

Corrective comes closest to our prediction and should be the correct answer

35) **Keyword** - habitual boasting about his wealth

Connector – as an example (same direction)

The sentence suggests that Tom keeps boasting about his wealth all the time.

Prediction – braggart, show off

Braggart matches our prediction and should be the correct answer

Two-Blank Sentences

36) **Keyword** - traits of every individual are stamped

Connector – None (same direction)

Prediction for Blank 1 – basic

Prediction for Blank 2 - permanently

Fundamental & *indelibly* come closest to our prediction and should be the correct answer

37) **Keyword** - thoughts which were to him too deep for prose expression

Connector – is actually the first blank

The sentence implies a contrast between essays and poetry, so the Connector has to bring this out

Prediction for Blank 1 – In addition to, Apart from

Prediction for Blank 2 – contained, mentioned

Besides & *embodied* come closest to our prediction and should be the correct answer

38) **Keyword** – None

Connector – not (contrast)

Because of the implied contrast, we need to find a pair of words that are opposite in meaning. Since the sentence doesn't have a Keyword as such, there will only be one such pair possible

Prediction for Blank 1 – None

Prediction for Blank 2 – None

The only possible combination of contrasting words is *iconoclastic* and *conventional*. These should be the correct answer

39) **Keyword** - many things to be said against

Connector – but (contrast)

Prediction for Blank 1 – criticism, complaint

Prediction for Blank 2 – acceptable, worthwhile

Indictment & *quashed* come closest to our prediction and should be the correct answer

40) **Keyword** - over-confident belief

Connector – point of view is a healthy reaction to the over-confident belief (contrast)

Start predicting from the 2nd blank. Since it is an over confident belief the word should be 'all' or something similar. Because of the implicit contrast, the first blank should be the opposite of this.

Prediction for Blank 1 – nothing

Prediction for Blank 2 – everything

Nothing and *everything* exactly match our prediction and should be the correct answer

41) **Keyword** - Successful government programs

Connector – but (contrast)

The Keyword indicates that the first blank should be positive and the second blank should contrast with this

Prediction for Blank 1 – counter, reduce

Prediction for Blank 2 – continue to

Abate and *still* come closest to our prediction and should be the correct answer

42) **Keyword** – 'paid news' and other ills

Connector – There is no clear Connector as such. However, social networking sites are uncontrolled and are, in that sense, opposite of media. Also the use of 'force' suggests that the second blank should contrast with the first (contrast)

The Keyword indicates that the first blank should be negative and the second blank should contrast with this

Prediction for Blank 1 – susceptible, dependent

Prediction for Blank 2 – countering

Vulnerable and *countervailing* come closest to our prediction and should be the correct answer

43) **Keyword** – None

Connector – None (same direction)

This sentence can be interpreted in two ways – either opponents of free internet have done something to pass new legislation or supporters of free internet have done something to stop new legislation. The options will only provide for one of these scenarios and that will be the correct answer

Prediction for Blank 1 – None

Prediction for Blank 2 – None

The only possible combination of contrasting words is *advocates* and *stall*. These should be the correct answer

44) **Keyword** - hope

Connector – None (same direction)

The use of 'hope' suggests that the situation is not very good currently

Prediction for Blank 1 – make up

Prediction for Blank 2 – poor, low

Compensate and *sluggish* come closest to our prediction and should be the correct answer

45) **Keyword** - proving the impossibility of airborne transmission

Connector – also (same direction)

The virus has basically proven several assumptions wrong

Prediction for Blank 1 – In addition to

Prediction for Blank 2 – proved

Apart from and *proven* come closest to our prediction and should be the correct answer

46) **Keyword** - struggling businesses

Connector – like (same direction)

Prediction for Blank 1 – reducing

Prediction for Blank 2 – reducing

Paring and *trimming* come closest to our prediction and should be the correct answer

47) **Keyword** - None

Connector – Although (contrast)

The two words need to be opposites, because of the contrast implied in the sentence

Prediction for Blank 1 – None

Prediction for Blank 2 – None

Ambivalent and *enthusiastic* come closest to our prediction and should be the correct answer

48) **Keyword** - were made obsolete by the invention of the cannon, fascinating relics of a bygone era

Connector – None, needs to be put in

The sentence suggests that even though cannons made castles redundant, castles still survive

Prediction for Blank 1 – Although

Prediction for Blank 2 – exist

Though and *survive* come closest to our prediction and should be the correct answer

49) **Keyword** - were became extinct as part of one single event, still

Connector – Even though (contrast)

Prediction for Blank 1 – acceptance, popularity

Prediction for Blank 2 – unclear, obscure

Credence and *inconclusive* come closest to our prediction and should be the correct answer

50) **Keyword** - halfway through the book

Connector – ; (same direction)

Prediction for Blank 1 – predictable, common

Prediction for Blank 2 – predict

Prosaic and *foresee* come closest to our prediction and should be the correct answer

51) **Keyword** - students' mischievous behaviour; their expression of remorse

Connector – Although (contrast)

Prediction for Blank 1 – angered, irritated

Prediction for Blank 2 – calmed, mollified

Vexed and *placated* come closest to our prediction and should be the correct answer

52) **Keyword** - great classical novels

Connector – So (same direction)

Prediction for Blank 1 – everlasting, important

Prediction for Blank 2 – outdated, useless

Enduring and *fossils* come closest to our prediction and should be the correct answer

53) **Keyword** - brief, it was instructive

Connector – None (same direction). Even though the sentence uses 'though' it is to show the contrast between brief and instructive and not between the two blanks

One of the blanks should mean brief and the other instructive

Prediction for Blank 1 – None

Prediction for Blank 2 – None

Succinct and *enlightening* come closest to our prediction and should be the correct answer

54) **Keyword** - social movement

Connector – Rather (contrast)

The two blanks should be the opposite of each other

Prediction for Blank 1 – None

Prediction for Blank 2 – None

Collaborative and *individualistic* come closest to our prediction and should be the correct answer

55) **Keyword** - of its vocabulary

Connector – ; (same direction)

The two blanks should have similar meanings

Prediction for Blank 1 – None

Prediction for Blank 2 – None

Rejuvenation and *novelty* are the only similar pair of words and should be the correct answer

56) **Keyword** - same size as the earth, and its gravitational field is only slightly weaker than the earth's

Connector – So (same direction); but (contrast)

The first blank has a same direction Connector so it should follow the thought expressed in the initial part of the sentence. The second blank should show a contrast because of 'but'

Prediction for Blank 1 – same

Prediction for Blank 2 – actually

Similar and *practically* come closest to our prediction and should be the correct answer

57) **Keyword** - it once was; still

Connector – Although (contrast)

The sentence basically states that even though the university's reputation has fallen, it is still a good university that produces good students

Prediction for Blank 1 – good

Prediction for Blank 2 – proud

Sterling and *proud* come closest to our prediction and should be the correct answer

58) **Keyword** - because the writing was too faint

Connector – Needs to be inserted

Because the writing was too faint, the researcher must not have been able to decipher the text. This was despite spending several hours at it, so the Connector will obviously have to show contrast

Prediction for Blank 1 – In spite of

Prediction for Blank 2 – unable

Despite and *unable* come closest to our prediction and should be the correct answer

59) **Keyword** - his approving smile

Connector – however (contrast)

Since the first part of the sentence states that the Prime Minister did not give his permission, the second part should obviously suggest (due to the implied contrast) that he did give his permission

Prediction for Blank 1 – permission

Prediction for Blank 2 – conveyed

Consent and *implied* come closest to our prediction and should be the correct answer

60) **Keyword** - It brought the Great Depression to an end

Connector – None (same direction)

Prediction for Blank 1 – very important

Prediction for Blank 2 – starting

Seminal and *beginning* come closest to our prediction and should be the correct answer

61) **Keyword** - people who proclaim liberating philosophies sometimes also engage

Connector – Needs to be inserted

The Keyword suggests that people tend to do two types of contrasting things, so the Connector should be a contrasting one. Also the word that goes in the second blank needs to contrast with liberating philosophies to show the antipodal views of these people

Prediction for Blank 1 – Contrastingly

Prediction for Blank 2 – conservative

Paradoxically and *repressive* come closest to our prediction and should be the correct answer

62) **Keyword** - take action

Connector – rather (contrast)

The Keyword suggests that the second blank should contrast with taking action. Also the first blank should describe such a person

Prediction for Blank 1 – lazy person

Prediction for Blank 2 – encourage

Procrastinator and *prolong* come closest to our prediction and should be the correct answer

63) **Keyword** - losing all his money in life

Connector – while (contrast)

The Keyword suggests that the novelist was financially wise in his fiction. Also the second blank should mean a contrast

Prediction for Blank 1 – wise, adept

Prediction for Blank 2 – a contrast

Astute and *an irony* come closest to our prediction and should be the correct answer

64) **Keyword** - led to a sustained uprising

Connector – None (same direction)

If it led to an uprising, the policy must have been negative.

Prediction for Blank 1 – any negative word

Prediction for Blank 2 – controlled, stopped

Contentious and *quelled* come closest to our prediction and should be the correct answer

65) **Keyword** - It is a myth

Connector – None (same direction)

The two words have to be of contrasting nature

Prediction for Blank 1 – None

Prediction for Blank 2 – None

The only possible combination of contrasting words is *abstractions* and *practical* and these should be the contract answer

66) **Keyword** - soaking in large amounts of sunlight was relatively harmless

Connector – however (contrast)

The second blank has to be negative to contrast with harmless in the first part of the sentence

Prediction for Blank 1 – thought

Prediction for Blank 2 – harmful

Believed and *deleterious* come closest to our prediction and should be the correct answer

67) **Keyword** - often debated

Connector – None (same direction)

The two blanks have to be of contrasting nature

Prediction for Blank 1 – None

Prediction for Blank 2 – None

Benediction and *bane* are the only possible pair of contrasting words and should be the correct answer

68) **Keyword** - because he is a very witty man

Connector – Even though (contrast)

Since John is a very witty man, the second blank should imply that nobody objects to his company. The contrast in the sentence then implies that the first blank has to be negative because in spite of negative remarks nobody objects to John's company

Prediction for Blank 1 – insulting, disparaging

Prediction for Blank 2 – objects to, minds

Vitriolic and *balks at* come closest to our prediction and should be the correct answer

69) **Keyword** - trucks will continue to carry

Connector – Until (contrast)

Prediction for Blank 1 – Till the time

Prediction for Blank 2 – faster, cheaper

Until and *efficacious* come closest to our prediction and should be the correct answer

70) **Keyword** - who find it almost impossible to make sense of

Connector – None (same direction)

Prediction for Blank 1 – esoteric, recondite

Prediction for Blank 2 – confusing, dense

Arcane and *baffling* come closest to our prediction and should be the correct answer

Three-Blank Sentences

71) **Keyword** - believing all is finished

Connector – None (same direction)

Prediction for Blank 1 – any negative word

Prediction for Blank 2 – any negative word

Prediction for Blank 3 – give themselves up

Unsparing, a punishment, and *resign* come closest to our prediction and should be the correct answer

72) **Keyword** - believing all is finished

Connector – But (contrast)

Prediction for Blank 1 – unless

Prediction for Blank 2 – warmly, excitedly

Prediction for Blank 3 – different

Unless, effusively, and *disparate* come closest to our prediction and should be the correct answer

73) **Keyword** - bring it home in the beak, without tasting it themselves

Connector – so (same direction)

Prediction for Blank 1 – Like, similar to

Prediction for Blank 2 – search

Prediction for Blank 3 – experts

Like, forage, and *pedants* come closest to our prediction and should be the correct answer

74) **Keyword** - rise of smaller nations

Connector – None (same direction)

Prediction for Blank 1 – an important

Prediction for Blank 2 – filled

Prediction for Blank 3 – sees

A telling, dominated, and *reflects* come closest to our prediction and should be the correct answer

75) **Keyword** - first attempt to use e-books in education

Connector – Indeed (same direction); But (contrast)

Prediction for Blank 1 – not

Prediction for Blank 2 – in existence

Prediction for Blank 3 – a small

Not, around, and *little* come closest to our prediction and should be the correct answer

76) **Keyword** - A brave and highly decorated officer

Connector – as (same direction)

Prediction for Blank 1 – considered, believed to be

Prediction for Blank 2 – against

Prediction for Blank 3 – corrupt, guilty

Revered, unexceptional, and *erring* come closest to our prediction and should be the correct answer

77) **Keyword** - recent wave of revolutions across the Arab world

Connector – None (same direction)

Prediction for Blank 1 – important

Prediction for Blank 2 – bringing out, expressing

Prediction for Blank 3 – unhappiness

Pivotal, articulating, and *ire* come closest to our prediction and should be the correct answer

78) **Keyword** - they work so well for college students; nor reduce behaviour problems

Connector – But (contrast)

Prediction for Blank 1 – memory

Prediction for Blank 2 – studying, preparing

Prediction for Blank 3 – improve

Concentration, cramming, and *augment* come closest to our prediction and should be the correct answer

79) **Keyword** - has become a super successful tycoon now

Connector – Needs to be inserted

The sentence structure indicates that the rise of the bus conductor has been surrounded by controversy so a contrasting Connector needs to be added to the sentence

Prediction for Blank 1 – Even though

Prediction for Blank 2 – success

Prediction for Blank 3 – controversy

Though, assent, and *controversy* come closest to our prediction and should be the correct answer

80) **Keyword** - many players must rely on loans

Connector – None (same direction)

Prediction for Blank 1 – high

Prediction for Blank 2 – rich

Prediction for Blank 3 – lower

Stratospheric, affluent, and *sap* come closest to our prediction and should be the correct answer

81) **Keyword** - millions of workers are paying the price

Connector – And (same direction)

Prediction for Blank 1 – any contrasting word

Prediction for Blank 2 – ignore

Prediction for Blank 3 – forgetfulness

However, forget, and *amnesia* come closest to our prediction and should be the correct answer

82) **Keyword** - had characters that would not

Connector – None (same direction)

Prediction for Blank 1 – get along

Prediction for Blank 2 – any negative word

Prediction for Blank 3 – too idealistic

Harmonize, irascible, and *quixotic* come closest to our prediction and should be the correct answer

83) **Keyword** - Conditions for journalism have never been better

Connector – : (same direction)

Prediction for Blank 1 – any positive word

Prediction for Blank 2 – any positive word

Prediction for Blank 3 – any positive word

Robust, strong, and *sophisticated* come closest to our prediction and should be the correct answer

84) **Keyword** – blatantly proud and bold

Connector – : (same direction)

Prediction for Blank 1 – arrogant/insolent

Prediction for Blank 2 – arrogant/insolent

Prediction for Blank 3 – very

Imperial, impudent, and *offensively* closest to our prediction and should be the correct answer

85) **Keyword** - could actually turn out to be boring

Connector – - (same direction)

Prediction for Blank 1 – deceptive

Prediction for Blank 2 – good, tempting

Prediction for Blank 3 – uninteresting

Misleading, great, and *trite* come closest to our prediction and should be the correct answer

86) **Keyword** - He began these tactics early in life

Connector – And (same direction)

Prediction for Blank 1 – avoiding

Prediction for Blank 2 – situation

Prediction for Blank 3 – skilled, good

Eschewing, predicament, and *adept* come closest to our prediction and should be the correct answer

87) **Keyword** - whenever they read or listen to any recital of the cruelties

Connector – None (same direction)

Prediction for Blank 1 – unaware

Prediction for Blank 2 – surprised

Prediction for Blank 3 – inflicted

Ignorant, incredulous, and *inflicted* come closest to our prediction and should be the correct answer

88) **Keyword** - at times she could be hard

Connector – Even though (contrast)

Prediction for Blank 1 – worshipped

Prediction for Blank 2 – any negative word

Prediction for Blank 3 – admired

Venerated, vindictive, and *loved* come closest to our prediction and should be the correct answer

89) **Keyword** - even during their lifetime, are usually known to the public only through

Connector – None (same direction)

Prediction for Blank 1 – made up, fake

Prediction for Blank 2 – media

Prediction for Blank 3 – separate, disparate

Fictitious, chamberlain, and *distinct* come closest to our prediction and should be the correct answer

90) **Keyword** - Few elected officials would ever dare say

Connector – But (contrast)

Prediction for Blank 1 – not

Prediction for Blank 2 – questioning

Prediction for Blank 3 – disproving

Less, challenging, and *questioning* come closest to our prediction and should be the correct answer

91) **Keyword** - museums across the world have done well to attract more visitors

Connector – Needs to be inserted

Prediction for Blank 1 – Any contrasting word

Prediction for Blank 2 – Any contrasting word

Prediction for Blank 3 – continue

Despite, but, and *replicated* come closest to our prediction and should be the correct answer

92) **Keyword** - flaws in present laws

Connector – None (same direction)

Prediction for Blank 1 – Pointing out

Prediction for Blank 2 – supporters

Prediction for Blank 3 – strengthen

Citing, proponents, and *bolster* come closest to our prediction and should be the correct answer

93) **Keyword** - the theory must be correct regardless of the facts

Connector – None (same direction)

Prediction for Blank 1 – opponents

Prediction for Blank 2 – disagree

Prediction for Blank 3 – belief

Critics, be discordant, and *prejudice* come closest to our prediction and should be the correct answer

94) **Keyword** - when someone reciprocates that point of view

Connector – Yet (contrast)

Prediction for Blank 1 – hypocrisy

Prediction for Blank 2 – always

Prediction for Blank 3 – angry

Contradiction, candidly, and *defensive* come closest to our prediction and should be the correct answer

95) **Keyword** - the consequences of such acts persist into the present

Connector – As a result (same direction)

Prediction for Blank 1 – any negative word such as atrocities

Prediction for Blank 2 – justify

Prediction for Blank 3 – relief

Injustices, account, and *redress* come closest to our prediction and should be the correct answer

96) **Keyword** - women's liberation movement began among students and professional women

Connector – Although (contrast)

Prediction for Blank 1 – together with

Prediction for Blank 2 – arouse

Prediction for Blank 3 – impact

Combined, mobilize, and *affect* come closest to our prediction and should be the correct answer

97) **Keyword** - another major event of the twentieth century that has not been

Connector – But (contrast)

Prediction for Blank 1 – understood

Prediction for Blank 2 – investigated, looked into

Prediction for Blank 3 – confusion

Comprehended, delved, and *confusion* come closest to our prediction and should be the correct answer

98) **Keyword** - essential contribution to natural history

Connector – None (same direction)

Prediction for Blank 1 – huge

Prediction for Blank 2 – create

Prediction for Blank 3 – fit into

Enormous, devise, and *slotted* come closest to our prediction and should be the correct answer

99) **Keyword** - we are reading together

Connector – None (same direction)

Prediction for Blank 1 – combined

Prediction for Blank 2 – watching

Prediction for Blank 3 – interaction

Shared, passive, and *exchange* come closest to our prediction and should be the correct answer

100) **Keyword** - some appreciation of its methodology

Connector – But (contrast)

Prediction for Blank 1 – untrue

Prediction for Blank 2 – appreciation

Prediction for Blank 3 – important

Exaggerated, respect, and *pertinent* come closest to our prediction and should be the correct answer

SECTION 3

Sentence Equivalence

Sentence Equivalence

In a Sentence Equivalence question, you will have a sentence given to you with only one blank. There will be six options provided to you from which you need to select TWO options, both of which can be separately inserted in the blank. The thing to keep in mind is that both of these words, when inserted in the blank, should give the same meaning to the sentence. No partial credit will be given; you will be marked correct only if you get both the words correct in a sentence.

Use your knowledge of Keywords and Connectors to make a prediction for the blank and go with whichever two options best match your prediction.

You will get 4 Sentence Equivalence questions in each verbal section of the GRE (i.e. 8 questions in the entire test)

Tips to keep in mind when attempting Sentence Equivalence Questions

Have an answer in mind before you look at the options – It is always a good idea to have an answer in mind before you look at the options. At least you should be able to predict whether the word will be a positive or a negative one or whether there should be a relation between the words in a multiple blank sentence.

This strategy will also help you assess whether you are able to understand the meaning of the sentences correctly. If your predictions are correct but your actual answer is wrong, then you need to work on your vocabulary but if your prediction itself is incorrect then, even if you know all the words, you will not get the answer right. In this case you will need to start working on your comprehension.

Don't look for Synonyms – Some students tend to think of Sentence Equivalence questions as synonym questions i.e. they go looking for a pair of synonyms in the options and mark this pair as the correct choice. However, it is quite possible that the two correct options may not be exact synonyms, yet give similar meaning to the sentence when inserted in the blank. Thus, instead of concentrating on looking for synonyms, concentrate on understanding the meaning of the sentence conveyed by both the options.

Sometimes it is possible that three words all make sense in the blank but only two of these will provide a similar meaning to the sentence. This could be used as an elimination strategy

Sentence Equivalence Practice Set

1. The accounts, even of the best of ancient writers, should not be ___________ without examination, and a careful comparison with other sources of information.

    A abhorred

    B repudiated

    C adopted

    D verified

    E embraced

    F derided

2. To ___________ the dangers and distresses to which the holy men were exposed, nine noble knights formed a holy brotherhood to protect the pilgrims through the passes and defiles of the mountains.

    A alleviate

    B compound

    C incinerate

    D allay

    E fabricate

    F rarefy

3. The young man wanted to enlist with the army but his mother ___________ him.

- A abdicated
- B venerated
- C dissuaded
- D consecrated
- E discouraged
- F parodied

4. The arbitrators, hoping to end the dispute between the two friends, proposed a ___________ .

- A compromise
- B battle
- C paradox
- D truce
- E servitude
- F tyro

5. The renowned author's ___________ disposition reflects his passion for life.

- A austere
- B animated
- C lugubrious
- D lethargic
- E enervating
- F effervescent

6. Cryptozoology is the study of still unknown animals whose existence hasn't been ____________ .

- A hypothesized
- B proven
- C assessed
- D reneged
- E validated
- F scarified

7. A model's transformation into the ____________ image on the cover page that helps to sell magazines begins with a photographer's vision and requires numerous photo and wardrobe assistants, stylists, etc.

- A alluring
- B repelling
- C captivating
- D denigrating
- E emancipating
- F apathetic

8. Toddlers become ____________ at walking by imitating their parents and other elders.

- A malignant
- B adept
- C scrupulous
- D adroit
- E exuberant
- F dogmatic

9. The salesperson was known for being very ___________ so his colleagues found his sudden lethargy surprising.

- A lackadaisical
- B apathetic
- C assiduous
- D jocose
- E reclusive
- F sedulous

10. Despite their ___________ and disappointment, the supporters of the anti-corruption movement continued to work for their cause.

- A euphoria
- B remonstrations
- C befuddlement
- D disillusionment
- E recrimination
- F disgruntlement

11. Almost all cultures throughout history have had their own creation myth, suggesting that the origin of life is a subject of ___________ interest.

- A mundane
- B universal
- C unconventional
- D catholic
- E blatant
- F radical

12. Even though the judge tried to negotiate a settlement between the two parties, he remained __________ of the outcome because the parties refused to compromise.

- A sanguine
- B sceptical
- C deleterious
- D blissful
- E doubtful
- F gullible

13. Though the movie has mainly received __________ reviews, industry experts believe it is too early to write it off as a complete failure.

- A critical
- B unbiased
- C demeaning
- D deprecatory
- E uproarious
- F piquant

14. The horse refused to eat and kicked over the bucket to express his __________ .

- A indolence
- B felicity
- C reluctance
- D ire
- E resentment
- F pomposity

15. Because of voltage fluctuations, machines ___________ throughout the factory, preventing all production.

A malfunctioned

B berated

C corroborated

D burgeoned

E broke down

F censured

16. The usually composed actor shocked his staff by severely overreacting to the ___________ comments made by one of his fans.

A disparaging

B jocular

C verbose

D benign

E droll

F desultory

17. Despite their ___________ backgrounds, the freedom fighters overcame their differences in a united effort.

A rebellious

B audacious

C disparate

D fundamental

E sentimental

F inconsonant

18. ___________ the music store already has a set of loyal buyers, its owner is trying to expand her clientele by having promotional sales.

- A Since
- B Even though
- C Because
- D Interestingly
- E Surprisingly
- F Although

19. Experts often cite yelling at children ___________ and a poor way to help them learn.

- A inefficacious
- B competent
- C loathsome
- D uncanny
- E astute
- F fruitless

20. The French revolution was a powerful and ___________ occurrence because continued oppression gave the peasants no choice but to fight against the government.

- A ineluctable
- B exultant
- C unfathomable
- D inevitable
- E insurmountable
- F fortuitous

21. The haunting ___________ of the new artist's music stood in stark contrast to the bouncy jubilance of earlier artists.

- A melancholy
- B fallacy
- C enigma
- D bemusement
- E debilitation
- F anguish

22. Though microwaves are used for many purposes, they are most ___________ to us as an energy source for cooking food.

- A surprising
- B beneficial
- C familiar
- D accustomed
- E innocuous
- F cogent

23. When a baby first learns to walk he will generally walk cautiously, placing one foot ___________ in front of the other while trying to find his balance.

- A cognitively
- B confidently
- C tentatively
- D reassuringly
- E hesitatingly
- F equivocally

24. Many scientists believe that the universe is illimitable in size and that it will continue to expand ____________ .

- [A] bizarrely
- [B] erroneously
- [C] exceptionally
- [D] interminably
- [E] infinitely
- [F] exigently

25. Even though the telecom company seems to have cornered a large share of the market, its CEO insists that the company has no ____________ on the industry.

- [A] monopoly
- [B] gainsay
- [C] obscurity
- [D] penchant
- [E] onus
- [F] patent

26. The doctor praised the patient's ____________ nature and stated that she seemed to have an unconquerable spirit.

- [A] indomitable
- [B] indubitable
- [C] poignant
- [D] insurmountable
- [E] prescient
- [F] florid

27. A male tiger views his territory as ___________ and often engages in confrontations with any other male tiger that may wander within his territory.

- A sacrosanct
- B unsanctified
- C blithe
- D extant
- E formidable
- F inviolable

28. Although its effectiveness is not scientifically ___________, rice is believed by some to have powerful medicinal properties.

- A validated
- B juxtaposed
- C gainsaid
- D corroborated
- E insinuated
- F obviated

29. According to statistics, each year hundreds of thousands of old people who have outlived their ____________ to drive must depend on alternative transportation systems.

- A obsolescence
- B aptitude
- C precedent
- D faculty
- E resonance
- F stint

30. Modern museums are earnestly trying all that they can do to shore up __________ attendance.

A vacillating

B wavering

C declining

D dwindling

E relegating

F static

31. Because of his __________, Jason's guests felt well at ease staying at his house for the wedding.

A conviviality

B hostility

C acrimony

D salutation

E hegemony

F sociability

32. Although the manager's suggestions may have been useful, his language was so __________ that the Board of Directors could not understand most of the things he said.

A cogent

B esoteric

C piquant

D recondite

E curt

F deriding

33. Climbing a mountain such as the Everest is ____________ task, requiring months of physical and mental preparation.

- A an arduous
- B a piddling
- C a gruelling
- D a facile
- E an insurmountable
- F a specious

34. Anthony was worried about visiting a foreign country for the first time but the amiable people he met there helped ____________ his fears.

- A garner
- B exacerbate
- C compound
- D dispel
- E allay
- F inveigh

35. The problem with conservationists is that they are more concerned with ____________ the protection of the environment than actually doing something about it.

- A advocating
- B assailing
- C railing
- D championing
- E impugning
- F obtruding

36. ___________ the general's heroic efforts, his country still suffered a devastating loss.

A Undeterred by

B Owing to

C Despite

D Validating

E As a result of

F Notwithstanding

37. Although the ancient scriptures were well preserved, archaeologists were ___________ to decipher what was written on these scriptures.

A unable

B successful

C zestful

D unabashed

E ineffectual

F voracious

38. No action will be taken against the student for his intentions were found to be ___________ .

A rapacious

B benign

C urbane

D suave

E germane

F congenial

39. While some people love roses because of the ___________ appeal of their leaves and petals, some others are enthralled by their olfactory properties.

- A aesthetic
- B atheist
- C altruistic
- D exquisite
- E noisome
- F aromatic

40. George's ___________ for Geography should prove useful during his studies to become a Geography teacher.

- A abhorrence
- B fondness
- C affinity
- D antagonism
- E estrangement
- F reticence

41. The group felt ___________ when the court supported its actions.

- A despondent
- B ambivalent
- C vindicated
- D indignant
- E exonerated
- F coerced

42. Jimmy's manifest lack of enthusiasm about the job made the interviewer extremely ___________ to hire him because the company was looking for motivated employees who enjoyed what they did.

- A relieved
- B reluctant
- C ecstatic
- D apprehensive
- E audacious
- F egregious

43. The students were an unhappy lot because the teacher's directions on how to complete their project reports were extremely ___________ and ambiguous.

- A nebulous
- B cogent
- C luminous
- D brittle
- E vague
- F eugenic

44. Despite her capricious impulses, the CEO was actually quite ___________ when it came to making business decisions.

- A ephemeral
- B pragmatic
- C vocal
- D whimsical
- E grandiose
- F practical

45. People's fear of shark attacks is greatly __________ because every year more people die from lightning strikes than from shark attacks.

- A exaggerated
- B deprecated
- C implausible
- D amplified
- E intrepid
- F irremediable

46. Despite cotton gin's __________ effect on American industry, the gin also played a role in causing the continuation of slavery in America.

- A propitious
- B deleterious
- C maladroit
- D virulent
- E sardonic
- F salubrious

47. Crop rotation is considered useful by agriculturists because it helps to preserve soil nutrients, control disease, and __________ weed growth.

- A ameliorate
- B deter
- C stultify
- D suffuse
- E tumefy
- F jeopardize

48. In recent years the demand for trained guards has declined owing to the ___________ of electronic devices, such as motion detection equipment, that can offer better protection.

A	proliferation
B	proclivity
C	impairment
D	insolence
E	burgeoning
F	predilection

49. The ___________ speaker bellowed and provoked the protesters at the rally.

A	sardonic
B	impassive
C	fervent
D	impassioned
E	robust
F	stolid

50. After several rejections, the actor was ___________, certain that he would never act in a movie.

A	dejected
B	devout
C	luminous
D	flamboyant
E	sedentary
F	crestfallen

51. Although initially he felt great ____________ about going skydiving, John was eventually able to overcome his fear.

A consternation

B abnegation

C trepidation

D euphoria

E tranquillity

F passion

52. To counter the recession, the company decided to ____________ with another firm, forming one of the largest conglomerates in the country.

A renege

B merge

C obloquy

D unify

E satiate

F pillory

53. If not for ____________ human efforts, the Kirtland's warbler would probably not exist today.

A sustained

B laconic

C parochial

D perfunctory

E diligent

F oracular

54. Despite an ongoing ___________ for immortality, the emperor died at the age of 49 while travelling.

- A martinet
- B quest
- C intransigence
- D impertinence
- E questioning
- F crusade

55. Evolution is a ___________ issue and has been the subject of debate for years.

- A infallible
- B amicable
- C polemical
- D imperious
- E contentious
- F inexpedient

56. Eager to shift jobs, Tegra accepted the proffered offer with ___________ .

- A melancholy
- B alacrity
- C anguish
- D sprightliness
- E apathy
- F fealty

57. Andre's ___________ approach towards work means that he is seldom able to meet his deadlines.

- A insolent
- B succinct
- C felonious
- D indolent
- E lackadaisical
- F turbid

58. Although at times extremely contemptuous of internal employees, companies are unwilling to treat external consultants with equal ___________ .

- A criticism
- B indifference
- C antipathy
- D torpor
- E veracity
- F imminence

59. The pessimistic political candidate's ideas are extremely ___________ .

- A sanguine
- B bleak
- C incorrigible
- D dreary
- E grandiloquent
- F heretical

60. Thousands, perhaps even millions, of people around the world are ___________ with a neurological condition called *synesthesia.*

- A placated
- B frustrated
- C afflicted
- D enunciated
- E plagued
- F disparaged

61. The employee was certain that his ___________ at the party would cause him to be fired.

- A zealousness
- B misdeeds
- C eccentricities
- D appellation
- E cognizance
- F transgressions

62. It is difficult to ___________ all the costs associated with starting a new venture so prospective entrepreneurs should always build up a certain level of flexibility in their business plans.

- A doubt
- B anticipate
- C galvanize
- D foresee
- E attenuate
- F fructify

63. In addition to advising freshmen who have just joined college, Mr. Patterson regularly _________ senior students as well regarding career opportunities available for them when they pass out.

- A counsels
- B reprimands
- C admonishes
- D inveighs
- E guides
- F maunders

64. The movie's plot was extremely ___________, with the numerous twists and turns making it impossible to comprehend for most people.

- A prolix
- B tortuous
- C pristine
- D convoluted
- E banal
- F prosaic

65. ___________ of the government complain that the policy makers are focusing on short-term goals while ignoring the long-term benefits of the citizens.

- A Sycophants
- B Zealots
- C Critics
- D Renegades
- E Allies
- F Antagonists

66. The senator was criticized for his inconsistency in the matter as he frequently ___________ from one side of the issue to the other.

- A pined
- B vacillated
- C inundated
- D wavered
- E waivered
- F reviled

67. The car had been ___________ so many times before it reached the assembly line that its original conception was no longer recognizable.

- A refurbished
- B proselytized
- C sanctioned
- D umbraged
- E rejuvenated
- F tethered

68. ___________ by the poor result, the student began to question his abilities.

- A vindicated
- B disconsolate
- C absolved
- D dejected
- E unabashed
- F tousled

69. John is ___________ and vituperative speaker, equally harsh towards both friends and foes.

- A an opprobrious
- B an intimidating
- C an unfathomable
- D a timorous
- E a solicitous
- F a contemptuous

70. The writer's novels are ___________ ; he uses long circumlocution when a simple sentence would suffice.

- A terse
- B succinct
- C prolix
- D subtle
- E sordid
- F verbose

71. The director's movies have an air of capriciousness: just when you think the story line is getting _________ , he suddenly takes a different direction.

- A bizarre
- B inexplicable
- C predictable
- D foreseeable
- E succulent
- F reprehensible

72. The aspiring candidate's performance in the debate ____________ any chance he may have had of winning the election.

- A sanctifies
- B nullifies
- C validates
- D abrogates
- E quarries
- F plagiarizes

73. Joanna is one of the most ____________ persons in the office, having a seemingly endless reserve of energy.

- A lethargic
- B generous
- C enervating
- D vivacious
- E benevolent
- F ebullient

74. Despite all its ____________ , a stint with the army is a life-changing experience.

- A pliability
- B tribulations
- C precursors
- D rigors
- E leniency
- F warmth

75. Man is by nature violent and any theory that fails to account for this fact is inherently __________ .

[A] awry
[B] flawless
[C] fulgent
[D] omnipotent
[E] mitigated
[F] fallacious

76. Although the buildings in the beach town appear __________ , the property values are quite high.

[A] majestic
[B] dilapidated
[C] obsequious
[D] pellucid
[E] lissome
[F] derelict

77. Though John claimed that all was well between him and his wife, his constant irritability __________ that claim.

[A] bolstered
[B] attested
[C] belied
[D] contradicted
[E] buttressed
[F] encapsulated

78. The rules of engagement ____________ deadly force unless all alternative actions have been exhausted.

- A proscribe
- B forbid
- C ridicule
- D embolden
- E rouse
- F condone

79. The people have become so ____________ to corruption that the recent financial scandal did not even make the front pages of newspapers.

- A entrenched
- B desensitized
- C benumbed
- D animated
- E enlivened
- F expiated

80. In current political times, it has become ____________ to discuss certain subjects lest one end up antagonizing the feelings of some group.

- A beguiling
- B loathe
- C phlegmatic
- D abhorrent
- E pragmatic
- F antediluvian

81. Although the stock market has shown a healthy growth over the past one year, there have been short periods in which the market has fallen ___________ .

A sharply
B gradually
C rarely
D ruefully
E precipitously
F imperviously

82. The teachers' stern ___________ towards the children was countered with plenty of love.

A insolence
B impuissance
C disposition
D equanimity
E deference
F demeanour

83. The public was surprised to hear the otherwise ___________ author make such a pompous remark.

A braggart
B modest
C uncouth
D unpretentious
E conceited
F egotistical

84. Despite being sympathetic to the cause, the judge showed no __________ in announcing his verdict.

A remorse

B impartiality

C partisanship

D bias

E reticence

F chagrin

85. Though Henry had a reputation for being __________, at times he could be quite serious.

A jocose

B melancholy

C grandiloquent

D verbose

E droll

F irascible

86. __________ a comprehensive study has yet to be done about the harmful effects of mobile phones, we don't even know the amount of time an average person spends talking on the mobile phone.

A Despite

B Because

C Since

D In spite of

E Hence

F So that

87. The army chief accused the senator of ___________ for suggesting that war was the only option available to them because the senator was unaware of the ground realities of the situation.

- A treason
- B collusion
- C naiveté
- D inexperience
- E artifice
- F felony

88. Though miserly towards his own needs, the philanthropist was always ___________ toward others.

- A pusillanimous
- B impecunious
- C parsimonious
- D magnanimous
- E cantankerous
- F munificent

89. The coach should not be held responsible for the ___________ performance of the team for no one could have predicted the complete failure on the part of the team's star players to perform during the tournament.

- A laudable
- B fortuitous
- C deplorable
- D indiscreet
- E execrable
- F impetuous

90. Although onion prices rose during the strike, suppliers actually reported ___________ in profits.

A an increase

B a wane

C a slump

D an inundation

E an ossification

F a proliferation

91. Once upon a time integration was ___________ to most Americans; now, however, most of them view it as desirable.

A an anathema

B a boom

C a benediction

D a utopia

E a malediction

F a travesty

92. An admirable person is one who overcomes his ___________ impulses and becomes good.

A commendable

B baser

C scrupulous

D sententious

E ignoble

F viscous

93. Although the war ended a decade ago, the two countries have been ___________ to develop more amiable relations.

- A reticent
- B open
- C vituperative
- D vying
- E xenophobic
- F hesitant

94. While tone defines the overall language used by a writer,___________ deals with the specific kinds of words and phrases that the writer uses.

- A iconoclasm
- B diction
- C valediction
- D verbiage
- E transient
- F shibboleth

95. Some people believe that students can learn better by studying ___________ at home rather than by studying in groups in schools or colleges.

- A independently
- B unwittingly
- C assiduously
- D solo
- E sporadically
- F languidly

96. Clichés are overused phrases that prevent one's writing from being fresh and ___________ .

A trite

B banal

C original

D interesting

E rancorous

F intrepid

97. Spending restrictions represent just one of the many ways that freedom is ___________ when purchasing a new home.

A buttressed

B bolstered

C reaffirmed

D curtailed

E restrained

F exculpated

98. Because competition can ___________ people better than anything else can, it is essential for a growing and thriving society.

A dissuade

B rouse

C disgruntle

D galvanize

E impede

F mitigate

99. The ___________ with speed has thrown modern society into such a frenzy that even the most technologically advanced equipment appears unsatisfactorily slow.

A indifference

B onus

C obsession

D obeisance

E paradox

F fixation

100. Although public figures should expect some ___________ into their lives, the media often goes overboard with its efforts to report the same.

A opprobrium

B pillage

C scrutiny

D recalcitrance

E interference

F quiddity

Sentence Equivalence - Answers & Explanations

Q No.	Answer	Q No.	Answer	Q No.	Answer	Q No.	Answer
1	C, E	26	A, D	51	A, C	76	B, F
2	A, D	27	A, F	52	B, D	77	C, D
3	C, E	28	A, D	53	A, E	78	A, B
4	A, D	29	B, D	54	B, F	79	B, C
5	B, F	30	C, D	55	C, E	80	B, D
6	B, E	31	A, F	56	B, D	81	A, E
7	A, C	32	B, D	57	D, E	82	C, F
8	B, D	33	A, C	58	A, C	83	B, D
9	C, F	34	D, E	59	B, D	84	C, D
10	D, F	35	A, D	60	C, E	85	A, E
11	B, D	36	C, F	61	B, F	86	B, C
12	B, E	37	A, E	62	B, D	87	C, D
13	A, D	38	B, F	63	A, E	88	D, F
14	D, E	39	A, D	64	B, D	89	C, E
15	A, E	40	B, C	65	C, F	90	B, C
16	B, E	41	C, E	66	B, D	91	A, E
17	C, F	42	B, D	67	A, E	92	B, E
18	B, F	43	A, E	68	B, D	93	A, F
19	A, F	44	B, F	69	A, F	94	B, D
20	A, D	45	A, D	70	C, F	95	A, D
21	A, F	46	A, F	71	C, D	96	C, D
22	C, D	47	B, C	72	B, D	97	D, E
23	C, E	48	A, E	73	D, F	98	B, D
24	D, E	49	C, D	74	B, D	99	C, F
25	A, F	50	A, F	75	A, F	100	C, E

1) **Keyword** - careful comparison with other sources of information
   Connector – None (same direction)
   Prediction – accepted, believed
   Adopted and *Embraced* fit in best with our prediction and should be the correct answers

2) **Keyword** - holy brotherhood to protect the pilgrims
   Connector – None (same direction)
   Prediction – reduce, rid
   Alleviate and *Allay* fit in best with our prediction and should be the correct answers

3) **Keyword** - wanted to enlist with the army
   Connector – But (contrast)
   Prediction – discouraged, stopped
   Dissuaded and *Discouraged* fit in best with our prediction and should be the correct answers

4) **Keyword** - hoping to end the dispute between the two friends,
   Connector – None (same direction)
   Prediction – ceasefire
   Compromise and *Truce* fit in best with our prediction and should be the correct answers

5) **Keyword** - reflects his passion for life
   Connector – reflects (same direction)
   Prediction – cheerful, vivacious
   Animated and *Effervescent* fit in best with our prediction and should be the correct answers

6) **Keyword** - unknown animals
   Connector – None (same direction)
   Prediction – proved, verified
   Proven and *Validated* fit in best with our prediction and should be the correct answers

7) **Keyword** - image on the cover page that helps to sell magazines
   Connector – None (same direction)
   Prediction – attractive, beautiful
   Alluring and *Captivating* fit in best with our prediction and should be the correct answers

8) **Keyword** - by imitating their parents
Connector – None (same direction)
Prediction – skilled
Adept and *Adroit* fit in best with our prediction and should be the correct answers

9) **Keyword** - sudden laziness
Connector – so (same direction)
Prediction – hard working, meticulous
Assiduous and *Sedulous* fit in best with our prediction and should be the correct answers

10) **Keyword** - continued to work
Connector – Despite (contrast)
Prediction – any negative word similar to disappointment
Disillusionment and *Disgruntlement* fit in best with our prediction and should be the correct answers

11) **Keyword** - all cultures
Connector – None (same direction)
Prediction – common, shared
Universal and *Catholic* fit in best with our prediction and should be the correct answers

12) **Keyword** - tried to negotiate a settlement
Connector – Even though (contrast)
Prediction – unsure, hesitant
Sceptical and *Doubtful* fit in best with our prediction and should be the correct answers

13) **Keyword** - it is too early to write it off
Connector – Though (contrast)
Prediction – poor, negative
Critical and *Deprecatory* fit in best with our prediction and should be the correct answers

14) **Keyword** - refused to eat and kicked over the bucket
Connector – None (same direction)
Prediction – unhappiness, anger
Ire and *Resentment* fit in best with our prediction and should be the correct answers

15) **Keyword** - preventing all production
Connector – Because of (same direction)
Prediction – failed
Malfunctioned and *Broke down* fit in best with our prediction and should be the correct answers

16) **Keyword** - usually composed actor shocked his staff
Connector – None (same direction)
Prediction – harmless, trivial
Jocular and *Droll* fit in best with our prediction and should be the correct answers
Note that while disparaging and desultory are also similar words with negative connotations, we cannot go with these because the staff members feel that the actor overreacted. If a comment was deprecatory or insulting, then the actor's reaction can hardly be called an 'overreaction'

17) **Keyword** - overcame their differences
Connector – Despite (contrast)
Prediction – different, varied
Disparate and *Inconsonant* fit in best with our prediction and should be the correct answers

18) **Keyword** - trying to expand her clientele
Connector – needs to be inserted. We need a contrasting Connector to indicate that even though the store already has buyers, it wants to attract even more buyers
Prediction – although, despite
Even though and *Although* fit in best with our prediction and should be the correct answers

19) **Keyword** - way to help them learn
Connector – None (same direction)
Prediction – useless, ineffective
Inefficacious and *Fruitless* fit in best with our prediction and should be the correct answers

20) **Keyword** - no choice but to fight
Connector – Because (same direction)
Prediction – unavoidable, inescapable
Ineluctable and *Inevitable* fit in best with our prediction and should be the correct answers

21) **Keyword** - bouncy jubilance
Connector – contrast (contrast)
Prediction – sad, gloomy
Anguish and *Melancholy* fit in best with our prediction and should be the correct answers

22) **Keyword** - used for many purposes
Connector – Though (contrast)
Prediction – useful, known
Familiar and *Accustomed* fit in best with our prediction and should be the correct answers

Note that 'beneficial' could also fit in the blank but there is no other word in the remaining options that means or comes close to meaning beneficial

23) **Keyword** - he will generally walk cautiously
Connector – None (same direction)
Prediction – carefully, cautiously
Tentatively and *Hesitatingly* fit in best with our prediction and should be the correct answers

24) **Keyword** - universe is illimitable in size
Connector – and (same direction)
Prediction – continuously, forever
Interminably and *Infinitely* fit in best with our prediction and should be the correct answers

25) **Keyword** - cornered a large share of the market
Connector – Even though (contrast)
Prediction – control, stronghold
Monopoly and *Patent* fit in best with our prediction and should be the correct answers

26) **Keyword** - an unconquerable spirit.

Connector – and (same direction)

Prediction – never say die

Indomitable and *Insurmountable* fit in best with our prediction and should be the correct answers

27) **Keyword** - engages in confrontations

Connector – And (same direction)

Prediction – sacred

Inviolable and *Sacrosanct* fit in best with our prediction and should be the correct answers

28) **Keyword** - to have powerful medicinal properties

Connector – Although (contrast)

Prediction – proven

Validated and *Corroborated* fit in best with our prediction and should be the correct answers

29) **Keyword** - must depend on alternative transportation systems

Connector – None (same direction)

Prediction – will, desire

Aptitude and *Faculty* fit in best with our prediction and should be the correct answers

30) **Keyword** - to shore up

Connector – None (same direction)

Prediction – falling, declining

Declining and *Dwindling* fit in best with our prediction and should be the correct answers

Note that vacillating and wavering are also synonyms but cannot be the answers because they mean changing so the numbers could both go up and down. However we want our sentence to mean that the numbers are continuously going down.

31) **Keyword** - felt well at ease staying at his house

Connector – Because of (same direction)

Prediction – friendliness, hospitality

Conviviality and *Sociability* fit in best with our prediction and should be the correct answers

32) **Keyword** - could not understand most of the things

Connector – Although (contrast)

Prediction – difficult, complex

Esoteric and *Recondite* fit in best with our prediction and should be the correct answers

33) **Keyword** - months of physical and mental preparation

Connector – None (same direction)

Prediction – difficult, challenging

Arduous and *Gruelling* fit in best with our prediction and should be the correct answers

34) **Keyword** - worried about visiting a foreign country

Connector – But (contrast)

Prediction – remove, rid

Allay and *Dispel* fit in best with our prediction and should be the correct answers

35) **Keyword** - than actually doing something about it

Connector – more….than (contrast)

Prediction – speaking about

Advocating and *Championing* fit in best with our prediction and should be the correct answers

36) **Keyword** - still suffered a devastating loss

Connector – Needs to be inserted. Since the country suffered a loss, the word has to be a contrasting one

Prediction – despite, inspite of

Despite and *Notwithstanding* fit in best with our prediction and should be the correct answers

37) **Keyword** - well preserved

Connector – Although (contrast)

Prediction – unable

Unable and *Ineffectual* fit in best with our prediction and should be the correct answers

38) **Keyword** - No action will be taken
Connector – for (same direction)
Prediction – good, honest
Benign and *Congenial* fit in best with our prediction and should be the correct answers

39) **Keyword** - enthralled by their olfactory properties
Connector – While (contrast)
Prediction – beauty
Aesthetic and *Exquisite* fit in best with our prediction and should be the correct answers

40) **Keyword** - prove useful
Connector – None (same direction)
Prediction – liking
Fondness and *Affinity* fit in best with our prediction and should be the correct answers

41) **Keyword** - the court supported its actions
Connector – None (same direction)
Prediction – proved right
Vindicated and *Exonerated* fit in best with our prediction and should be the correct answers

42) **Keyword** - lack of enthusiasm
Connector – because (same direction)
Prediction – wary, unwilling
Reluctant and *Apprehensive* fit in best with our prediction and should be the correct answers

43) **Keyword** - were an unhappy lot
Connector – because (same direction)
Prediction – any pair of negative words with similar meanings
Nebulous and *Vague* fit in best with our prediction and should be the correct answers

44) **Keyword** - capricious impulses
Connector – Despite (contrast)
Prediction – practical, rational
Pragmatic and *Practical* fit in best with our prediction and should be the correct answers

45) **Keyword** - more people die from lightning strikes than from shark attacks.
Connector – Because (same direction)
Prediction – not correct, blown out of proportion
Exaggerated and *Amplified* fit in best with our prediction and should be the correct answers

46) **Keyword** - causing the continuation of slavery
Connector – Despite (contrast)
Prediction – beneficial, positive
Salubrious and *Propitious* fit in best with our prediction and should be the correct answers

47) **Keyword** - considered useful
Connector – Because (same direction)
Prediction – prevent, discourage
Deter and *Stultify* fit in best with our prediction and should be the correct answers

48) **Keyword** - demand for trained guards has declined
Connector – owing to (same direction)
Prediction – increase
Proliferation and *Burgeoning* fit in best with our prediction and should be the correct answers

49) **Keyword** - bellowed and provoked the protesters
Connector – None (same direction)
Prediction – effective, rousing
Fervent and *Impassioned* fit in best with our prediction and should be the correct answers

50) **Keyword** - certain that he would never act
Connector – None (same direction)
Prediction – sad, disappointed
Dejected and *Crestfallen* fit in best with our prediction and should be the correct answers

51) **Keyword** - eventually able to overcome his fear.
Connector – Although (contrast)
Prediction – fear, nervousness
Consternation and *Trepidation* fit in best with our prediction and should be the correct answers

52) **Keyword** - forming one of the largest conglomerates

Connector – None (same direction)

Prediction – combine, merge

Merge and *Unify* fit in best with our prediction and should be the correct answers

53) **Keyword** - would probably not exist today

Connector – not (contrast)

Prediction – dedicated, continuous

Sustained and *Diligent* fit in best with our prediction and should be the correct answers

54) **Keyword** - emperor died at the age of 49

Connector – Despite (contrast)

Prediction – search, desire

Quest and *Crusade* fit in best with our prediction and should be the correct answers

55) **Keyword** - subject of debate

Connector – None (same direction)

Prediction – argumentative, controversial

Polemical and *Contentious* fit in best with our prediction and should be the correct answers

56) **Keyword** - Eager to shift jobs

Connector – None (same direction)

Prediction – enthusiasm

Alacrity and *Sprightliness* fit in best with our prediction and should be the correct answers

57) **Keyword** - he is seldom able to meet his deadlines

Connector – None (same direction)

Prediction – casual, lazy

Indolent and *Lackadaisical* fit in best with our prediction and should be the correct answers

58) **Keyword** - extremely contemptuous of internal employees

Connector – Although (contrast)

Prediction – contempt

Criticism and *Antipathy* fit in best with our prediction and should be the correct answers

59) **Keyword** - pessimistic political candidate's ideas
Connector – None (same direction)
Prediction – pessimistic, negative
Bleak and *Dreary* fit in best with our prediction and should be the correct answers

60) **Keyword** - neurological condition
Connector – None (same direction)
Prediction – suffer from
Afflicted and *Plagued* fit in best with our prediction and should be the correct answers

61) **Keyword** - cause him to be fired
Connector – None (same direction)
Prediction – negative actions
Misdeeds and *Transgressions* fit in best with our prediction and should be the correct answers

62) **Keyword** - prospective entrepreneurs should always build up a certain level of flexibility
Connector – so (same direction)
Prediction – estimate
Anticipate and *Foresee* fit in best with our prediction and should be the correct answers

63) **Keyword** - advising freshmen
Connector – In addition (same direction)
Prediction – gives advice to, assists
Counsels and *Guides* fit in best with our prediction and should be the correct answers

64) **Keyword** - numerous twists and turns making it impossible to comprehend
Connector – None (same direction)
Prediction – complex, confusing
Tortuous and *Convoluted* fit in best with our prediction and should be the correct answers

65) **Keyword** - complain
Connector – None (same direction)
Prediction – Opponents
Critics and *Antagonists* fit in best with our prediction and should be the correct answers

66) **Keyword** - inconsistency in the matter
Connector – for (same direction)
Prediction – changed, shifted
Vacillated and *Wavered* fit in best with our prediction and should be the correct answers

67) **Keyword** – its original conception was no longer recognizable
Connector – None (same direction)
Prediction – redesigned, changed
Refurbished and *Rejuvenated* fit in best with our prediction and should be the correct answers

68) **Keyword** - question his abilities
Connector – None (same direction)
Prediction – Disappointed, sad
Disconsolate and *Dejected* fit in best with our prediction and should be the correct answers

69) **Keyword** - equally harsh
Connector – None (same direction)
Prediction – any negative word similar in meaning to vituperative
Opprobrious and *Contemptuous* fit in best with our prediction and should be the correct answers

70) **Keyword** - he uses long circumlocution
Connector – ; (same direction)
Prediction – lengthy, long
Prolix and *Verbose* fit in best with our prediction and should be the correct answers

71) **Keyword** - have an air of capriciousness
Connector – : (same direction)
Prediction – common, predictable
Predictable and *Foreseeable* fit in best with our prediction and should be the correct answers

72) **Keyword** - chance he may have had of winning the election
Connector – None (same direction)
Prediction – removed
Nullifies and *Abrogates* fit in best with our prediction and should be the correct answers

73) **Keyword** - seemingly having an endless reserve of energy
Connector – None (same direction)
Prediction – lively, energetic
Vivacious and *Ebullient* fit in best with our prediction and should be the correct answers

74) **Keyword** - is a life-changing experience
Connector – Despite (contrast)
Prediction – difficulties, problems
Tribulations and *Rigors* fit in best with our prediction and should be the correct answers

75) **Keyword** - theory that fails to account for this
Connector – And (same direction)
Prediction – wrong
Fallacious and *Awry* fit in best with our prediction and should be the correct answers

76) **Keyword** - property values are quite high
Connector – Although (contrast)
Prediction – in a poor condition
Dilapidated and *Derelict* fit in best with our prediction and should be the correct answers

77) **Keyword** - all was well between him and his wife
Connector – Though (contrast)
Prediction – falsified
Belied and *Contradicted* fit in best with our prediction and should be the correct answers

78) **Keyword** - all alternative actions have been exhausted

Connector – None (same direction)

Prediction – stop, prohibit

Proscribe and *Forbid* fit in best with our prediction and should be the correct answers

79) **Keyword** - financial scandal did not even make the front pages

Connector – so....that (same direction)

Prediction – immune, used to

Desensitized and *Benumbed* fit in best with our prediction and should be the correct answers

80) **Keyword** - one end up antagonizing the feelings

Connector – None (same direction)

Prediction – improper, incorrect

Loathe and *Abhorrent* fit in best with our prediction and should be the correct answers

81) **Keyword** - has shown a healthy growth

Connector – Although (contrast)

Prediction – sharply

Precipitously and *Sharply* fit in best with our prediction and should be the correct answers

82) **Keyword** - with plenty of love

Connector – countered (contrast)

Prediction – behaviour

Demeanour and *Disposition* fit in best with our prediction and should be the correct answers

83) **Keyword** - such a pompous remark

Connector – Not a clear Connector as such but the use of the words 'surprised' and 'otherwise' suggests that there has to be a contrast between 'pompous' and the word that goes in the blank (same direction)

Prediction – modest, unassuming

Modest and *Unpretentious* fit in best with our prediction and should be the correct answers

84) **Keyword** - sympathetic to the cause

Connector – Despite (contrast)

Prediction – partiality, favouritism

Partisanship and *Bias* fit in best with our prediction and should be the correct answers

85) **Keyword** - could be quite serious

Connector – Though (contrast)

Prediction – funny, carefree

Jocose and *Droll* fit in best with our prediction and should be the correct answers

86) **Keyword** - we don't even know

Connector – Needs to be inserted. The sentence implies a causal relationship between the parts before and after the comma. Hence we need to go with a same direction Connector

Prediction – Because

Because and *Since* fit in best with our prediction and should be the correct answers

87) **Keyword** - the senator was unaware

Connector – Because (same direction)

Prediction – ignorance

Naiveté and *Inexperience* fit in best with our prediction and should be the correct answers

88) **Keyword** - miserly towards his own needs

Connector – Though (contrast)

Prediction – generous

Magnanimous and *Munificent* fit in best with our prediction and should be the correct answers

89) **Keyword** - no one could have predicted the complete failure

Connector – For (same direction)

Prediction – poor

Deplorable and *Execrable* fit in best with our prediction and should be the correct answers

90) **Keyword** - onion prices rose

Connector – Although (contrast)

Prediction – fall, reduction

Wane and *Slump* fit in best with our prediction and should be the correct answers

91) **Keyword** - most of them view it as desirable

Connector – However (contrast)

Prediction – curse, a hated thing

Anathema and *Malediction* fit in best with our prediction and should be the correct answers

92) **Keyword** - admirable person is one who overcomes

Connector – None (same direction)

Prediction – negative

Ignoble and *Baser* fit in best with our prediction and should be the correct answers

93) **Keyword** - war ended a decade ago

Connector – Although (contrast)

Prediction – unwilling

Reticent and *Hesitant* fit in best with our prediction and should be the correct answers

94) **Keyword** - specific kinds of words and phrases

Connector – None (same direction). The contrasting 'while' at the beginning of the sentence can be ignored because the meaning of the word that goes in the blank is already given to us in form of the keyword

Prediction – proper use of words

Diction and *Verbiage* fit in best with our prediction and should be the correct answers

95) **Keyword** - by studying in groups

Connector – rather than (contrast)

Prediction – alone, independently

Independently and *Solo* fit in best with our prediction and should be the correct answers

96) **Keyword** - are overused phrases

Connector – None (same direction)

Prediction – original

Original and *Interesting* fit in best with our prediction and should be the correct answers. All other options are actually negative and hence can be eliminated

97) **Keyword** - Spending restrictions

Connector – None (same direction)

Prediction – cut down, limited

Restrained and *Curtailed* fit in best with our prediction and should be the correct answers

98) **Keyword** - it is essential for a growing and thriving society

Connector – Because (same direction)

Prediction – encourage, motivate

Rouse and *Galvanize* fit in best with our prediction and should be the correct answers

99) **Keyword** - thrown modern society into such a frenzy

Connector – None (same direction)

Prediction – preoccupation

Obsession and *Fixation* fit in best with our prediction and should be the correct answers

100) **Keyword** - media often goes overboard

Connector – Although (contrast)

Prediction – interference

Scrutiny and *Interference* fit in best with our prediction and should be the correct answers

SECTION 4

Reading Comprehension

Reading Comprehension

As the name suggests, Reading Comprehension (RC) questions will test students on their understanding or comprehension of unfamiliar texts from short or long passages. Each passage will be followed by a few questions related to that passage. On an average, students will see 10 Reading Comprehension questions in each verbal reasoning section spread across 5 passages. Most of the passages appearing on the GRE will be short passages of approximately 80-150 words though students may see one or two long passages as well comprising 300-400 words.

How much Time should you spend on each Passage?

You will need to complete 20 questions in 30 minutes in each verbal section. Thus you have roughly one and a half minutes for each question. However, RC questions will take you a little longer to answer so you must save on time while answering Sentence Equivalence and Text Completion questions.

Ideally you should take at the most one minute for each Sentence Equivalence and Text Completion question, which will leave you with 20 minutes to answer the 10 Reading Comprehension questions.

Nature of Passages

The passages that you see on the GRE will primarily be from the following subject areas:

- Physical Sciences
- Social Sciences
- Humanities
- Business & Economics

The passages will not always be interesting or fun to read; as a matter of fact some of them will be downright boring and difficult to understand. The language of the passages will be similar to what you are likely to see in publications such as The Economist and The Wall Street Journal. Generally, passages from Physical Sciences and Business & Economics subject areas tend to be more detail-oriented and easier to understand than passages from Social Sciences and Humanities, which mostly tend to be of an abstract nature.

The problem most students face on RC is that they have to go through text from areas they aren't conversant with and answer questions based on this. The moment you see a passage from an unfamiliar area such as American History or Women's Suffrage, you immediately start telling yourself that you will do badly on this passage because you have no idea about the subject area. If you start with this negative thought process, things will obviously only go downhill for you.

Please keep in mind that you are not expected to have any prior knowledge of the topic in the first place. All the information that you need to answer the questions is given to you in the passage. You just need to comprehend the passage and select the correct answer from the options provided. In fact there is a negative aspect of getting passages from your comfort area which will be discussed later in this book.

How NOT to Approach RC Passages

Whenever we read some text, it is human tendency to focus on the facts provided. We tend to focus on specific details, numbers, and dates but in the process end up missing out on the big picture, which provides the answer to the question 'WHY'. Why has the author provided these figures or details? This is the purpose of the author in writing this paragraph. If you concentrate on the details and miss out on this 'WHY' aspect, then you will always struggle to answer RC questions correctly.

This is because most questions will not directly ask you something that is clearly mentioned in the passage; rather the questions will be more roundabout and indirect in nature. The answer to most of the questions will not be clearly stated in the passage so it does not make sense to spend valuable time trying to absorb all the details mentioned in the passage.

Make a Passage Map

A good way of approaching a passage, especially a long one, is to make a map of the passage. A passage map is nothing but one or two lines for every paragraph in the passage, highlighting *why* the author has written that paragraph. Note that the passage map does not have to highlight *what* the author has written but rather *why* has he written what he has written, which means that the points in your passage map should always start with verbs such as *describe, explain, praise, criticize, condemn,* etc. Most of the time you will find this information in either the first or the last sentence of each paragraph. Students often tend to focus on the middle part of paragraphs (which contains all the details) so please make a conscious effort to go back and read the first and the last sentence of every paragraph so as to keep a perspective of why the author is writing what he is writing.

Topic, Scope and Purpose

Apart from the passage map, there are three more things you need to be absolutely clear about before you look at the first question – The Topic, the Scope and the Purpose of the passage.

The topic of the passage is nothing but a word or a phrase that captures the essence of the passage. The topic tells you what subject matter the entire passage revolves around. The GRE will rarely ever ask you to identify the topic of the passage; this is more for your understanding of the passage.

The scope of the passage basically tells you what aspect of the topic is the passage concerned with. The understanding of the scope becomes important because this helps you eliminate incorrect options quickly.

The purpose is the most important part of the passage and will answer the question – *why did the author write the entire passage?* When thinking about the purpose, think on three lines – is the author positive i.e. is he trying to praise or support something, is the author negative i.e. is he trying to criticize something, or is the author simply neutral i.e. is he just describing or explaining something. Obviously this will also clarify the tone of the passage for you. If you are clear about the purpose of the passage, you will not have to keep referring back to the passage to check each option; rather you will be able to eliminate a lot of the options just by looking at them because they contradict the author's primary purpose.

For example, if you know that the main purpose of the author is positive and there is a question asking you, to select from five options, that one option the author would most likely agree with; then you can immediately eliminate options with negative connotations because the author has a positive agenda. Thus, identifying the purpose correctly will save you a lot of time on GRE RC and also make you more confident of your eliminations.

The GRE will often ask you to identify the main purpose of the passage, so it's all the more important that you be clear on this aspect. We'll discuss this more in the section on Global questions.

Even though most RC passages on the GRE will be just one paragraph long, it still makes sense to be clear on the topic, scope, and purpose of the passage.

Avoid making this mistake

A common mistake students make while preparing a passage map is to make notes for every sentence in a paragraph. They will read one sentence and make a note for that sentence and then come back and read the next sentence and again make a note for it and so on. Needless to say this is an absolute waste of time and beats the purpose of making the passage map in the first place.

As we said earlier, the passage map should answer the *why* and not the *what*. We do not want you to write any details in the passage map. The details are already there in front of you on your screen and you can refer to them whenever a question requires you to do so. We will go as far as to suggest that you should not even try to understand everything that is written in the paragraph, as long as you are able to understand why the author has written what he has written.

For example, a paragraph could start by stating that there are two theories put forward by economists to explain how the foreign exchange markets work. The rest of the paragraph could go into explaining these two theories out of which one you may not have understood. This is fine; do not waste your time re-

reading the paragraph, just move on to the next paragraph. If there is any question on this particular theory then you can always come back and read this part again, else you would have saved yourself valuable time. It is this kind of street-smartness that will be rewarded on the GRE.

Do not confuse the author's views with his statements

While reading the passage, be careful to differentiate between when the author is stating something and when is the author attributing a comment to somebody else. For example, if the author were to make a statement such as *'Critics of the Theory of Relativity believe that the theory is incorrect'* – do not construe this as the author criticizing anything. The author is merely providing you the opinion of the critics and is neutral by himself.

This is especially true in the case of passages in which the author is reviewing the work of some other author or individual. In such passages make sure that you also read the questions properly because some questions could be from the point of view of the author of the passage while some others could be from the point of view of the author or scholar whose work is being evaluated.

Engage with the Passage – Do not read Passively

While reading, try to engage with the passage. This will also help prevent your concentration from wandering. The best way to get yourself involved with the passage is to try to predict what will come next in the passage. When you do this, you are essentially putting yourself in the author's shoes and thinking like him, which will help you get a great understanding of the passage. Use the last sentence of a paragraph to predict what will come in the next paragraph.

For example, if the paragraph ends by stating that scientists have proposed a solution for a problem, the next paragraph will most probably provide you with the details of this solution. Once you see that most of your predictions are turning out to be correct, you will find it more fun to read the passage and you'll also notice an increase in your confidence levels as you go about tackling the passage.

Make Use of Transition words

While making a passage map or generally reading a passage, try to make use of transition words to understand the overall structure of the passage and also to predict what will happen next in the passage. For example, if the author starts a paragraph with the words *Similarly* or *Likewise*, then you immediately know that whatever he has described in the earlier paragraph, the same thought process will continue in this paragraph as well.

Contrastingly, if the author is praising something in a paragraph, and the next paragraph starts with the words *However* or *Despite*, then you immediately know that the author will now talk about some negative or contrasting aspect of that thing. Transition words will make it very easy for you to understand the broad structure of a passage; these will mostly be found in the first and the last sentence of a paragraph, so pay attention to these sentences

GRE Reading Comprehension Question Pattern

The RC questions on the GRE will appear in the following three patterns:

1. **Multiple choice questions (select one out of five options)** – These are regular RC questions where a question has five options and students need to select one correct option from these. These include the Critical Reasoning type questions, which will be discussed in a separate section in this book.

2. **Multiple choice questions (select all that are correct from three options)** – This is a variation of the above pattern in which a question will have only three options. The catch is that more than one of these options could be correct. A student is required to mark all the options that are correct which could be one, two, or all three options. Generally these questions tend to be more difficult than the regular multiple choice RC questions.

3. **Highlight in the passage** – These questions do not provide any options to students, rather students are required to actually click on a specific sentence within the passage that answers the question asked. By definition, these questions will almost always be *Detail* questions. Read on to know more about 'Detail' and other question types.

GRE Reading Comprehension Question Types

1. Global Questions

Global questions are questions that cannot be answered by reading from the passage i.e. the answer is not written in the passage. The main purpose/primary concern type questions will fall under this question type. Note that the passage will never tell you what is its main purpose. However, if you have made a good passage map then you should not have much difficulty in answering these questions.

Keep in mind that, since the answer is not given in the passage, you don't really need to go back to the passage to answer a Global question. This will also save you time.

A trick to answering Global questions is to make use of the fact that each of the options in such questions will start with a verb, which will have a positive, negative, or neutral connotation. Thus if you are clear on the author's tone, you should be able to eliminate two or three options immediately just by looking at the first word of every option.

For example, if you know that the author's tone is neutral, then options that start with words such as *arguing, praising, criticizing,* etc. will never be correct because these have either a positive or a negative connotation. The correct answer in this case would start with neutral words such as *describe, explain, analyze, etc.*

Example:

What is the main purpose of the author in writing the passage?

What is the primary concern of the 3rd paragraph in the passage?

How to identify Global Questions - Global questions will always contain phrases such as *primary purpose, main idea, main concern,* etc.

How to Approach Global Questions

- Read the question critically to understand whether it is asking for the primary purpose of the entire passage or of some specific paragraph
- Predict an answer before going through the options. If the question is asking for the main purpose of a particular paragraph you may want to refer to your passage map or even take a quick look at the relevant paragraph

- Look at the first word of every option and match it with your prediction. Eliminate the ones that are inconsistent with your prediction
- By this time you should have managed to come down to two options. Read both the options completely and try to eliminate one of them. At this point be careful of options that appear half correct and half incorrect

Common Traps to watch out for in Global Questions

— Make sure you read the question correctly. Students often assume that a primary purpose question will always ask for the primary purpose of the entire passage, whereas sometimes the question may ask you for the primary purpose of only one particular paragraph. To confuse you further, the options will contain choices that explain the primary purpose of a different paragraph or of the entire passage.

— Another common trap used by the test maker is to give options that contain details or facts mentioned in the passage, so you'll be tempted to mark these as the answer because you can see the fact mentioned in the passage. However, remember that the answer to a global question will never be mentioned in the passage. The author obviously did not write the entire passage just to provide you with some fact or detail; rather he must have had a broader agenda, which you need to identify. So, on global questions, if you see options containing details from the passage, you can be rest assured that these will not be the correct answer.

2. Detail Questions

As the name suggests, Detail questions will ask you questions related to what is explicitly mentioned in the passage. In that sense they are the opposite of Global questions as the answer to these questions will always be stated in the passage. So make sure that you go back and read the answer from the passage before selecting an option. This is where a good passage map comes in handy while tackling long passages because you don't have to waste time trying to find the answer in the entire passage.

Examples:

Which of the following is provided by the author as an example of reverse osmosis?

Each of the following is mentioned in the passage as a side effect of medicine EXCEPT:

How to identify Detail Questions - Detail questions will use language such as *the passage states that,* or *explicitly stated in the passage.* To answer Detail questions you will obviously have to refer back to the passage. In fact we strongly suggest that you do so because a lot of students tend to go with hunches on these questions, simply because they are too lazy to go back and compare their answer with the information in the passage, and they end up getting the answer wrong as a result.

How to Approach Detail Questions

- Try to identify keywords from the question stem and match these keywords with your passage map to identify which paragraph you need to refer to in order to answer the question correctly
- Go back to the passage and research the relevant information. Do not assume that you remember the answer from the passage
- Analyze each option with a critical eye, not just for keywords but also for the thought that the option is trying to convey because the answer will mostly come from here

Use of EXCEPT on Detail questions

Since the answer to a Detail question is always written in the passage, it might seem that these questions would be relatively easier to answer. However, the test-maker has a way of making these questions confusing and lengthy by the use of words such as 'EXCEPT'.

For example, a question may state that *'According to the passage, each of the following is true of a steam turbine EXCEPT'*. In this case four of the options will be mentioned in the passage and you will need to identify that fifth option that is not mentioned in the passage. Thus, you need to check each of the options against the information in the passage, which makes the entire exercise take longer than would a regular question.

Also, the wording of the options is confusing, in the sense that there won't be that one option that contains words that have never been mentioned in the passage (thereby making it easy for you to identify this as the correct answer). Rather, all the options will contain keywords from the passage; it's just that one of them will convey some incorrect information about the keyword. Thus, make sure that you read every option with a critical eye.

Common Traps on Detail Questions

— Watch out for options that distort details from the passage, so if you are just trying to match keywords between the options and the passage you might think that this particular option is mentioned in the passage. However, the meaning conveyed by the option could be completely different from that conveyed in the passage. For this reason we do not recommend the strategy of matching keywords, especially when you are down to two options. Read both the options completely and figure out which option conveys the same meaning as the passage.

— As explained earlier, watch out for the use of EXCEPT or NOT on Detail questions. If the question states '*The passage states each of the following EXCEPT*', a common tendency on the part of students is to forget the 'except' and go with the option that contains something stated in the passage (which is obviously the wrong answer).

3. Vocabulary in Context Questions

These questions will ask you to identify the meaning of a word or a phrase as used in the passage. The keyword here is *in context* i.e. the answer always has to be with reference to the passage. The dictionary meaning of the word will rarely be the correct answer; in fact this is one of the most common wrong answer traps.

To answer these questions correctly, go back and read the sentence which contains this word or phrase (since the GRE passages do not contain line numbers, the word or phrase will be highlighted in the passage to make it easy for you to locate the same). Then read one or two sentences before and after this sentence to get an idea of the context. Now look at each option and eliminate.

Example:

What is the meaning of the word 'explosion' as used in the passage?

The word 'cynosure', as used in the passage, is closest in meaning to

Tip: The answer to a vocabulary-in-context question will almost never be the literal or dictionary meaning of the word so look out for such traps

4. Function Questions

Function questions will ask you to identify the function of a word, a sentence, a paragraph, a punctuation mark, etc. in the context of the overall passage. These are essentially *Why* questions i.e. they will ask you why the author uses a particular word or sentence in the passage. To answer these questions correctly, you will need to put yourself in the author's shoes and think like the author.

Obviously the understanding of the main purpose of the passage becomes crucial while answering these questions.

Please remember that the question is not asking you for your opinion on something as this is what students end up providing most of the time. It is asking you for the author's rationale behind doing something in the passage.

There is a unique problem students face when a Function question asks them to identify the function of a paragraph in the passage - they invariably end up marking the option that best describes what is contained in the passage as the correct answer. However, this gives the answer to the question *What is contained in the paragraph* whereas we need to answer the question *Why has the author written what he has written*. Please appreciate the difference between the *What* and the *Why*. To answer the *why* correctly, you will need to go back to the main purpose of the overall passage and link your answer from this.

Function questions will either start with the interrogative *Why* or they will end with the phrase *in order to – The author provides the example of the atomic clock in order to OR why does the author provide the example of the atomic clock?*

For example:

> *Why does the author use the lines 'the early bird gets the worm' in the passage'*
>
> *What is the function of the 3rd paragraph in the passage? (same as asking Why does the author use the 3rd paragraph in the passage)*

The answer to these questions will once again not be mentioned in the passage. These questions need to be answered keeping in mind the overall purpose and tone of the passage. Also remember to answer the question in a very specific manner. For example, if the question is asking you for the function of a sentence in the 3rd paragraph then the answer to that question cannot be the function of the entire 3rd paragraph. Answer only for the specific line or word that has been quoted in the question.

Tip: To answer logic questions correctly, students need to put themselves in the author's shoes and understand why the author is doing something. Remember that the question is not asking for the student's opinion on something.

5. Inference Questions

The dictionary meaning of the term 'Inference' is to derive by reasoning and this is exactly what you will be required to do on Inference Questions – arrive at an answer that is not explicitly stated in the passage but that can be definitely concluded given the information in the passage. So, Inference questions will require you to arrive at an answer that can be concluded or stated based on the information provided in the passage. The answer to these questions will never be directly stated in the passage.

Inference is the most important question type on GRE Reading Comprehension and is also the question type on which students make the most mistakes. This is because students often tend to read too much between the lines i.e. they end up over-inferring from the passage. While reading between the lines may be a good quality in our day to day life (some may even say a desirable one), it's best if you avoid doing so on the GRE. Hence, make it a point to avoid strongly worded or extreme sounding options – options containing words such as *must be true, always be the case, never be the case, cannot be determined, etc.* - and go with more open ended and vague options – options containing words such as *usually, sometimes, possibly, might be true, etc.*

For example:

> *Which of the following is implied by the author in the 4th paragraph?*
>
> *Which of the following options would the author of the passage most likely agree with?*

<u>How to Identify Inference Questions</u>

Inference question stems will use subjective words such as *imply, infer, suggest, most likely agree, least likely agree, etc.* Notice the subtle difference between an Inference and a Detail question in that an Inference question uses the term *suggests* whereas a Detail question uses the term *states* (to imply that the answer is mentioned in the passage).

<u>How to Approach Inference Questions</u>

- Read the question critically. Inference questions can often be worded in a tricky manner. Make sure you've correctly understood whose point of view you need to answer from. For example, a question may ask you which of the options would the author of the passage most likely agree with, while another might ask you which of the options a particular character in the passage would most likely agree with.

- Once you've read the question, quickly take a look at each of the options and try to eliminate two or three that are surely incorrect because they talk about things that aren't even discussed in the passage.

- Once you have come down to two or three options, eliminate the ones that sound extreme i.e. ones that use very strong words. In case you are still stuck between two options, read each option critically and select the one that can definitely be inferred from the passage.

Common Traps on Inference Questions

- At all costs avoid making use of outside information while answering Inference questions. A common wrong answer is one that looks perfectly logical by itself but cannot be inferred from the information in the passage.

- Always avoid the tendency to over infer or to read too much between the lines. Never go with extreme options on Inference Questions.

Critical Reasoning Questions

Apart from the above five question types, the new GRE will also test you on a sixth one – Critical Reasoning questions. These questions are heavily inspired from the critical reasoning section of the GMAT (remember the GRE is now competing with the GMAT as the preferred test for B-school admissions) and involve working with arguments.

Every Critical Reasoning question that you see on the GRE will have three parts to it:

1. **The Stimulus** – This is the main body of the argument

2. **The Question Stem** – This is the one or two lines in the middle that actually tell you what you have to do – find the assumption, strengthen, weaken, etc. In *Provide a Logical Conclusion* question type, this tends to be before the stimulus.

3. **The Options** – Each question will have five options from which you will need to identify the correct one.

The stimulus will usually appear in two forms – as an argument or as several statements of facts. To understand the difference between the two, let's look at what makes up an argument. Most arguments will have the following three parts – *Conclusion, Evidence, and Assumption.*

Conclusion, Evidence, and Assumption

Let's try to understand these terms with an example:

> *People don't like to visit the Evergreen wildlife park in the rainy season. This year the park authorities have reconstructed all the roads inside the park, so people will like to visit the Evergreen Park in the rainy reason this year.*

Conclusion – This is the point of the argument and answers the question *What* i.e. what is the argument basically stating - *that people would like to visit the Evergreen Wildlife park in the rainy season this year.*

Conclusions usually follow signalling words such as *thus, so, hence, therefore, etc.* In case there are no such words in the argument, try to paraphrase the entire argument in one sentence. This sentence would almost always be the conclusion of the argument.

Evidence – While the Conclusion tells you *What* the argument is saying, the Evidence tells you *Why* the argument is concluding what it is concluding. So in the above argument, why does the author conclude that people will like to visit the Evergreen Park this year? Because the park authorities have reconstructed all the roads inside the park, so this becomes your evidence.

Evidence usually follows signalling words such as *because, since, as a result of, etc.*

So the conclusion tells you the ***what*** of the argument and the evidence tells you the ***why*** of the argument. Another way of looking at conclusion and evidence is that a conclusion will almost always be *an opinion* whereas the evidence will almost always be *a fact*. In the above argument it is a fact that the roads have been reconstructed but it is the author's opinion that people will like to visit the Evergreen Park this year.

Assumption - Now, going back to the above argument, notice that from the given evidence we cannot necessarily arrive at the stated conclusion. The argument only states that people don't want to visit the Evergreen Park during the rainy season; it never states why people don't like to do so. So the author *assumes* that the only reason people don't like to visit the park is because of the poor road conditions within the park. If this is not assumed then the argument will fall apart.

For example, if the real reason why people do not visit the Evergreen Park was the fact that there are hardly any animals in the park, then even if the roads were made of velvet people will not visit the park because bad roads was not the reason for people not visiting the park in the first place. So, for the author to conclude that people will want to visit the park this year, he has to assume that the only reason people did not visit the park earlier was the poor road condition inside the park.

So, now that you know what components make up an argument, let's look at the relation among these. All arguments will have the following structure:

EVIDENCE + ASSUMPTION = CONCLUSION

In essence you can think of the assumption as unstated evidence or as a bridge between the evidence and the conclusion. If this bridge collapses, then you cannot arrive at the conclusion from the given evidence.

Here it is very important to note that the assumption is always *unstated* evidence i.e. it will never be written in the argument. It has to be assumed in the mind. So in a *find an assumption* question, if one of the options restates what is already mentioned in the argument, then this cannot be the assumption.

So, to summarize, with reference to the above argument:

> ***The Conclusion*** - people would like to visit the Evergreen Wildlife Park in the rainy season this year

The Evidence - the park authorities have reconstructed the roads within the park.

The Assumption – the only reason people do not visit the Evergreen National park in the rainy season is because of the poor roads within the park

One mistake students make is to assume that the last sentence of the argument will always be the conclusion. Nothing could be farther from the truth. The conclusion can be at the beginning of the argument, in the middle of the argument, or at the end of the argument.

Argument with conclusion at the beginning:

The Wind Wane project is an excellent one for Sihora County. The project will generate employment for the local population and also provide the residents with energy at low costs. In addition it will also lead to the opening up of new schools and colleges in Sihora County.

Argument with conclusion in the middle:

The Wind Wane project will generate employment for the local population in Sihora County and also provide the residents with energy at low costs. *So, the Wind Wane project is an excellent one for Sihora County.* In addition, the project will also lead to the opening up of new schools and colleges in Sihora County.

Argument with conclusion at the end:

The Wind Wane project will generate employment for the local population in Sihora County and also provide the residents with energy at low costs. In addition it will also lead to the opening up of new schools and colleges in Sihora County. *So, the Wind Wane project is an excellent one for Sihora County.*

So if the conclusion can be anywhere in an argument, how do you identify it. The answer is simple – by applying the *What and Why method* we discussed earlier.

What is the author saying (Conclusion) – The Wind Wane project is an excellent one for Sihora County

Why is the author saying so (Evidence) – Because the Wind Wane project will generate employment for the local population in Sihora County, provide them with energy at low costs, and also lead to the opening up of new schools and colleges in Sihora County.

So there you have your conclusion and evidence. The *What and Why* method is especially useful because it will actually force you to understand the meaning of the argument as a whole.

Stimulus with a set of Facts

As stated earlier, some question stimulus' will contain arguments but some may just contain statements of facts without any conclusion.

For example

> The sale of automobiles has increased by more than 100% in Vino city in the last one year. Out of this increase, more than 70% comprise Multi utility vehicles and Sports utility vehicles. Hatchbacks comprise the rest of the 30% sales figure.

As you can see the above stimulus just gives you some facts or data without arriving at any conclusion as such.

So a stimulus can be in the form of an argument or it may just comprise a set of facts. This will to a large extent be determined by the question type that you get. For example, in a *find the assumption* question the stimulus will always be in the form of an argument and for an *Explain the Contradiction* question the stimulus will always contain facts.

Initial Steps to approach Critical Reasoning questions on the GRE

- Always start by reading the stimulus. Some students prefer reading the question stem first but to us it's a waste of time because you'll read the question stem, then read the stimulus, and then invariably read the question stem again.

- Read the stimulus critically. Pay attention to every word. In the end summarize everything in your own words. If the stimulus is in the form of an argument be clear on *What* the stimulus is stating and *Why* it is stating so.

- Read the Question stem and use the strategy to tackle that particular question type, as described in the subsequent chapters of this book

- You should take an average of two minutes to answer each Critical Reasoning question. This is an average figure, so some questions may take you longer and some may be completed in less than two minutes

Note: Critical Reasoning questions will always require students to select one correct answer from five options.

Critical Reasoning Question Types

There will primarily be the following question types that will be tested by the GRE:

1. Assumption
2. Strengthen
3. Weaken
4. Flaw
5. Explain
6. Bold faced

1) Assumption Questions

Assumption is the most important of all the Critical Reasoning concepts/question types. This is because assumption will give you the answer to four question types – *Find the Assumption questions (but of course), Strengthen questions, Weaken questions, and Flaw questions.* We will see the connection between assumptions and each of these question types later but first let's take a look at assumptions themselves.

As we discussed in the previous chapter, an assumption is basically the unstated evidence that must be true for the argument's conclusion to be true. The most important thing to keep in mind while trying to arrive at the assumption is that the author's conclusion is true, even if it is the most absurd of conclusions. A lot of the times the problem students face is that they end up questioning the logic or validity of the author' argument. Leave that thought process for Weaken or Flaw questions. For Assumption questions you must take the author's conclusion to be absolutely one hundred percent true.

So, if the author concludes that aliens will arrive next week then you must agree with this fact; only then will you be able to arrive at the assumption correctly. For example, in this case one assumption may be that the shiny object in the sky is a space ship commanded by aliens. While it is extremely unlikely that the GRE will give you an argument such as the alien one, the reason we picked such an extreme example is to drive home the point that whatever the author states has to be taken as the truth by you. Never question the conclusion; instead focus your energies on identifying what else needs to be true for the author's conclusion to be true and you would have arrived at the assumption.

Over the last six years, most of the students in Tupac city have regularly attended colleges in the neighbouring Mekon city to pursue their graduate degrees. However, according to a recent change in the education policies of Mekon city, the colleges in Mekon city are expected to increase their fees to almost the same level as those charged by colleges in Tupac city. Therefore it can be safely concluded that colleges in Tupac city will see a surge in the number of students enrolling with them to pursue their graduate degrees

Which of the following is an assumption on which the argument depends?

A. The teachers at colleges in Mekon city are generally considered superior to those at colleges in Tupac city

B. Tupac city does not have good quality colleges

C. The low fees charged by colleges at Mekon city is the primary reason why students from Tupac city move to these colleges

D. Students who study at colleges in Tupac city do not perform better than those who study at colleges in Mekon city

E. Mekon city does not have more colleges than Tupac city

Always start an assumption question by paraphrasing the conclusion and the evidence.

Conclusion (What is the author saying) – that there will be a surge in the enrolments at colleges in Tupac city

Evidence (Why is the author saying this) – because students in Tupac city who earlier used to move to Mekon city to pursue their graduate degrees will now not do so as the colleges in Mekon city will charge them the same fees as the colleges in Tupac city do.

Note that that conclusion is an opinion of the author but the evidence is a fact because the colleges in Mekon city are definitely looking at increasing their fees.

The Importance of Predicting the Assumption

On assumption questions, it always helps if you already have a rough answer in mind before you look at the options as this can prevent you from getting confused between or among very close choices.

For example, given the above conclusion and evidence set, in order to arrive at the conclusion from the given evidence what must the author of the argument be assuming?

The author must be assuming that the low fees charged by colleges in Mekon city is the single most important factor why students from Tupac city have been moving to colleges in Mekon city. If he does not assume this, the argument will fall apart.

For example, if students have been shifting to Mekon city because the teachers in Mekon city colleges are better than those at Tupac city colleges then, even if the fees at colleges in Mekon City go up, students will keep on moving to Mekon city because the reason for the shift is the better quality of teachers.

So for the author's conclusion to be true, he has to assume that the only reason students have been shifting to colleges in Mekon city is the low fees charged by colleges in Mekon city. Option (C) states this best and hence is the correct answer.

However, just to get more clarity, let's take a look at the other options as well:

A. As we saw above, this fact actually weakens the argument because in this case the students will keep on shifting to colleges in Mekon City

B. Quality of colleges is outside the scope of the argument because the argument is only concerned with the fees charged by colleges. In fact, just like option (A), (B) could also weaken the argument by suggesting that lower fees is not the reason why students might be moving to colleges in Mekon city

C. The correct answer

D. This may or may not be the case but doesn't have to be the case for the author's conclusion to be true

E. The number of colleges in each city is irrelevant to the argument

The Denial/Negation Rule for Assumption questions

On Assumption questions, in case you are confused between two or more options, an effective way to eliminate incorrect options is by applying the Negation rule to the answer choices. The Negation or Denial rule is based on the principle that the assumption has to be true for the argument's conclusion to be true. As a corollary to this, if the assumption is denied or negated, then the argument must fall apart.

Hence, under the Negation rule, all you do is try to deny or negate each option and check whether the argument's conclusion can still be true. If it can be true then this option is not the assumption. Likewise if denying an option makes the conclusion fall apart then this option has to be the assumption.

Let's try the denial rule with each of the options in the Tupac city vs. Mekon city question discussed above:

A. The teachers at colleges in Mekon city are generally NOT considered far superior to those at colleges in Tupac city

   Negation this option does not help in any way because the argument is never about the quality of teachers in the first place. In its original wording this option was weakening the argument, now it is not doing anything.

B. Tupac city does ~~not~~ have good quality colleges

   Since this option already contains the word *not*, the ideal way to negate this is to remove the *not*. Again this does not explain why students have been shifting in the first place and quality of colleges is never the issue anyway.

C. The low fees charged by colleges at Mekon city is NOT the primary reason why students from Tupac city move to these colleges

   Negating this option definitely makes the argument fall apart because in this case the students will keep on shifting to colleges in Mekon City even after the increase in fees. Then, there will be no surge in enrolments at colleges in Tupac city. So this option has to be the assumption.

D. Students who study at colleges in Tupac city ~~do not~~ perform better than those who study at colleges in Mekon city

   Again strike out the *do not* from this option to negate it. Like option B, if this were to be the case then the students wouldn't have been shifting from Tupac city to Mekon city in the first place

E. Mekon city does ~~not~~ have more colleges than Tupac city

   The number of colleges in either city is irrelevant to our argument.

So you can see the denial or the negation rule can come in very handy when you are confused between options. However ***don't apply this rule on all the five options*** and waste your time. Two or three options can usually easily be eliminated; apply this rule to the remaining options.

Active and Passive Assumptions

Active assumptions are those assumptions that actively support the argument. These are the predictions you come up with when you are trying to pre-phrase an assumption. Active assumptions must be true for the argument to be true.

However, do notice the fact that the moment you assume that something must be true in an argument, you automatically assume that the other possibilities must NOT be true. It is these other possibilities that we call Passive Assumptions.

For example, in the Tupac city vs. Mekon city argument discussed earlier, the moment the author assumes that the primary reason students have been moving to colleges in Mekon city is the low fees charged by these colleges, he automatically assumes that other factors (such as better quality of teachers or better infrastructure) cannot be the reason for this shift. So the following can also be the assumptions in that argument:

- The better quality of teachers at colleges in Mekon city is *not* the primary reason why students have been shifting to colleges in Mekon city

- The better infrastructure at colleges in Mekon city is *not* the primary reason why students have been shifting to colleges in Mekon city

- The large number of clubs and entertainment centres in Mekon city is *not* the primary reason why students have been shifting to colleges in Mekon city

Notice that denying any of the above assumptions will make the original argument fall apart.

As you can see we can keep on making as many passive assumptions as we want. This is the biggest difference between active and passive assumptions. There can only be one active assumption in an argument but there can be several passive assumptions. It is precisely for this reason that you cannot predict a passive assumption whereas you can predict an active assumption.

You may have noticed that all the passive assumptions written above contain the word ***not***. This is the best way to identify passive assumptions since by definition they will always contain some negating word, most often *not*.

Let's look at one final example to understand active and passive assumptions.

> It takes four hours to cover the distance between Aston and Torin cities by bus. John has boarded a bus at Aston city that is scheduled to depart for Torin city at 10:00 a.m. If the bus departs on its correct time, John will reach Torin city well in time to attend his interview scheduled for 4:00pm that afternoon.
>
> **Active Assumption** – The bus will not get delayed on the way from Aston to Torin.
>
> **Passive Assumptions**
>
> - The bus will not have a flat tie or all four flat tires
> - The bus will not be struck by lightning
> - The bus will not be attacked by gunmen
> - The bus driver will not decide to go to some other city, etc.

So the active assumption gives you one general assumption and the passive assumption gives you several, each of which refutes the possibility of the active assumption not being true.

Author's note: *Do not get unnecessarily confused between active and passive assumptions since on the GRE nobody will ask you to distinguish between or identify the two. Just know that there is something like a passive assumption so that when you see it on a question you don't end up eliminating it immediately because it may actually be the correct answer.*

So try this question then:

> Eating unhygienic food always results in cases of stomach infection or food poisoning. Dominic is currently suffering from food poisoning, so he must have eaten unhygienic food in the last few days.
>
> Which of the following is an assumption on which the argument depends?
>
> (A) Eating unhygienic food will most definitely lead to food poisoning
>
> (B) Dominic does not have a weak immune system that makes him prone to food poisoning

(C) Dominic can make out the difference between hygienic and unhygienic food

(D) Eating unhygienic food is the only way to get food poisoning

(E) Unhygienic food contains harmful bacteria and other pathogens that lead to food poisoning

The Conclusion – Dominic must have eaten unhygienic food in the last few days

The Evidence – Eating unhygienic food always leads to food poisoning and Dominic is currently suffering from food poisoning

The Assumption – The argument states that eating unhygienic food will always lead to a person getting food poisoning. There can be no question about this fact since this is given to us as evidence. However the argument never states that this is the *only* way to get food poisoning. There could also be other ways of getting food poisoning such as drinking impure water or eating hygienic food with dirty hands.

So for the author's conclusion to be true, he has to assume that the only way to contract food poisoning is by consuming unhygienic food. (D) states this best and should be the correct answer.

Let's look at the other options as well;

(A) This is clearly stated in the argument so cannot be the assumption. In fact this is part of the evidence. Remember that an assumption will never be stated, it is always assumed

(B) This option is a trap because it has been worded in the form of a passive assumption (notice the use of the word *not*). However even if Dominic does have a weak immune system, he may still have contracted food poisoning from some source other than unhygienic food.

(C) Whether Dominic is able to make out this difference is irrelevant. In fact it is possible that he could not make out this difference, which is why he ended up having unhygienic food in the first place

(D) The Correct Answer

(E) How unhygienic food leads to food poisoning is not the concern of the argument.

The following can be Passive Assumptions in the argument:

- Drinking impure water cannot lead to food poisoning, (*because if it can then maybe this is how Dominic contracted food poisoning and not by consuming unhygienic food)*
- Eating with dirty hands cannot lead to food poisoning, (*because if it can then maybe this is how Dominic contracted food poisoning and not by consuming unhygienic food)*

The wording of Assumption Questions

Assumption questions most often directly ask you to identify the assumption in the argument. However sometimes they can be worded in the form of *must be true* questions.

Here is an example:

Which of the following must be true for the above argument to be true?

This shouldn't come as a surprise because conceptually an assumption must be true for an argument to be valid.

How to Approach Assumption Questions

1. Read the argument and be clear on the evidence and the conclusion
2. Know that since this is an assumption question, there has to be some piece of evidence missing from the argument
3. Try to predict this missing piece of evidence. In a *Find the Assumption* question, you must always have an answer in mind before you look at the options
4. Eliminate two or three options because they definitely appear to be incorrect. Possible wrong answer choices can be those that are outside the scope of the argument, that repeat what is stated in the argument, or that can be inferred from the argument.
5. If stuck between two or more options try the denial or negation rule

2) Strengthen Questions

Strengthen questions, as the name suggests, will require you to strengthen whatever it is that an argument is stating. However, do keep in mind that strengthen does not mean to confirm an argument. Even if an option can provide a small point in favour of the argument it is strengthening the argument. Similarly even if an option can remove a small doubt from your mind about the argument, it is again strengthening the argument.

Notice that to strengthen a stimulus, it is imperative that the stimulus have a conclusion. So strengthen questions will always contain a stimulus that is in the form of an argument.

Of all the laptops available for sale in Ireland, those manufactured by Ivy Infotech must have the fastest processors. Over the last six months Ivy Infotech has sold three times as many laptops as its closest competitor. Additionally Ivy Infotech's order books are full for the next 12 months.

Which of the following options, if true, most strengthens the argument?

A. Ivy Infotech is the oldest manufacturer of laptops in Ireland

B. Ivy Infotech has the largest market share in laptop sales in Ireland for the past five years

C. Ivy Infotech sources its processors from the company which is the world's biggest manufacturer of laptop processors

D. All the laptops available for sale in Ireland are same in every aspect except for their processors

E. The Irish populace prefers laptops with faster processors

Since this is a strengthen question, you know that the stimulus will be worded in the form of an argument. So the first step is to identify the conclusion and the evidence of this argument.

Conclusion (What is the argument stating) – Laptops manufactured by Ivy Infotech have the fastest processors.

Evidence (Why is the argument stating this) – Because Ivy Infotech has sold the maximum number of laptops in the last six months in Ireland.

But does this make sense? Can't there be some other plausible reason why the people in Ireland are buying Ivy Infotech's laptops?

Maybe these laptops have a very sleek design, maybe they have a very long batter life, or maybe they are the cheapest laptops in the market. There can be several other reasons (other than fast processors) why the Irish are buying laptops manufactured by Ivy Infotech. This brings us to the assumption. Remember that since the stimulus is in the form of an argument, it must contain an assumption.

Assumption (the unstated evidence) – So let's try to predict the assumption. It will be something on the lines of 'the only difference among the different laptops available in Ireland is the speed of the processor; the laptops are the same in every other aspect', because then if the people are still buying Ivy Infotech's laptops then these laptops must have the fastest processors, else people would be buying some other company's laptops.

Strengthener – So now that we have identified the conclusion, the evidence, and the assumption, the option that best tells us that the assumption is true has to strengthen the argument. (D) does this best and should be the correct answer.

For clarity, let's also take a look at the other options:

A. The argument is only concerned with processor speeds accounting for high sales. It has got nothing to do with how old a company is.

B. Again this option doesn't tell us why Ivy Infotech has the largest market share. Is it the processor speed or some other reason?

C. Very well but it is possible that the other competitors of Ivy Infotech also source their processors from this same company

D. The correct answer. If the only difference among the laptops is the processor speed and if people are still buying laptops manufactured by Ivy Infotech, then these laptops must have the fastest processors.

E. The option uses the word 'prefers' which doesn't tell you anything. You could prefer flying by a private jet to flying by a commercial airline but you mostly still have to fly by a commercial airline. So the Irish could prefer laptops with faster chips but might buy some other laptop which has a slightly slower processor but a much longer battery life or which is much cheaper in price.

Strengtheners and Assumptions

Did you notice something interesting in the above question – the correct answer is almost a paraphrase of the assumption that we had predicted earlier i.e. the strengthener is the same as the assumption. If you think about it, conceptually this has to be the case. An assumption is unstated evidence that strengthens an argument so if this unstated evidence is stated in the form of an option, then it will obviously strengthen the argument. So a strengthener will either be the assumption itself or it will supply some evidence that will make it more likely for the assumption to be true.

Thus the answer to a strengthen question will a lot of the times be the assumption, though you may not consciously realize this all the time.

Active and Passive Strengtheners

Since strengtheners follow from the assumption, it is but obvious that, just like we had active and passive assumptions, we'll also have active and passive strengtheners. An active strengthener will give you a positive point i.e. a point in favour of the argument whereas a passive strengthener will remove one or more of the negative points from the argument.

The following can be some passive strengtheners for the Ivy Infotech example:

- Sleek design is not the reason why the Irish are buying Ivy Infotech's laptops
- A longer battery life is not the reason why the Irish are buying Ivy Infotech's laptops
- The fact that Ivy Infotech's laptops are the cheapest laptops available in the market is not the reason why the Irish are buying Ivy Infotech's laptops

Notice that all these passive strengtheners again use the word *not*, just as passive assumptions do.

So a passive strengthener, in essence, removes a doubt from your mind about the argument whereas an active strengthener gives you some supporting point in favour of the argument

Always strengthen the connection between the Evidence and the Conclusion

While strengthen questions are generally easy, there is one folly that you must guard against – you must, at all times, try to strengthen the connection between the evidence and the conclusion. Never strengthen the conclusion in isolation (even if the argument asks you to strengthen the conclusion).

> I read in the newspaper this morning that in the last one month 20 children have been kidnapped in Sodham County, when they stepped out of their house alone at night. So I conclude that if you are a child

staying in Sodham County, it is unsafe for you to step out alone at night.

Which of the following two options strengthens my argument?

1. I read this article in a newspaper that is a very trustworthy newspaper known for its honest credible reporting.

2. Two child kidnappers, who have recently been released from prison, have been seen loitering around in Sodham County at night over the last month.

While a lot of you may have gone with option two as the correct answer, it is in fact incorrect. Why am I concluding that if you are a child in Sodham County it is unsafe for you to step out alone at night? Not because I know something about the child kidnappers, but because I read something in the newspaper.

Another person could very well come and tell me that the newspaper is known for false reporting and for sensationalising things, facts which would weaken my argument. The opposite facts, as stated in option one, will then obviously strengthen my argument because my evidence is the newspaper article.

So the takeaway is that you always try to strengthen the link between the evidence and the conclusion. The evidence is there for a purpose and you must make use of it.

How to Approach Strengthen Questions

1. Read the argument and be clear on the evidence and the conclusion

2. Try to predict the assumption because the strengthener will, in some way, be linked to this

3. Go through the options and eliminate those that weaken the argument or are otherwise outside the scope of the argument

4. Remember to take into consideration the evidence as well; don't just strengthen the conclusion in isolation

3) Weaken Questions

Weaken questions, as the name suggests, will require you to weaken or raise doubts about whatever it is that an argument is stating. In that sense these are the exact opposite of Strengthen questions that you saw in the previous chapter.

Do keep in mind that weaken does not mean to negate an argument. Even if an option can raise a small doubt in your mind about the validity of the argument, it is weakening the argument. Similarly if an option removes a strengthener from an argument, it is again weakening the argument.

Notice that to weaken a stimulus, it is imperative that the stimulus have a conclusion. So weaken questions will always contain a stimulus that is in the form of an argument.

For conceptual clarity, let's look at the same example that we saw in the previous chapter but with different options.

> Of all the laptops available for sale in Ireland, laptops manufactured by Ivy Infotech must have the fastest processors. Over the last six months Ivy Infotech has sold three times as many laptops as its closest competitor. Additionally Ivy Infotech's order books are full for the next 12 months.
>
> Which of the following options, if true, most weakens the argument?
>
> A. Ivy Infotech was severely criticised last year for manufacturing laptops with slow processors
>
> B. Apart from laptops, Ivy Infotech also manufactures desktops and tablets, sales of which have declined drastically in the last six months
>
> C. At the same time last year, Ivy Infotech had sold 60% more laptops than it has this year
>
> D. All the laptop manufacturers in Ireland, including Ivy Infotech, source their processors from the same company
>
> E. Due to production bottlenecks, the production of laptops by Ivy Infotech's rival companies has fallen by more than 60% in the last six months

Since this is a weaken question, you know that the stimulus will be worded in the form of an argument. So the first step is to identify the conclusion and the evidence of this argument.

Conclusion (What is the argument stating) – Laptops manufactured by Ivy Infotech have the fastest processors.

Evidence (Why is the argument stating this) – Because Ivy Infotech has sold the maximum number of laptops in the last six months in Ireland.

But does this make sense? Can't there be some other plausible reason why the people in Ireland are buying Ivy Infotech's laptops? Maybe these laptops have a very sleek design, maybe they have a very long batter life, or maybe they are the cheapest laptops in the market. There can be several other reasons (other than fast processors) why the Irish are buying laptops manufactured by Ivy Infotech. This brings us to the assumption. Remember that since the stimulus is in the form of an argument, it must contain an assumption.

Assumption (the unstated evidence) – So let's try to predict the assumption. It will be something on the lines of 'the only difference among the different laptops available in Ireland is the speed of the processor; the laptops are the same in every other aspect', because then if the people are still buying Ivy Infotech's laptops then these laptops must have the fastest processors, else people would be buying some other company's laptops.

Weakener – So now that we have identified the conclusion, the evidence, and the assumption, the option that best tells us that the assumption may NOT be true has to weaken the argument. In essence, this option will provide us with some other reason (other than faster processors) why the sales of Ivy Infotech's laptops have been very high. (E) does this best and should be the correct answer.

For clarity, let's also take a look at the other options:

A. This was last year while the increase in sales has been this year. It is very much possible that because of this criticism Ivy Infotech equipped its laptops with faster processors. So by no stretch does this option weaken the argument.

B. Desktops and tablets are outside the scope of the argument. The fact remains that Ivy Infotech's laptops have outsold those of its rivals by a large margin. We need to show that this was not because of the faster processors and this option fails to do so.

C. This option states that overall Ivy Infotech has performed worse this year than it did last year but we are not concerned with this. The fact remains that Ivy Infotech's laptops have outsold those of its rivals by a large margin. We need to show that this was not because of the faster processors and this option fails to do so.

D. Looks good but doesn't necessarily weaken the argument. All the companies in Ireland source their processors from the same company does not mean that the processors are all the same. Those sourced by Ivy Infotech could very well be faster than those sourced by its rival firms.

E. This option gives you an alternative reason why Ivy Infotech has sold more laptops than its rivals. It was not because of demand side issue but because of supply side constraints. Because of the production bottlenecks at its rival companies' plants, Ivy Infotech's laptops were probably available in the market in much larger numbers than those of its rivals, which is why they sold more. Hence this option weakens the argument by providing you with an alternative explanation to the one mentioned in the stimulus.

Weakeners and Assumptions

Common sense dictates that the only way in which an option can weaken an argument is by raising doubts about the validity of its assumption. When you make an assumption, you immediately deny the possibility of any other scenario being true. The weakener will provide you with these alternate scenarios and hence raise doubts in your mind as to which explanation is the correct one.

Remember that an option will never weaken the argument by questioning its evidence or by trying to negate its evidence. The evidence is a fact so it can never be questioned. What can be questioned however is the conclusion that is arrived at by using this evidence. You can't question facts but you can always question an opinion.

So the answer to a weaken question will usually be the option that provides you with alternatives to what has been assumed in the argument.

Always weaken the connection between the Evidence and the Conclusion

Just like strengthen questions, on weaken questions also you must, at all times, try to weaken the connection between the evidence and the conclusion. Never weaken the conclusion in isolation (even if the argument asks you to weaken the conclusion).

According to a recent survey conducted in Unitown City, people who drove SUV's were much more likely to flout traffic rules than people who drove regular sedans. Hence, if the government wishes to reduce the incidence of road accidents, it should ban the sale of SUVs in the city.

Which of the following two options most weakens the argument?

1. The road condition in Unitown City is very poor, and it is much easier to drive SUVs on these roads than regular sedans.

2. The survey size comprised 5% of the population of Unitown City.

The conclusion of this argument is based on the evidence of the recent survey. The only way to weaken this argument is by questioning the integrity of this survey. Notice that you cannot state that the survey was never conducted, you can only question its integrity.

Option two states that the survey only comprised a very small population of Unitown City so it may not be representative of the entire population of Unitown City. For example, it is possible that people drive rashly in the neighbourhood where this survey was conducted, but the people in the rest of the city are safe drivers. Thus, option two definitely weakens the argument.

As against this, option one provides you with a reason why people should be allowed to drive SUVs. But if driving SUVs is going to lead to more accidents, then this may not be a good enough reason not to ban the sale of SUVs in the city. Hence this option is outside the scope of the argument.

So the takeaway is that you always try to weaken the link between the evidence and the conclusion. The evidence is there for a purpose and you must make use of it.

How to Approach Weaken Questions

1. Read the argument and be clear on the evidence and the conclusion

2. Try to predict the assumption because the weakener will, in some way, try to convince you that this assumption may not be valid

3. Go through the options and eliminate those that strengthen the argument or are otherwise outside the scope of the argument

4. Remember to take into consideration the evidence as well; don't just weaken the conclusion in isolation

4) Flaw Questions

Flaw questions will ask you to identify a flaw in the author's reasoning. Keep in mind that all arguments have the same fundamental flaw – that they rely on one or more unstated assumptions. So in a flaw question you basically need to question the assumption made by the author.

Ronald scored 600 on the GMAT while Derek scored 338 on the GRE. So Ronald performed much better than Derek did.

Which of the following is the most serious flaw in the argument?

(A) The argument does not take into account the possibility that Ronald's score could be a fluke

(B) The argument does not take into account the past academic records of Ronald and Derek

(C) The argument arrives at an extreme conclusion on the basis of unverified data

(D) The argument assumes that standardised test scores are the best predictor of future success of an individual

(E) The argument discounts the possibility that the GRE and the GMAT may have different scoring scales

Since this is a flaw question, you know that the stimulus will be worded in the form of an argument. So the first step is to identify the conclusion and the evidence of this argument.

Conclusion (What is the argument stating) – Ronald has performed better than Derek.

Evidence (Why is the argument stating this) – Ronald scored 600 on the GMAT and Derek scored 338 on the GRE, and since 600 is more than 338, Ronald must have performed better.

But does this make sense? Those of you who are aware of the GMAT scoring pattern would obviously know that a 338 (out of 340) on the GRE is a much better score than a 600 (out of 800) on the GMAT. However the argument does not assume that you will know this or need you to know this.

For all you know the GRE could be scored out of 1000 and the GMAT could be scored out of 2000. The important thing is to notice that the argument does not mention this fact, which will then take you to the assumption.

Assumption (the unstated evidence) – The assumption now is fairly easy to predict – that the GRE and the GMAT are scored on the same scoring scale. Only if this is assumed can the argument conclude what it is concluding; if you negate this fact then the argument will fall apart.

Flaw – The flaw will always question the assumption. It will raise doubts in your mind as to what if the assumption was not true. Out of the five options in the above argument, (E) does this best and hence is the correct answer. The argument does not take into account the possibility that the GRE and the GMAT may have different scoring scales and that a 338 on the GRE may actually be a better score than a 600 on the GMAT.

For clarity, let's also take a look at the other options:

A. It really doesn't matter how Ronald arrived at that particular score as long as there a possibility that this score could still be worse than Derek's score

B. Past academic records are irrelevant because the argument is only concluding for the current tests taken by Ronald and Derek. The argument does not make a conclusion that Ronald in general is a better student than Derek.

C. There is nothing in the argument to suggest that the data is unverified.

D. The argument does not make any conclusions about how successful will the two candidates be in future.

E. The correct answer.

Flaw and Assumptions

As we have seen, the answer to a flaw question will always be linked to the assumption of the argument. In essence, the flaw is the fact that the argument is relying on an assumption in the first place. So a flaw will simply end up questioning the assumption at all times.

The wording of the Flaw Question stem

A flaw question will either directly ask you to identify the flaw in the argument or it could also make use of terms such as *vulnerable to the objection* or *vulnerable to the criticism*. Here are some common ways of wording flaw questions:

- The argument is flawed primarily because
- Which of the following most strongly indicates that the logic of the above argument is flawed?
- The argument is most vulnerable to which of the following criticisms/objections?

How are Flaw Questions different from Weaken Questions

So are flaw questions the same as weaken questions? The answer is that the two are similar but not the same.

There is one big difference between the two – a flaw is always from within the argument; it is simply the assumption stated in some other words and will never mention additional evidence. As against this a weakener will almost always mention additional evidence that can question the validity of the argument's assumption. You can only weaken an argument by bringing in an additional point whereas the flaw will always be inherent in the argument.

Because of this fact an option that mentions a flaw will always be worded in the form of a question or a doubt whereas an option that mentions a weakener will always be worded in the form of a fact or evidence.

For example, in the Ronald vs. Derek argument, the following can be a possible weakener:

- The GRE is scored out of 340 whereas the GMAT is scored out of 800

Now do you notice how this option is different from the one that mentioned the flaw? The flaw was just raising a doubt that the two scoring scales may be different whereas this option provides a fact that confirms that the two scoring scales are different.

Typical Flaws present in Arguments

There are some typical flaws that the GRE likes to test students on. Let's take a look at some of them:

i. **Mistaking Correlation for Causation** – In such cases, the argument will state that X and Y take place together or one after the other, so X is the cause of Y i.e. what appeared to be a simple correlation is actually a cause and effect relation.

> The days on which Kevin wears a black shirt, he performs much better in his practice tests than he does on days on which he wears a shirt of some other colour. So on the day of the final test, Kevin must ensure that he wears a black shirt.

ii. **Confusing you with Absolute numbers and Percentages** – In such arguments, the author will try to confuse you by providing absolute numbers as evidence and concluding for a percentage or vice versa. You've already seen an example of this in the argument at the beginning of this chapter (Ronald vs. Derek). Here's another one:

> 10% of the total houses in London are for sale and 30% of the total houses in New York are for sale. So there are more houses for sale in New York than in London.

iii. **Representativeness** – In such arguments the author will assume a small sample size to be representative of a much larger population or group.

> The mayor of Rodham City does not seem to be very popular with the city's residents. Out of the 20 people that I spoke to this afternoon, as many as 15 said that they hated the mayor.

You'll see each of these argument types in much more detail later in this book when we discuss some typical argument patterns tested on the GRE.

How to Approach Flaw Questions

1. Read the argument and be clear on the evidence and the conclusion

2. Try to predict the assumption because the flaw will always question the assumption in some manner

3. Look for some typical flaws based on the wording of the argument. If the argument mentions numbers, look for a correlation-causation problem; if it mentions a survey, look for a problem of representativeness, etc.

4. Remember not to confuse a flaw with an option that weakens the argument. If confused, go with the option that is directly connected to the argument's assumption

5) Explain Questions

Explain questions will ask you to provide the most logical explanation for the situation described in the stimulus. This stimulus will usually contain a contradiction or an anomaly i.e. a contrary to fact situation. Also the stimulus will always contain facts and won't be in the form of an argument.

Leading book publishers had predicted that the rampant illegal sharing of books online would have a detrimental impact on the sales of their physical books. However, the more illegal online sharing sites increase in popularity, the more physical books are being sold.

Which of the following options best explains why the sales of physical books have been increasing with the increase in online piracy?

A. The illegal sharing of books online has not become as popular as was expected

B. People in general find it more difficult to read books on a computer screen than reading a physical book

C. Book publishers have, in the last few years, invested heavily in advertising their books

D. A lot of people have discovered new authors through online book sharing sites and subsequently bought other books written by these authors because it is easier to read a physical book

E. The government has introduced heavy fines for those downloading books from online sharing sites

An explain question will never contain an argument so don't waste your time looking for the conclusion, evidence, and assumption. Instead try to quickly paraphrase the contradiction in the stimulus – it was expected that people will stop buying physical books because they could now download books for free from illegal online book sharing sites. However, as the free illegal book sharing sites gain popularity, the sales of physical books has also been growing similarly.

The correct option needs to explain why this has been the case. So let's take a look at each option in the question above:

A. This option directly questions a fact mentioned in the stimulus, which is something that can never be done on any CR question. The arguments states that illegal online book sharing is becoming more and more popular and we need to accept this fact as it is. We just need to show the connection between this fact and the fact that the sales of physical books have also been growing similarly.

B. This looks very good. However notice that it just provides you with a reason why people may not want to read books online. So in this case the sales of physical books should have remained unaffected or declined marginally. Then why have the sales been increasing? This option doesn't explain this fact. Remember that the correct answer has to explain both sets of facts and not just one of them.

C. This again addresses one part of the contradiction – why have the sales of books been increasing. But this option does not show the link between increase in illegal online sharing of books and the increase in sales of physical books.

D. The correct answer. This choice correctly identifies a link between the two sets of facts mentioned in the stimulus. People discover new authors through online book sharing sites, they like the book that they have read, and so they subsequently buy other books by these authors in the physical format because it is easier to read in this form.

E. Like B, in this case also the sales of physical books should have remained steady or changed slightly but what explains the increase in sales of physical books?

Based on the above analysis we can arrive at certain tips to keep in mind while attempting *Explain the Contradiction questions*.

Tips for Explain questions

— **Make sure you have identified the discrepancy in the argument before looking at the options** – A lot of times students rush to the options without realising what exactly they have to explain. As a result they go through all the five options and are not able to eliminate anything, so they go back and again read the stimulus to understand the discrepancy. Then they once again go through all the options leading to wastage of precious time.

— **Never explain just one side of the stimulus** – As you saw in some of the options above, the correct answer has to explain both sides of the contradiction and not just one side.

— **Never deny the evidence** – This applies to all Critical Reasoning question types. Never try to negate or question the evidence or facts provided in the stimulus. Take this as true at all times

— **The answer will always be from the outside** – The answer to an explain question will always be a new point that somehow explains the contradiction in the stimulus, so don't eliminate an option just because it contains terms that have not been mentioned in the stimulus. As long as it explains the discrepancy, it could very well be the correct answer

Common wrong answer choices on Explain questions

- Options that explain only one side of the contradiction
- Options that negate or question the validity of the facts/evidence provided in the stimulus

How to approach an Explain Question

1. Read the stimulus. If it contains an argument then it most likely will not be an explain question. However if it contains a discrepancy/contradiction/anomaly, then it has to be an *Explain* question
2. Read the question stem to confirm that you are indeed looking at an *Explain* question
3. Don't bother making a prediction because there are several possibilities that can explain the situation. Quickly scan through the options eliminating the common wrong answer types discussed above
4. By this time you should have come down to two choices, if not arrived at the correct answer. If confused go back and read the stimulus to understand the stimulus better. Restate the contradiction or discrepancy in your own words and check which option is best explaining both sides of it. Select this option and move on.

6) Bold Faced Questions

In bold faced questions, two complete sentences or parts of sentences are highlighted in bold. The question will usually ask you to identify the role being played by the two bold or highlighted parts in the overall context of the argument or passage.

The difficulty with bold faced questions is that while you have to read the entire stimulus to understand what it is trying to state, you have to answer only for the bold part. A common trap the test maker uses is to give you options that describe the role played by the non-bold parts of the stimulus so as to trick you into going with these options.

The stimulus of a bold faced question will usually be in the form of an argument because only then can different sentences play different roles. In fact the stimulus will usually contain several arguments and counter arguments so as to make it difficult for you to grasp what exactly the parts in bold are doing.

Bold faced questions are generally regarded by test takers as one of the most (if not the most) difficult question types on the CR section. There are two reasons why these questions appear to be more difficult than the others:

1) You only have to answer for the bold parts

2) The confusing language of the options. All the options will use abstract language such as *the first is the opposition of the supposition assumed in the argument*

The options that you see on bold faced questions will always be worded in the form of *the first is doing x and the second is doing y*, further highlighting the fact that you only have to answer for the bold parts.

There is not one good reason for granting men paternity leave from work, while there are several good reasons to deny. For one, it would be an additional expense to businesses. Businesses are already facing tough times all over the world, so adding additional overhead is not an option. If the father acts like a father, he and the child will bond. **If the father doesn't act like a father, he and the child will not bond, regardless of whether he is at home or at work.**

In the argument given, the two portions in boldface play which of the following roles?

(A) The first is the primary conclusion of the argument and the second is a secondary conclusion

(B) The first is the advocacy of the argument and the second raises doubts about this advocacy

(C) The first provides evidence as to why a policy should not be adopted by businesses and the second further strengthens this evidence

(D) The first is a conclusion that the argument disagrees with; the second provides the reasoning behind this disagreement

(E) The first is the primary conclusion of the argument and the second provides reasoning supporting the primary conclusion

The argument provides reasons why men should not be granted paternity leave. The first bold part states the overall conclusion of the argument, and the second provides a reason in support of this conclusion. (E) states this best and is the correct answer.

Let's also look at the other options for more clarity:

A. While the first is indeed the primary conclusion of the argument, the second is not a secondary conclusion. In fact the second supports the primary conclusion of the argument by providing a reason why paternity leave is not required

B. While the first can be considered an advocacy, the second does not by any stretch raise doubts about this advocacy

C. The first bold part does not provide any evidence, it just provides the conclusion. The evidence is in the rest of the argument

D. The argument in fact agrees with the first bold part

E. The correct answer as described in option (A)

List of Common roles played by the bold parts

- **Final Conclusion** – This is the point that argument is trying to make
- **Intermediate Conclusion** – This often contrasts with the final conclusion
- **Counterpoint** – This is a statement that opposes something stated earlier in the argument
- **Background information** – This provides some context for the issue described in the argument

- **Prediction** – This will always be an opinion and talk about something happening in the future
- **Objection** – Questions or doubts something stated in the argument

On bold faced questions, once you've read the stimulus and before you look at the options, make a rough assessment of what exactly is the connection between the two parts of the argument in bold. This need not be a very precise relation, even something on the lines of *the first and the second are saying opposite things* or *the first is an evidence or a cause and the second is the conclusion or the effect* will do as this will help you eliminate incorrect options.

Remember that on bold faced questions you may not always be able to select the answer; rather you will often end up eliminating wrong answer choices to arrive at the correct answer. For example you could be stuck between two options both of which may look fine to you. Then you'll have to get down to reading every individual word in the shortlisted options and try to eliminate the incorrect ones.

For example if you know that the argument is neutral (i.e. it does not take any sides) and one of the options mentions the phrase *the author advocates* you immediately know that this cannot be the answer because the author is not advocating anything in the entire stimulus.

Approach to Bold faced questions

1. Read the stimulus/passage and try to understand its overall meaning. The stimulus of bold faced questions usually tends to be long, so spend some time on this. As you read try to make out what role each sentence may be playing from the list of common roles that you saw earlier in this chapter

2. Once you've read the entire argument go back and just read the bold parts and try to identify the relation between them.

3. Quickly scan through all the options eliminating ones which are clearly incorrect. For example, if you have identified that the first bold part is an evidence, any option that states that the first bold part is a conclusion can immediately be eliminated.

4. Once you've narrowed down your choices to two or three, go through every word of the options and try to spot something that contradicts what is stated in the argument

Now let's also take a look at some typical argument structures that the GRE uses. The questions will still be the same as we saw in the preceding chapters; nobody will ask you to identify the structure of the argument. It's just that if you spot the structure of the argument, it'll become very easy for you to arrive at the correct answer because you will know what exactly you are looking for even before you look at the options. You've already seen some of these in the Flaw chapter; now we'll take a more in-depth look at them.

1) Cause and Effect Arguments

These arguments basically state that just because two things happen together or one after the other, one is the cause of the other. Let's take a look at a very simplified example,

Jason is very intelligent because he studied at Harvard.

Cause – The fact that Jason has studied at Harvard

Effect – Jason becoming intelligent

If you look at this argument in terms of facts and opinion, the facts are that Jason is intelligent and that he has studied at Harvard. However the opinion is the connection between these two facts – that Jason is intelligent *because* he studied at Harvard.

Assumption – When the author concludes that the reason for Jason's intelligence is the fact that he studied at Harvard, he automatically assumes that nothing else could be responsible for Jason's intelligence except the fact that he studied at Harvard.

Cause and Effect Arguments and Weaken questions

On most occasions whenever you get cause and effect type of arguments, the question stem will require you to weaken the argument. There are two ways of weakening cause and effect type of arguments:

i) By providing another reason for the effect – As we saw above, in a cause and effect argument the author assumes that nothing else could be responsible for the effect in question. So if we can show that another cause could also lead to the same effect, then the argument is immediately weakened because we don't know what is leading to the effect for sure.

For example, the following can be a weakener for the Harvard argument above:

Both of Jason's parents are geniuses.

So then maybe Jason is very intelligent because of genetic reasons and not because he went to Harvard.

ii) By showing that the cause and effect could actually be upside down – This is a slightly more difficult to spot method of weakening cause and effect arguments. Even if two things happen together and we know that there definitely is a cause and effect relation between them, how do we know which of the two is causing the other; is X causing Y or is Y causing X. So if the argument concludes that X is causing Y, one way of weakening the argument is to show that it is actually Y that may be causing X.

For example

Because Jason was very intelligent, he got admitted into Harvard.

So it's is not that Jason became intelligent after going to Harvard but rather that he was intelligent which is why he could go to Harvard in the first place.

So if the argument in the stimulus is of the form A is causing B, then it can be weakened in the following two ways:

i) By showing that C can also lead to B

ii) By showing that it is not A that is causing B, but B that is causing A

Let's look at a proper example now.

A study has found that new ventures that are funded through bank loans are more likely to succeed than those funded by an entrepreneur's friends and relatives. The reason for this is not difficult to fathom. The obligation to pay a fixed instalment to the bank every month prevents the entrepreneur from getting complacent and increases his motivation to succeed.

Which of the following raises the strongest doubt on the above argument?

(A) Banks only fund those business ventures that have a very high probability of succeeding

(B) The study also showed the some ventures that had been funded by an entrepreneur's friends and relatives were extremely successful

(C) Most entrepreneurs agree that the pressure of repaying the bank loans acts as a positive stimulus for them

(D) It is an accepted fact that only those entrepreneurs opt for bank funding who are unable to generate funds from personal sources

(E) According to a different study, there is a strong correlation between an entrepreneur's educational background and the nature of his business venture

It's best to summarise cause and effect arguments in the form of a cause and an effect:

The Cause – Funding through bank loans

The Effect – A high probability of success for a new venture

As we saw there are two ways of weakening cause and effect arguments – either provide some other cause for the same effect or reverse the cause and the effect.

Option (A) reverses the cause and effect in the argument and is the correct answer. This option states that the cause was the business venture's high probability of success and the effect was funding provided by the bank. Had the bank felt that the venture may not succeed, it would not have funded the venture in the first place. So it is not because of the bank funding that the venture succeeded but because the venture was going to succeed that the banks funded it in the first place.

Let's look at the other options for clarity.

(A) The Correct Answer

(B) This doesn't tell you anything because of the use of the word *some*. Some ventures were successful and some were not. Had the option stated that *most* such ventures are very successful then it could have negated the argument (but this won't be the case because in that case the argument would be questioning the evidence itself, which can never be the case)

(C) This option actually strengthens the argument

(D) Under what conditions an entrepreneur opts for bank funding is irrelevant to the argument

(E) The nature of the entrepreneur's business venture is of no consequence to the argument.

2) Representativeness

Representativeness arguments will involve arriving at a generalized conclusion for a large population based on a sample or survey of a small sub set of the population.

For example,

> In response to a recent survey conducted by a newspaper in Quantos city, 70% of the respondents stated that they are very happy with the performance of the mayor and 20% stated that they are reasonably happy with the performance of the mayor. Only 10% of the respondents stated that they were unhappy with the mayor's performance. So, it seems safe to say that the residents of Quantos City are in general happy with the mayor's performance.

The Conclusion - The residents of Quantos City are in general happy with the mayor's performance.

The Evidence – The majority of respondents to a survey have expressed satisfaction with the mayor's performance.

The Assumption – The assumption is where the representativeness factor will come into play. What if this survey was conducted only amongst the economically well off residents? It is possible then that the poorer residents of Quantos City may actually be unhappy with the mayor's performance but their views haven't been taken into consideration at all in this survey.

So for the argument to hold true, the author of the argument has to assume that the survey mentioned in the argument is representative of the opinion of the entire population of Quantos city.

In general, whenever you see the terms *survey, poll, research, study, etc* mentioned in the evidence of any argument, immediately question whether this survey/poll/research is representative of the larger population as a whole. This will always be the assumption in the argument.

Then if you have to strengthen the argument, you will have to show that the survey/poll/research is indeed representative of the larger population whereas if you have to weaken the argument you will have to show that the survey/poll/research may not be representative of the larger population.

A strengthener for the above argument could be

> *The survey gave adequate importance to all demographic groups in Quantos City*

And a weakener could be

> *The survey comprised only 10% of the total population of Quantos City*

Notice that the strengthener and the weakener do not confirm or negate the argument. The strengthener simply removes one doubt from your mind and the weakener plants a doubt in your mind.

3) Number Arguments

Number Arguments are a mix of Maths and reasoning questions. These arguments will typically try to confuse you with their use of numbers.

For example

> Last year 300 undergrad students of Villa College managed to gain admission to the top ten graduate schools in the country. However, only 100 undergrad students of Havary College managed to gain admission to these schools. Thus, if you wish to study in the country's top ten graduate schools, your chances are higher if you pursue your undergrad degree from Villa College than from Havary College.

The Evidence – 300 undergrad students of Villa College gained admission into the country's top ten schools whereas only 100 undergrad students of Havary College gained admission to these schools

The Conclusion – A student's chances of gaining admission into one of the country's top ten graduate schools are higher if he attends Villa College than if he attends Havary College

On the face of it this argument looks very plausible. After all 300 is a much greater number than 100. However what if the total number of applicants at Villa College to the country's top ten graduate schools is 1000? Then the probability of a student getting into one of these top schools is 0.3 or 30%. And what if the total number of applicants at Havary College to the country's top ten graduate schools is 200? Then the probability of a student getting into one of these top schools is 0.5 or 50%.

So the chances of a Havary College student getting into a top graduate school are higher than those of a Villa College student. But this fact will make our argument fall apart. This leads us to the assumption in the argument.

The Assumption – The assumption has to be that the number of applicants to the country's top graduate schools from Villa College and Havary College is the same. Only then can 300 reflect a higher probability than 100.

So as you can see, number questions can be extremely confusing because the argument may appear completely logical to you at face value. It would help if you knew some common traps that the test maker uses to create number argument questions:

i. **A higher percentage could lead to a lower number and vice versa**

You can only make sense of percentages when you have a total number given to you. Looking at percentages in isolation can distort your perception of the data.

For example, in Year 1 the total radio sales in country X were 100000 units and in Year 2 the total sales came down to 60000 units. In Year 1, 40 % of all radio sets sold were of Company A and in Year 2 this percentage increased to 60%

So you notice that even though Company A's share of the total radio sales increased from 40% to 60%, the total number of radio sets sold by Company A actually fell from 40000 in Year 1 to 36000 in Year 2.

ii. **A higher number could lead to a lower percentage and vice versa**

Again looking at absolute numbers, without taking into consideration the relevant percentages, can distort your perception of the data.

For example, 10 students who study from Professor Roberts scored in the 90th percentile in their tests whereas 60 students who study from Professor Brown scored in the 90th percentile in the same test.

From the above data you may infer that Professor Brown is perhaps a better teacher than is Professor Roberts. However such an inference will be extremely erroneous because we don't know the total number of students taught by each of the Professors.

For example, if Professor Roberts taught only 20 students, then 50% of his students scored in the 90th percentile, and if Professor Brown taught 300 students, then only 20% of his students scored in the 90th percentile.

Tips for making Inferences from Number Arguments:

- For any number argument question you need three details – the total number, the absolute number and the percentage
- If the stimulus contains percentages, avoid answer choices that contain absolute numbers
- If the stimulus contains absolute numbers, avoid answer choices that contain percentages

Importance of Certain terms on Critical Reasoning Questions

1. The use of some, many, most, and majority

While you may think that there is not much difference between these terms, there actually is a big difference. *Some* or *few* means more than one but *most* means more than 50%. This can have a huge bearing when you get down to eliminating incorrect options.

> Four out of five students who study from Professor Larry score above 75% in their exams. So the credit for their excellent performance must go to Professor Larry.
>
> Which of the following two options most strongly weakens the argument?
>
> 1. Some students who study from Professor Larry also take additional tuitions in the subject from Professor James
>
> 2. Most students who study from Professor Larry also take additional tuitions in the subject from Professor James

The argument is in the form of a cause and effect argument where the cause is Professor Larry and the effect is students getting excellent scores in their exams. The easiest way to weaken such arguments is to provide an alternative explanation (cause) for the effect.

Both the above options provide you with an alternative explanation – the fact that students also took classes from Professor James so maybe Professor James is the cause and not Professor Larry. So does this mean that both the options weaken the argument?

No it doesn't.

Option one states that *some* students who study from Professor Larry also take classes in the same subject from Professor James. However, this fact doesn't tell you anything relevant because some students maybe taking these extra classes and some may not. For example, say the total number of students who take classes from Professor Larry is 100 and 5 of them also take classes from Professor James.

Now the argument tells you that on an average 80 out of these 100 students (four out of five) score 75% or above in their exams. Then even if the 5 students who studied from Professor James scored well because of Professor James' teaching, how do you account for the remaining 75 students. It is still very probable that they performed well because of Professor Larry's teaching. So the use of *some* does not take you to the answer.

However *most* means more than 50% so out of the 100 students who study from Professor Larry, if 51 also take classes from Professor James , then it definitely raises a doubt as to whether these students are doing well because of Professor Larry or Professor James. Thus this option weakens the argument by providing an alternate explanation for the stated conclusion.

The takeaway is that words such as *some, many, and few* will rarely give you the answer; instead look out for words such as *most, majority, etc.*

However don't follow this strategy as a blind rule. There is a situation in which *some* can give you the answer. Say an argument concludes that nobody in America uses wood fired stoves anymore. Now if one of the options were to say that a *few or some* people in America still use these stoves, then this option would definitely weaken the argument.

2. The use of 'not' in the options

This will be relevant only for Assumption questions. As you saw earlier in the chapter on Assumptions, the use of *not* in one or more options is an indicator that you may be looking at a passive assumption. Let's take a look at the earlier argument once again:

> Four out of five students who study from Professor Larry score above 75% in their exams. So the credit for their excellent performance must go to Professor Larry.
>
> Which of the following is an assumption in the argument?
>
> 1. The fact that they study from Professor Larry is the only reason that his students do well in the exam
>
> 2. The fact that most of the students who take classes from Professor Larry also take classes from Professor James is **not** the reason why these students perform well in the exams

Option one is definitely assumed in the argument because there can be several other reasons why these students perform well in their exams – maybe they refer to several additional books, maybe they do more research on their own, etc. So for the argument to conclude that the cause of the students' good scores is Professor Larry, it has to assume that nothing else could be the cause of this.

How about option B? Interestingly, option B is also an assumption in the argument. This option logically follows from the earlier assumption. If the argument assumes that the only reason students do well is because they attend Professor Larry's classes, then it automatically also assumes that any other explanation for the said fact cannot be correct. Option B negates the possibility of one such explanation being true, so it is also an assumption in the argument.

Basically option A is an active assumption and option B is a passive assumption.

3. The use of EXCEPT in the Question stem

If we were to ask you what is the opposite of a strengthen option what will you say? Most likely 'weaken'. It is this thought process that you will have to guard against in EXCEPT questions. Technically, the opposite of a strengthen option will be an option that does not strengthen. The fact that this option does not strengthen does not necessarily imply that it will weaken the argument. It may just be an irrelevant fact, or it may be an inference, etc.

So, if the question stem tells you that *each of the given options strengthens the argument EXCEPT* then you need to identify four options that strengthen the argument and the remaining fifth option will be the answer – this option may or may not weaken the argument.

Hence, in EXCEPT questions, when you encounter an option that looks irrelevant don't eliminate it since this may be the correct answer; in fact this option will most likely be the correct answer.

Reading Comprehension Strategies

Now that you have seen all the question types that will be tested on the GRE Reading Comprehension section, let's go some key strategies and points to remember that will greatly help improve your accuracy rate on the RC section of the GRE. Go through this section every time you take a full length test until all these strategies become ingrained in your mind.

The passage is not supposed to be entertaining

A lot of students complain that they find it extremely boring to practice RC passages and that doing so puts them to sleep. It is then not surprising at all that one of the biggest reasons why students perform poorly in the RC section is because they haven't practiced enough passages. Please keep in mind that the purpose of the passage is not to entertain you but to provide you with text that is dense, tedious, and difficult to comprehend. Do not go into the passage expecting to be entertained. You will see that if you go into the test expecting (and fully prepared) to read boring passages, this mindset itself will make you feel more in charge while attempting passages.

Be very careful if the passage is from your area of interest

Always remember to stick to what is mentioned in the passage and to not use outside information or your own knowledge of the subject area to answer questions. This is especially true of passages which are from your area of expertise. For example, say you get a passage about black holes, a subject about which you have considerable knowledge from before. A common trick used by the test maker is to give you an option that you know is the best answer because of your extra knowledge about black holes. However, this will be the wrong answer because it will not be supported by the limited information provided in the passage. For this reason it's best that you get a passage from an unfamiliar topic so that you can approach it objectively and without any preconceived notions.

Do not re-read sentences in the passage

A very common reason why students tend to spend a lot of time on the first read of the passage is because of their tendency to read every sentence in the passage twice or thrice. Part of the reason for this is lack of concentration. You are thinking about something else while reading a sentence so that by the time you finish the sentence you realize that you haven't understood a word of what you have read. So you go back and read the sentence again and then maybe a third time as well. Thus, you end up wasting valuable time.

However, the problem is not always that of concentration. A lot of the times the problem is more psychological in that students have developed this as a habit over the years and have convinced themselves that unless they read the text 3-4 times, they will not understand what it is trying to convey. So, on the first read they don't even make an attempt to understand what is written.

If you are also facing this problem of having to re-read sentences, try this approach - tell yourself that you will read the text only once; however, you can read as slowly as you want. It's fine even if you read at the rate of 50 words per minute as long as you do not re-read any sentence. Initially you may think that this is affecting your capacity to comprehend text (though this really shouldn't be the case since you can read as slowly as you want) but gradually you will see that you are breaking out of the habit to re-read sentences and, here is the best part, without having to sacrifice your reading speed.

Skim but don't skip

Students often ask us whether it is a good idea to read only parts of the passage and omit reading the irrelevant parts. If you notice, this question itself is illogical because you need to read all of the passage to be able to make out what is relevant and what is not. But what if you decide to follow the strategy of reading just the first and the last sentence of every paragraph and skipping the rest of it? We would not recommend that you do this because, while you will be able to answer global questions correctly, you will most likely struggle to answer Inference questions and definitely struggle to answer Detail questions, using this strategy.

For example, a question may ask you *'Which of the following is true of Sulphur according to the passage'?* Now if you have only read the first and the last sentence of each paragraph, you may not have even come across sulphur if it is mentioned in the middle of some paragraph. Then you will end up having to go back and read the entire passage all over again, trying to locate where sulphur is mentioned in the passage. All this obviously leads to wastage of precious time.

So, we think it is a bad idea to skip parts of the passage. However we also think it's a bad idea to try to understand every detail mentioned in the passage. What we recommend is that you skim the passage i.e. read the passage to understand the main idea of every paragraph without getting bogged down by the specific details mentioned in each paragraph. So, while you read everything in the passage (which will make life easier for you on Detail questions), you don't try to understand all of it completely.

Remember the Common Wrong answer traps

While going through the options, you must consciously make an attempt to look for and avoid common wrong answer traps. Here are a few of these traps:

- An option containing a specific detail from the passage will never be the answer to a Global/Primary purpose of the passage question

- Extreme answers must always be avoided on Inference questions

- The answer to a Function question will be the *Why* and not the *What*

Do not get over analytical/mechanical

It is usually advised that students do not get too involved with the passage by trying to understand the meaning of every word in the passage as this could lead to a *missing the woods for the trees* kind of situation. However, the other extreme must also be avoided. What some students do is attempt the passage in an extremely mechanical manner. They get so bogged down in following a process or structure that they completely miss out on the overall meaning of the passage. What we recommend is that you follow a balanced approach – try not to focus too much on every sentence in the passage while at the same time make sure you are clear on the main idea and main purpose of the passage by the time you are done reading it.

Do not get lost in Technical Jargon

Some passages, especially those from the fields of science or law, can be extremely jargon heavy in that they make use of lots of complex technical terms. Do not let this weigh you down. Jargon is the *what* of the passage, but remember that you have to focus on the *why* – why is the author providing you with all this jargon?

So the more complex a passage, the less you should try to focus on the details mentioned in it.

Do not get into the habit of underlining or writing next to the passage in the textbook

A lot of students, instead of jotting down the passage map on a separate piece of paper, prefer to simply underline the important points in the passage itself, or take notes next to the passage in the textbook. This is a very bad habit to get into because you will not be able to underline or write on the computer screen on the actual test. In fact this can completely catch you off guard and ruin your comprehension ability as well as your timing.

Try to eliminate down to two options

On a lot of questions, especially the high difficulty ones, you will often end up eliminating wrong answer choices rather than selecting the correct one. This is true not just for RC questions but for all other question types on the GRE as well. There is nothing wrong with this approach. In fact we encourage students to start by eliminating wrong answer choices. The first time you read through the options, try to eliminate two or three that make absolutely no sense in context of the passage. This shouldn't be very difficult if you have understood the passage correctly because it is very difficult for the test makers to provide you with four or five equally confusing choices.

So, the first time you go through the options, try to come down to two possible answers. Once you do this, you have increased your chances of getting the answer correct from 20% to 50%, which are very good odds. Once you have narrowed down to two possibilities, go through each of these options and try to identify the one that better answers the question asked. It might also be a good idea to re-read the question once again at this stage, as students often tend to misread questions on the test.

Figure out which strategy works best for you

Reading Comprehension is one topic on which the same approach will not work for all students. One student may prefer to take notes while reading whereas another may prefer to do so mentally. Even for the same student, the approach could differ based on the subject area of the passage. I may want to take notes on abstract passages whereas I may not want to do so on relatively simpler detail-oriented passages.

So you need to know which strategy works best for you. The only way to do this is by trying different strategies on several passages. Here are some strategies that you could try:

- Skim through the passage while spending more time on the questions and going back and forth between the questions and the passage
- Spend more time on the first read of the passage and less time on answering each question by avoiding going back to the passage too much.
- Read the passage quickly; then go back and re-read the first and last sentence of each paragraph and try to identify the structure of the passage
- Concentrate on transition words while reading the passage while ignoring most of the details mentioned in the passage.
- Read the first paragraph. Then read only the first and the last sentence of the remaining paragraphs and try to identify the main idea and the purpose of the passage

A difficult passage does not mean difficult questions and vice versa

Just because a passage is difficult to understand does not necessarily mean that the questions from this passage will also be difficult to answer. We've come across several instances in which even if you did not understand half of the passage you could still answer most of the questions correctly by simply elimination options. On the other hand, we have also come across passages which are very easy to comprehend but which provide you with such close options that you can't help getting confused.

What we are trying to highlight is that the moment students see a tough passage, such as one on Philosophy, they tend to assume that this is a very difficult passage and that they will struggle to get the questions right. By starting with this negative mindset, students drastically reduce their chances of success and will end up marking even the simple questions incorrectly.

Easier passage with tricky options provide a different problem – one in which students think they are doing everything correctly whereas they are actually being tricked into going with the wrong options. A lot of students complain after the test that they thought they were marking everything correctly, yet they got a low score. The reasoning described earlier can explain this sort of situation.

In fact we think it is much better if you get tough passages because they keep you on your toes. You'll not get lax and you will recheck each option before marking one. Contrastingly, an easy passage lulls you into a false sense of security and makes you complacent and careless, thereby lowering your score.

Do not worry about your Reading Speed

Some students ask us whether they should join a speed reading course or buy books on the subject. Even some experts suggest that students get into the habit of reading fast. We just recommend that students get in the habit of reading, period!

GRE RC is not a test of reading speed but of comprehension. The average reading speed of humans is around 250 words per minute and the average GRE passage contains around 150 words. So it should take an average person less than one minute to read a GRE passage. However, the problem is comprehension, which is a function of things other than the reading speed.

How to improve Comprehension

To improve your comprehension levels in general, it would be a good idea to go through the following publications on a regular basis. However, do not expect this to show magical results. Reading a dozen issues of the Reader's Digest will not make you an RC expert overnight.

- The Economist
- The Wall Street Journal
- The Reader's Digest
- The National Geographic Magazine
- The Scientific American

In addition to these, it would be a good idea to read one general and one business newspaper every day, with special focus on the Editorial section of the newspapers because it contains more opinionated articles.

Practice, Practice, and more Practice

As we stated at the beginning of this book, there is no great path-breaking strategy that one can use for Reading Comprehension. While basic ideas such as not concentrating too much on every detail in the passage and finding out the main idea and primary purpose obviously remain, the best and perhaps the only way to improve RC is by practicing more and more passages, especially those from outside your comfort area. For this reason we have provided you with 100 RC practice questions in this book. This should be enough to provide you with a thorough workout of all the different subject areas which passages could come from, and of the difficulty levels and question types that could be tested.

Reading Comprehension Practice Set

Passage 1

Because the livelihood of many citizens is linked to the management of national parks, local politicians often encourage state involvement in federal planning. But, state legislatures have not always addressed the fundamental policy issues of whether states should protect park wildlife. Timber harvesting, ranching and energy exploration compete with wildlife within the local ecosystem. Priorities among different land uses are not generally established by current legislation. Additionally, often no mechanism exists to coordinate planning by the state environmental regulatory agencies. These factors limit the impact of legislation aimed at protecting park wildlife and the larger park ecosystem. Even if these deficiencies can be overcome, state participation must be consistent with existing federal legislation. States lack jurisdiction within national parks themselves, and therefore state solutions cannot reach activities inside the parks, thus limiting state action to the land adjacent to the national parks.

1. The passage provides support for which of the following assertions?

    A. Timber harvesting and ranching are the main activities that are responsible for the decline of national parks.
    B. The federal government has been selling national park land to state governments in order to raise money for wildlife conservation.
    C. The actions of state governments have often failed to promote the interests of national park wildlife.
    D. Local politicians want the federal government to turn control of national parks over to state governments.
    E. States have the authority to control the harmful activities being carried out inside national parks

2. Select the sentence in the passage which highlights some of the activities that are harming national parks.

Passage 2

In the third decade of the nineteenth century, Americans began to define their character in light of the railroads that had just been introduced. They liked the idea that it took special people to foresee and capitalize on the promise of science. Railroad promoters, using the steam engine as a metaphor for what they thought Americans were and what they thought Americans were becoming, frequently discussed parallels between the locomotive and national character, pointing out that both possessed youth, power, speed, single-mindedness, and bright prospects.

However, these metaphors also had their dark side. A locomotive was quite unlike anything Americans had ever seen. It was large, mysterious and dangerous; many thought that it was a monster waiting to devour the unwary. There was a suspicion that a country founded upon Jeffersonian agrarian principles had bought a ticket and boarded a train pulled by some iron monster into the dark recesses of an unknown future.

To ease such public apprehensions, promoters, poets, editors, and writers alike adopted the notion that locomotives were really only iron horses, an early metaphor that lingered because it made steam technology ordinary and understandable. Iron horse metaphors assuaged fears about inherent defects in the national character, prompting images of a more secure future, and made an alien technology less frightening, and even comforting and congenial.

For the following question, consider each of the choices separately and select all that apply.

3. From the information in the passage, which of the following can be inferred about the railroads?

   A. Some Americans viewed the introduction of the railroads with scepticism
   B. The railroads proved extremely beneficial for Americans in general
   C. Many prominent people of that time supported the introduction of railroads

4. Which of the following assertions is not consistent with the information in the passage?

   A. Railroads created trepidation in the minds of a lot of Americans
   B. Americans viewed the inventors of the railroad with respect
   C. Parallels were drawn between the railroads and the character of the American people to project the railroads in a positive light
   D. The railroads helped to remove the inherent defects in the national character
   E. The railroads were introduced in America the nineteenth century

5. Select the sentence in the passage that mentions one of the things that was done to allay the fears of people with regards to railroads.

Passage 3

While leaks are generally defended by media officials on the grounds of the public's right to know, in reality they are part of the Washington political power game, as well as part of the policy process. The "leaker" may be currying favour with the media, or may be planting information to influence policy. In the first case, he is helping himself by enhancing the prestige of a journalist; in the second, he is using the media as a stage for his preferred policies. In either instance, it closes the circle: the leak begins with a political motive, is advanced by a politicized media, and continues because of politics. Although some of the journalists think *they* are doing the work, they are more often than not instruments of the process, not prime movers. The media must be held accountable for their activities, just like every other significant institution in our society, and the media must be forced to earn the public's trust.

For the following question, consider each of the choices separately and select all that apply.

6. Which of the following can be inferred from the information in the passage?

   A. Media leaks are a part of the American government's policy
   B. The primary purpose of media leaks is to influence public policy
   C. There needs to be accountability among media with regards to its actions

7. What does the passage state about journalists who believe that they are the prime movers behind media leaks?

   A. Their belief is correct because media leaks can make or break governments
   B. Their belief is correct because they are the link between the public and the government
   C. Their belief is incorrect because more often than not they are just being used to serve somebody else's larger purpose
   D. Their belief is incorrect because at times the public may not chose to believe them
   E. Their belief is incorrect because they are as accountable to the people as any other institution in the society

Passage 4

In the decades following World War II, American business had undisputed control of the world economy, producing goods of such high quality and low cost that foreign corporations were unable to compete. But in the mid-1960s the United States began to lose its advantage and by the 1980s American corporations lagged behind the competition in many industries. In the computer chip industry, for example, American corporations had lost most of both domestic and foreign markets by the early 1980s.

The first analysts to examine the decline of American business blamed the U.S. government. Still later analysts blamed the American workforce, citing labour demands and poor productivity as the reasons American corporations have been unable to compete with Japanese and European firms. Finally, a few analysts even censured American consumers for their unpatriotic purchases of foreign goods. **The blame actually lies with corporate management, which has made serious errors based on misconceptions about what it takes to be successful in the marketplace**. These missteps involve labour costs, production choices, and growth strategies.

8. What is the relation between the highlighted parts of the passage?

   A. The first is a premise of the author and the second is the main conclusion of the author
   B. The first is an intermediate conclusion made by the author and the second provides evidence to justify this conclusion
   C. The first provides the opinion of one particular group and the second provides the contrasting conclusion of the author
   D. The first provides evidence that undermines the author's conclusion and the second strengthens the author's conclusion
   E. The first is a strategy adopted that failed and the second is a strategy adopted that succeeded

For the following question, consider each of the choices separately and select all that apply.

9. Which of the following can be concluded from the information in the passage?

   A. American consumers are partly responsible for the decline in the global standing of American corporates
   B. American businesses functioned extremely efficiently in the period following World War II
   C. Poor production choices made by the leaders of American companies are partly to be blamed for the decline in the stature of these companies

10. What is the main purpose of the passage?

    A. To blame American corporate leaders for making poor growth strategies
    B. To provide an alternative explanation for an event
    C. To justify the taking place of an event
    D. To repudiate the claim that the corporate management was responsible for the decline in American industry during the 80s
    E. To analyze several interpretations of an event and to support one of them

Passage 5

Though he left us with numerous great works and, to be sure, is widely regarded as America's first internationally renowned author, Washington Irving's sometimes enigmatic tendencies and techniques have left literary critiques and academics to ponder his motives more than 140 years after his death. One such trait that raises the proverbial eyebrow of the community of readers and critiques is Irving's repeated, and varied, use of pseudonyms throughout his career.

11. Which of the following can be inferred from the information in the passage?

    A. Irving never wrote under his own name
    B. All great authors have some eccentricities related to them
    C. Several centuries have passed since Irving died
    D. Irving was criticized by people of his time for writing under different pseudonyms
    E. There are aspects of Irving's personality that remain unexplained

Passage 6

The 1960s and 1970s witnessed a new boomtown era in the West. The typical contemporary boomtown is fuelled by a quest for energy in the form of a fossil-fuelled electric generating plant, a hydroelectric dam or a new mine. The energy project is typically located near a small community or is forced to start a community from scratch. Often, the boomtown is poorly planned and under-financed. Long-time residents find their community changed for the worse and newcomers find the town an undesirable place to live.

The boomtown is characterized by inadequate public services, undesirable labour conditions, confusion in community structure, and deterioration of the quality of life arising from rapid population growth due to a major economic stimulus. Accelerated growth is the most distinguishing characteristic of a boomtown.

12. Select the sentence in the passage that explains what can accelerate the process of setting up of boomtowns?

For the following question, consider each of the choices separately and select all that apply.

13. According to the passage, which of the following can be a characteristic of a boomtown?

    A. Poor planning and infrastructure
    B. Sluggish economy and a low growth rate
    C. Lack of finances

Passage 7

In a now-famous study, Stephen Kosslyn asked subjects to imagine an animal, such as a rabbit, next to either an elephant or a fly. When the image was formed, Kosslyn would ask whether or not the target animal had a particular attribute. For example, Kosslyn might say, "elephant, rabbit," and then "leg." He found that it took subjects longer to answer when the target animal was next to the large animal than when it was next to the small animal. Kosslyn interpreted this to mean that subjects had to zoom in on the image to detect the particular feature. Just as one has difficulty seeing details on small objects, so the subjects could not simply mentally "see" details on the smaller object in their mental image.

14. If the experiment discussed in the passage were to be recreated then, as per the information in the passage, in which of the following situations would a person take the least time to answer?

    A. If the target was next to an object of the same size
    B. If the target was next to a larger object
    C. If the target had a unique distinguishing mark
    D. If the target was of a different shape than the other objects
    E. If the target was next to a smaller object

15. Select the sentence in the passage that leads to Kosslyn's interpretation that subjects have to zoom in on an image.

Passage 8

Artistic movies are composed of a multitude of 'shots' or discrete scenes usually lasting only 6 to 20 seconds; together the hundreds of individual scenes combine to make up the movie. For each shot the director has many options on how to film the same. For example, imagine that the movie's script calls for two actors to speak a fixed dialogue in a specified location. Even while the director stays true to the script, he has considerable leeway in how to film the scene. He may film an 'extreme long shot', with the camera far away. This tends to show the setting in a panorama, emphasizing the background while underplaying the actors, and is used primarily in outdoor scenes where the backdrop is particularly impressive. Or, he may employ the 'long shot', which brings the camera close enough to capture the actor's entire bodies, together with some of the setting. And finally there is the 'close-up', where the camera is brought in close enough to focus on the actors' heads and faces and has the effect of spotlighting a particular actor while hiding the setting and other actors.

16. The passage discussion most clearly suggests that the most important aspect of filmmaking is

    A. figuring out what moviegoers are going to love
    B. deciding how to make a movie artistic
    C. using a good director
    D. signing a top actor for the lead role
    E. using a great cameraman

For the following question, consider each of the choices separately and select all that apply.

17. Which of the following can be inferred from the information in the passage?

    A. For a scene in which it is important to highlight the facial expression of an actor, it is best to use the close up shot
    B. A director shooting a movie in Zurich for its beautiful locales should use a lot of extreme long shots
    C. A fight scene between two actors in a nondescript setting should be best filmed in a long shot

Passage 9

In spite of the conventional interpretation, a survey of source material reveals that the image of the plains as Desert was restricted in 1825 to certain portions of the country and to certain segments of the population. Analysis of newspapers and periodical literature indicates that the Desert image was strongest in the rural areas of the Northeast and weakest in the rural areas of the South and trans-Appalachian West. Acceptance of the Desert concept was more likely among the well-educated elite, particularly in the Northeast, and acceptance of a "Garden" notion was greater among the rural populations, particularly in the South and West.

American historians have argued that the myth of the Great American Desert dominated the pre-Civil War view of the Great Plains. It was this conception of the plains as Desert, according to the traditional interpretation, that caused the American folk migration westward to leap over the region during the 1840's and the 1850's. This conventional understanding is neither completely invalid nor necessarily incorrect; but it is too simplistic to be fully satisfying. To claim the universal acceptance of stereotyped images of the Great Plains is to ignore the presence of a considerable array of data to the contrary.

18. Which of the following can most likely be inferred from the passage?

    A. The conventional view holds that the Great Plains were in fact largely a desert
    B. People in the South west were much less likely to think of the Great Plains as a desert
    C. During the American migration mentioned in the passage, people moved from the Great Plains to more urban areas

19. Select the sentence in the passage that provides the reason why migrants did not settle down in the Great Plains.

For the following question, consider each of the choices separately and select all that apply.

20. Which of the following would the author of the passage most likely agree with?

    A. Educated and well-off people were more likely to believe in the concept of the Desert than the rural people
    B. The myth of the Great American Desert dominated the pre Civil War view of the Plains
    C. The conventional view of the of the Plains as a Desert is not entirely incorrect

21. Which of the following can be inferred from the last sentence of the passage – *"To claim the universal acceptance of stereotyped images of the Great Plains is to ignore the presence of a considerable array of data to the contrary."*

   A. The Great Plains was in fact not a desert
   B. There is considerable data available that could prove that the Great Plains was much more than what stereotyped images make it out to be
   C. It is almost universally accepted that the Great Plains were in fact a Desert
   D. The reason migrants decided to skip over the Great Plains is because they thought of this area as a desert
   E. Not everyone in America believed in the notion that the Great Plains was a Desert

Passage 10

Scientists study reef fishes not only because of the diverse sampling of species but also because of the range of behaviours and relationships between species and other animals that is available for analysis. Intense competition and predation have caused fishes to carve out special niches. Mimicry and camouflage offer just two ways for species to blend in with their surroundings. Symbiotic relationships between fish and other organisms also occur with frequency on coral reefs. The anemonefish share their habitat with sea anemones in a symbiotic relationship that scientists have yet to unravel completely. The defensive nematocysts of the anemone are used to stun prey, but the anemonefish are resistant to these stinging cells. Researchers believe that the fish secrets a mucous coating that mimics that of the anemone allowing for chemical signals to prohibit the firing of the cells. One theory holds that the fish obtain these chemicals by rubbing against the sea anemone's tentacles. The benefits, if any, to the anemone for having these fish live with them are not clear.

For the following question, consider each of the choices separately and select all that apply.

22. Which of the following options provides the rationale behind why scientists study reef fishes?

   A. Scientists want to study the anemonefish, which is only found in reefs
   B. The reefs provide scientists with a wide variety of fish species in one place
   C. The reefs provide scientists with several examples of interdependence between different species

23. Select the sentence in the passage that explains how species in coral reefs can blend in with their environment.

Passage 11

Because we have so deeply interiorized writing, we find it difficult to consider writing to be an alien technology, as we commonly assume printing and the computer to be. **Most people are surprised to learn that essentially the same objections commonly urged today against computers were urged by Plato in the *Phaedrus*, against writing.** Writing, Plato has Socrates say, is inhuman, pretending to establish outside the mind what in reality can be only in the mind. Secondly, Plato's Socrates urges, writing destroys memory. Those who use writing will become forgetful, relying on external resource for what they lack in internal resources. Thirdly, **a written text is basically unresponsive, whereas real speech and thought always exist essentially in a context of give-and-take between real persons.**

24. Which of the following would the author of the passage most likely agree with?

    A. Writing can at times appear as inhuman
    B. A negative aspect of writing is that it could destroy memory
    C. Writing can at times fail to provide the right context
    D. Writing is more important than other cognitive skills
    E. There have been people in the past who have opposed the technology of writing

25. What is the relation between the highlighted lines in the passage?

    A. The first is the main thesis of the author and the second provides explanation for the main thesis
    B. The first is the primary conclusion of the passage and the second provides an alternate contradictory conclusion
    C. The first is a rebuttal of Platos's argument and the second is Plato's main argument
    D. The first is the main thesis of the author and the second contradicts the main thesis of the author
    E. The first is a point made in opposition of the advocacy of a truth and the second is that truth

Passage 12

Arguments abound over whether marijuana should be legalized. Medical research has repeatedly provided evidence that marijuana use causes permanent physical, psychological, and thus emotional damage to those who regularly use it. Studies at the University of Maryland and UCLA indicated that the regular smoking of only two marijuana cigarettes a day would tend to promote toe fungus and thrush. But over the years, much stronger claims have surfaced: heavy marijuana users perform poorly at work or school, are more likely to be delinquent and develop psychiatric problems, or have abnormal brain waves. *Repeatedly, however, such studies encounter the same objection: are the problems caused by smoking marijuana, or is it just that people with problems are more likely to end up using marijuana heavily?*

For the following question, consider each of the choices separately and select all that apply.

26. Which of the following questions is most similar in structure to the one contained in the highlighted lines in the passage?

    A. Recently several bridges have collapsed in Tycho city for which the architects' poor design has been blamed. But couldn't the bridges have collapsed because of some other reason beyond the control of the architects, such as use of poor quality construction material?
    B. Students who get scholarships tend to perform better than students who don't. However is it because of the scholarships that the students perform better or is it that the students were good students because of which they got the scholarship in the first place?
    C. It has been noticed that children who play basketball are much taller than other children, so parents should encourage their children to play basketball if they want them to become tall. However is it that the children are tall because they play basketball or is it that they play basketball because they are tall?

27. Which of the following options best summarizes the passage as a whole?

    A. According to experts, there are several harmful effects of using marijuana
    B. There are people who believe that the use of marijuana should be legalized
    C. Poor performance at work and psychiatric problems could be the result of marijuana use
    D. At the moment there is no consensus on whether marijuana's benefits outweigh its harmful effects or vice versa
    E. Marijuana use should not be legalized as it can have serious deleterious effects

Passage 13

The simple statement that the universe had a beginning in time is by now so obvious to astrophysicists that few give it a second thought. Yet it is a statement that has profound implications. Most civilizations embrace one of two opposite concepts of time. Linear time has a beginning, a duration, and an end; cyclical time, as its name suggests, continues around and around forever. In a universe that functions through cyclical time, the question of creation never arises; the universe always was and always will be. The minute you switch to linear time you immediately confront the vexing question not only of creation, but also of the Creator. Although there is no logical reason for the assumption, many people believe that if something comes into existence, it must do so in response to the actions of some rational being. Because of that belief, astronomers, even though they resist becoming involved in theological discussion, find themselves in one when they posit the Big Bang universe. It puts them squarely in the middle of an age-old debate.

28. Each of the following is suggested by the passage EXCEPT

   A. Astronomers in general support the Big Bang model
   B. Linear time and cyclical time are contradictory in nature
   C. The belief that the universe had a beginning in time can lead to some difficult to answer questions
   D. The Big Bang model is not based on sound logical reasoning
   E. Astronomers typically avoid getting into debates about the existence of god

Passage 14

The value of old maps as documents useful for historicity depends necessarily on to what degree they depict and on how accurately. For virtually all periods of pre-modern history some maps have survived to serve as historiography, depicting, however imperfectly, certain features of past geography. The work of Claudius Ptolemy—who lived in the 2nd century A.D.—for centuries provided the basis for maps of the known world and its major regions. Although many were drawn on the scientific basis which he provided, they nevertheless embodied many errors—of location, distance, and the shape of areas of land and sea. The medieval portolan charts of the Mediterranean Sea and the later charts which provided sailing directions, produced in Holland, were accurate enough to be useful in practical navigation. However, few of the early maps approach modern standards, which require accurate representation of distances and of heights above mean sea-level and the use of carefully distinguished symbols. This is because it was not until the 18th century that cartography, as an exact science, was born.

29. The author of the passage would most likely agree with which of the following?

    A. Ancient maps are almost as accurate as modern maps
    B. It is not necessary that a map be completely error free to be useful
    C. Claudius Ptolemy's was the most famous map maker of his era
    D. Cartography is a modern field of study
    E. Information provided by ancient maps is most often incorrect

Passage 15

As formal organizations, business corporations are distinguished by their particular goals, which include maximization of profits, growth, and survival. Providing goods and services is a means to this end. If, for example, a number of individuals (outsiders or even insiders) believe that a company's aggressive marketing of infant formula in third world countries is morally wrong, the company is unlikely to be moved by arguments based on ethos alone as long as what it is doing remains profitable. But if those opposed to the company's practice organize a highly effective boycott of the company's products, their moral views will soon enter into the company's deliberations indirectly as limiting operating conditions. They can, at this point, no more be ignored than a prohibitive increase in the costs of certain raw materials.

For the following question, consider each of the choices separately and select all that apply.

30. According to the information in the passage, which of the following business corporations is achieving its primary goal?

    A. A business corporation that takes every possible step to ensure that its customers are satisfied
    B. A business corporation that spends a lot of money in hiring external consultants to devise growth strategies for the business
    C. A business corporation that gives top-most priority to profitability

For the following question, consider each of the choices separately and select all that apply.

31. Suppose a company is indulging in some unethical practice. Then, according to the information in the passage, under which of the following conditions is the company most likely to correct this practice?

    A. If a group of consumers were to file a court case against the company
    B. If a newspaper ran a campaign encouraging citizens not to purchase the products of the company
    C. If the actions of the company were to lead to it being criticized in the international media

Passage 16

What is the biggest lesson from the Great Depression? In my view, it is that monetary policy and the financial sector play a crucial role in economic development. One important component of the monetary policy is the financial market, more specifically the banking sector.

Why are financial markets and the banking sector so important? Banks fulfil a very important role in the economy by matching borrowers and lenders. When we deposit $100 in a bank, the bank keeps, at most, two to three dollars in its vaults (some of this is actually kept with the central bank), the remaining $98 or so are lent to a borrower.

Most businesses require loans for their normal operations. When the banking sector does not work properly, businesses cannot get loans and they have to curtail their production and lay off workers. As they curtail production, they demand fewer products from their suppliers and therefore their suppliers have to reduce their output and fire workers. If manufacturers cannot sell their goods because the firm downstream does not need as many products as before, they cannot generate enough revenue to repay their earlier loans. Businesses go bankrupt and banks experience further problems as their balance sheet deteriorates due to non-performing loans. At this point, banks want to lend even less because of the uncertainty generated from bankruptcies. As they lend less, the vicious circle continues – with producers cutting production and firing workers. On top of this, depositors start worrying about their deposits because the non-performing loans have made some banks go belly up – your bank has lent out your money to borrowers who cannot return it. Depositors start withdrawing their cash and banks have even fewer possibilities for lending as they have to hoard cash in case there is a run on the bank. If the financial sector does not work, the real economy can go into a deadly spiral and shrink by 30 per cent as during the Great Depression.

One would have thought that this fact would be obvious to all the policy makers. However all the lessons from the Great Depression seem to have been lost within three-quarters of a century. It seems, to paraphrase Marc Bard, that politics (especially of the petty and partisan variety) eats policy for lunch seven days a week.

32. What is the main purpose of the author in writing the passage?

    A. To explain how banks and other financial institutions function
    B. To discuss the lessons learnt from the Great Depression
    C. To argue that banks and manufacturing businesses are interdependent
    D. To criticize a group of people for not learning from the lessons of the Great Depression
    E. To conclude that people give preference to politics over policies

33. According to the information in the passage, which of the following can be inferred?

   A. Banks are short of cash most of the time
   B. Banks do not like to keep money with the central bank.
   C. Banks do not like to keep large amounts of money in their vaults.
   D. Banks usually keep some money with the central bank.
   E. Banks actually fool the customers

34. In the last paragraph, the tone of the author is

   A. Adulatory
   B. Optimistic
   C. Critical
   D. Analytical
   E. Ridiculing

For the following question, consider each of the choices separately and select all that apply.

35. Which of these could be a result of the banking system not functioning properly?

   A. The economy can go into a depression.
   B. Workers of manufacturing companies can be fired.
   C. Businesses can find it difficult to get loans.

Passage 17

During the late 1990s, HP, the second largest computer manufacturer in the world, faced major challenges in an increasingly competitive market. In 1998, while HP's revenues grew by just 3%, competitor Dell's rose by 38%. Also HP's share price remained more or less stagnant, while competitor IBM's share price increased by 65% during 1998. Analysts said HP's culture, which emphasized teamwork and respect for co-workers, had over the years translated into a consensus-style culture that was proving to be a sharp disadvantage in the fast-growing Internet business era. Analysts felt that instead of Lewis Platt, HP needed a new leader to cope with rapidly changing industry trends. Responding to these concerns, in July 1999, the HP board appointed Carleton S. Fiorina (Fiorina) as the company's CEO.

Fiorina implemented several cost-cutting measures to streamline the company's operations. Some of the measures included forced five-day vacation for workers and postponement of wage hikes for three months in December 2000. Even though the employees protested vociferously against such measures, Fiorina did not relent in implementing the same.

The steps taken by Fiorina surprised analysts. They said that these steps were a major departure from HP's organizational culture - 'The HP Way' of promising lifelong employment and employee satisfaction. According to the company insiders, though change was necessary, employees' morale had suffered badly.

36. According to the passage, the consensus-style culture of HP was

    A. The most important factor responsible for the fall in HPs revenues
    B. A Cost saver
    C. Passive towards changing market conditions
    D. Out of sync with the competitor's strategies
    E. A Quality booster

For the following question, consider each of the choices separately and select all that apply.

37. Which of the following can be inferred from the passage?

    A. Dell had a much stronger brand image as compared to HP
    B. Share price of a company can be an indicator of its success.
    C. Fiorina favoured cost cutting even at the cost of employee morale.

Passage 18

To account for the conformation of the Alps, two hypotheses have been advanced, which may be respectively named the hypothesis of fracture and the hypothesis of erosion. The former assumes that the forces by which the mountains were elevated produced fissures in the earth's crust, and that the valleys of the Alps are the tracks of these fissures; the latter maintains that the valleys have been cut out by the action of ice and water, the mountains themselves being the residual forms of this grand sculpture.

I had heard the Via Mala cited as a conspicuous illustration of the fissure theory — the profound chasm thus named, and through which the Hinter-Rhein now flows, could, it was alleged, be nothing else than a crack in the earth's crust. To the Via Mala I therefore went in 1864 to instruct myself upon the point in question. The gorge commences about a quarter of an hour above Tusis and, on entering it, the first impression certainly is that it must be a fissure. This conclusion, in my case, was modified as I advanced because the signs I saw thereupon left no doubt in my mind that this gorge was created due to river action.

38. What is the function of the first sentence of the second paragraph - *'The gorge commences......it must be a fissure'*?

    A. It is a hypothesis that the author later disagrees with
    B. It is a hypothesis that the author goes on to prove right
    C. It is a neutral observation made by the author
    D. It confirms the author's initial belief
    E. It is the first step in the author's experiment

For the following question, consider each of the choices separately and select all that apply.

39. Which of the following can be inferred from the information provided in the passage?

    A. It is now absolutely clear what led to the formation of the Alps
    B. According to the hypothesis of erosion, the valleys in the Alps have been created by the action of ice and water
    C. The Via Mala is the name of a river that flows through the Alps

Passage 19

Among the men and women prominent in the public life of America there are but few whose names are mentioned as often as that of Emma Goldman. Yet the real Emma Goldman is almost quite unknown. The sensational press has surrounded her name with so much misrepresentation and slander, it would seem almost a miracle that, in spite of this web of calumny, the truth breaks through and a better appreciation of this much maligned idealist begins to manifest itself. There is but little consolation in the fact that almost every representative of a new idea has had to struggle and suffer under similar difficulties. Is it of any avail that a former president of a republic pays homage at Osawatomie to the memory of John Brown? Or that the president of another republic participates in the unveiling of a statue in honour of Pierre Proudhon, and holds up his life to the French nation as a model worthy of enthusiastic emulation? Of what avail is all this when, at the same time, the LIVING John Browns and Proudhons are being crucified? The honour and glory of a Mary Wollstonecraft or of a Louise Michel are not enhanced by the City Fathers of London or Paris naming a street after them—the living generation should be concerned with doing justice to the LIVING Mary Wollstonecrafts and Louise Michels. Posterity assigns to men like

Wendel Phillips and Lloyd Garrison the proper niche of honour in the temple of human emancipation, but it is the duty of their contemporaries to bring them due recognition and appreciation while they live.

40. Select the sentence in the passage that most accurately describes the primary concern of the author in writing the passage.

41. Why does the author mention *'the President of another country'* in the passage?

A. To assert that every proponent of a new idea has had to face difficulties in the past
B. To state that Pierre Proudhon had been unfairly treated by his contemporaries when he was alive
C. To demonstrate that a situation discussed earlier in the passage is prevalent in all countries
D. To provide an example of an incident in which the good work of a person was appreciated only after his death
E. To demand that Pierre Proudhon be given some compensation for the unjust treatment meted out to him when he was alive

For the following question, consider each of the choices separately and select all that apply.

42. With which of the following statements would the author most likely agree?

A. The press is primarily responsible for the negative reception that new ideas are greeted with
B. Emma Goldman's contemporaries are partly to be blamed for the way she was treated when she was alive
C. Nobody knows the real Emma Goldman

Passage 20

Although the Great Plains country of the West was the natural home of the American Bison, where it flourished most abundantly, it also wandered south across Texas to the burning plains of North-eastern Mexico, westward across the Rocky Mountains into New Mexico, Utah, and Idaho, and northward across a vast treeless waste to the bleak and inhospitable shores of the Great Slave Lake itself. It is more than probable that had the bison remained unmolested by man and uninfluenced by him, he would eventually have crossed the Sierra Nevadas and the Coast Range and taken up his abode in the fertile valleys of the

Pacific slope. It is also very likely that, had the bison remained for a few more centuries in undisturbed possession of his range and with liberty to roam at will over the North American continent, several distinctly recognizable varieties would have been produced. The individuals inhabiting the extreme north, in the vicinity of Great Slave Lake, for example, would have developed still longer hair, and taken on more of the dense hairiness of the musk ox.

43. The passage mentions each of the following as a negative impact of man's activities on the American bison EXCEPT

   A. The bison could not inhabit the valleys of the Pacific slope
   B. Certain new varieties of the bison could not be produced
   C. The bison could not cross the Sierra Nevada
   D. There was a drastic fall in the bison population
   E. The bison's ability to roam at will was curtailed

For the following question, consider each of the choices separately and select all that apply.

44. Which of the following can be inferred from the information provided in the passage?

   A. The American bison is a long-haired animal
   B. The American bison has now become extinct
   C. The Rocky Mountains was not the natural habitat of the American bison

45. Select the sentence in the passage that points out one physical characteristic of the American Bison.

Passage 21

A relic I still have in my possession amongst my naval memorabilia is a black, mourning armband issued to us when King George VI died on February 6, 1952. It was dispatched by Messrs Gieves of Old Bond Street in London, the naval tailors 'By appointment to the King'. I recall listening to the last Christmas day broadcast of King George VI, with his consort by his side, while having dinner with a friend in Surrey. Then a few weeks later we were to receive news of his death while we were at sea on board our training cruiser HMS Devonshire headed for the Caribbean. As we proceeded to drop anchor in Barbados harbour, we were struck first, by the magnificent sight of flying fish which kept darting across the placid blue waters, and then, by the great alacrity with which mourning bands were delivered to us for the funeral ceremonies. Inevitably, we were billed by 'Messrs Thieves' for five shillings, a princely sum then, because our pay was four shillings a day.

46. At the end of the passage, the author refers to 'Messrs Gieves of Old Bond Street' as 'Messrs Thieves'. This most likely suggests that the author

    A. did not appreciate being charged a high price for the black armbands that he did not order for voluntarily
    B. believed that 'Messrs Gieves' had shown a lot of alacrity in delivering the armbands on time
    C. thought that he was underpaid for his work in the army
    D. was miserly by nature
    E. was not in favour of elaborate funeral ceremonies

47. Select the sentence in the passage that identifies the author's location when King George VI died.

Passage 22

It is one of the disadvantages of reading books about natural scenic wonders that they fill the mind with pictures, often exaggerated, often distorted, often blurred, and, even when well drawn, injurious to the freshness of first impressions. Such has been the fate of most of us with regard to the Falls of Niagara. There was little accuracy in the estimates of the first observers of the cataract. Startled by an exhibition of power so novel and so grand, emotion leaped beyond the control of the judgment, and gave currency to notions which have often led to disappointment.

48. Which of the following would the author of the passage most likely agree with?

    A. One should never read books about natural scenic wonders
    B. Reading books about natural scenic wonders can prevent a person from having an unbiased viewing of that wonder
    C. The Niagara Falls have been described incorrectly in books
    D. The Niagara Falls are actually not grand and novel
    E. Emotional descriptions of natural wonders are always exaggerated

Passage 23

The purpose of mechanics is to describe how bodies change their position in space with time. I should load my conscience with grave sins against the sacred spirit of lucidity were I to formulate the aims of mechanics in this way, without serious reflection and detailed explanations. Let us proceed to disclose these sins.

It is not clear what is to be understood here by "position" and "space." I stand at the window of a railway carriage which is travelling uniformly, and drop a stone on the embankment, without throwing it. Then, disregarding the influence of the air resistance, I see the stone descend in a straight line. A pedestrian who observes the misdeed from the footpath notices that the stone falls to earth in a parabolic curve. I now ask: Do the "positions" traversed by the stone lie "in reality" on a straight line or on a parabola? Moreover, what is meant here by motion "in space" ? From the considerations of the previous section the answer is self-evident. In the first place we entirely shun the vague word "space," of which, we must honestly acknowledge, we cannot form the slightest conception, and we replace it by "motion relative to a practically rigid body of reference." The positions relative to the body of reference (railway carriage or embankment) have already been defined in detail in the preceding section. If instead of "body of reference " we insert " system of co-ordinates," which is a useful idea for mathematical description, we are in a position to say: The stone traverses a straight line relative to a system of co-ordinates rigidly attached to the carriage, but relative to a system of co-ordinates rigidly attached to the ground (embankment) it describes a parabola. With the aid of this example it is clearly seen that there is no such thing as an independently existing trajectory, but only a trajectory relative to a particular body of reference.

49. What can be inferred about the author from the first paragraph of this passage?

A. The author agrees with the definition of a term as mentioned in the first line of the passage
B. The author wants to reflect on the definition of a term as mentioned in the first line of the passage
C. The author believes that concepts such as 'space' cannot be defined in absolute terms
D. The author does not completely agree with the definition of a term as mentioned in the first line of the passage
E. The author is a physics expert

50. If a stone were to be dropped on a platform 20 feet below, from the window of a moving vehicle, which of the following must be true, according to the information in the passage?

A. To a person sitting in the vehicle the stone would appear to fall in the shape of a parabola
B. To a person sitting in another vehicle 500 metres behind, the stone would appear to fall in a straight line
C. To a person standing on the platform the stone would appear to fall in a straight line
D. To a person standing on the platform the stone would appear to fall either in a straight line or in the shape of a parabola
E. To a person standing on the platform the stone would appear to fall in the shape of a parabola

For the following question, consider each of the choices separately and select all that apply.

51. The passage implies that scientists should refrain from doing which of the following?

A. Coming up with theoretical definitions without judging the practical veracity of the same
B. Considering concepts in the field of physics in absolute terms
C. Attempting to define terms from the realm of Physics in the relative sense rather in absolute terms

52. The author conducts an experiment in the passage. Select the sentence in the passage that highlights one qualifier that the author gives in his experiment.

Passage 24

The Cyclopses, according to mythology, were a race of bad-tempered and rather stupid one-eyed giants. Not, perhaps, a great portend for a new generation of robots. But Andrew Davison, a computer scientist at Imperial College, London, thinks one eye is enough for a robot, provided its brain can think fast enough. For a robot to work autonomously, it has to understand its environment. Stereoscopic vision, integrating the images from two "eyes" looking at the same thing from different angles, is one approach to achieve this, but it involves a lot of complicated computer processing. The preferred method these days, therefore, is SLAM (Simultaneous Localization and Mapping), which uses sensors such as laser-based range finders that "see" by bouncing beams of light off their surroundings and timing the return.

For the following question, consider each of the choices separately and select all that apply.

53. Which of the following assertions can be made from the information in the passage?

    A. A Robots with two eyes is most likely making use of stereoscopic vision
    B. Cyclopses were mythical beings with one eye and small stature
    C. SLAM is probably simpler than Stereoscopic vision

Passage 25

The sole use and sole object of existence is enjoyment or pleasure, which two words will here be treated as synonymous; happiness, also, though not quite identical in meaning, being occasionally substituted for them. Enjoyment, it must be observed, is of various kinds, measures, and degrees. It may be sensual, or emotional, or imaginative, or intellectual, or moral. It may be momentary or eternal; intoxicating delight or sober satisfaction. It may be unmixed and undisturbed, in which case, however short of duration or coarse in quality, it may in strictness be called happiness; or it may be troubled and alloyed, although of a flavour which would be exquisite if pure, and if there were nothing to interfere with the perception of it. Understood, however, in a sufficiently comprehensive sense, enjoyment or pleasure may be clearly perceived to be the sole object of existence. The whole value of life plainly consists of the enjoyment, present or future, which life affords, or is capable of affording or securing. Now, the excellence of all rules depends on their conduciveness to the object they have in view. The excellence of all rules of life must, therefore, depend on their conduciveness to the sole object which life has in view, viz., enjoyment. But the excellence of rules of life, or of conduct or modes of acting, would seem to be but another name for their morality, and the morality of actions obviously depends on their conformity to moral rules. Whence, if so much be admitted, it necessarily follows that the test of the morality of actions is their conduciveness to enjoyment.

54. What is the main purpose of the author in writing the passage?

    A. To define a term by giving examples
    B. To put forward a point of view and explain its implication
    C. To describe several interpretations of a belief
    D. To present an unusual interpretation of a well known fact
    E. To evaluate two competing beliefs

55. The author of the passage would agree with each of the following EXCEPT

A. Pleasure always leads to happiness
B. Pleasure can be of different types
C. Enjoyment is no different from pleasure
D. Unmixed enjoyment cannot strictly be called enjoyment
E. The sole purpose of life is the quest for happiness

For the following question, consider each of the choices separately and select all that apply.

56. The passage provides information in support of which of the following assertions?

A. An act of crime cannot be considered an immoral act if a person derives enjoyment from that act
B. The morality of actions cannot solely be judged by their perceived enjoyment
C. The excellence of all rules of life depends on their morality

Passage 26

Progress became a theme in European thought in about 1750. The thinkers of the Enlightenment wanted to replace the Biblical account of time (Genesis, Creation, Fall, Redemption) with a myth which put Man, not God, at the centre of the story. The narrative of human progress was understood to be both a material and a moral process; not just changing our technologies, but altering our instincts, and for the better.

We now live in ironic, anti-heroic times. Do we still believe in the story of progress? It sits in the attic of our minds like a glorious Victorian antique, as magnificent as a stuffed moose head and just as useless. Perhaps worse than useless. Modern political correctness has lodged a suspicion in our mind about the Ascent of Man. What do you mean, Man? What about Woman? And which Man? Surely not the European conquerors? And Ascent? Surely you're not implying that western civilization is superior to everything that's gone before? And so on. The Ascent of Man may be an idea we had better do without.

57. The author mentions the thinkers of the Enlightenment in order to

    A. assert that the Bible was an impediment in the way of progress.
    B. demonstrate that Man is superior to God
    C. affirm that human progress is akin to mastery over the world.
    D. illustrate the transformation in man's approach towards the concept of 'progress'
    E. conclude that the Ascent of Man is an obsolete idea.

58. Select the sentence in the passage that highlights the primary difference between the Modern and the Biblical accounts of time.

Passage 27

Woman's demand for equal suffrage is based largely on the contention that a woman must have equal rights in all affairs of society. Needless to say, I am not opposed to woman suffrage on the conventional ground that she is not equal to it. I see no physical, psychological, or mental reasons why a woman should not have the equal right to vote with man. But that cannot possibly blind me to the absurd notion that a woman will accomplish that wherein man has failed. If she would not make things worse, she certainly could not make them better. To assume, therefore, that she would succeed in purifying something which is not susceptible of purification, is to credit her with supernatural powers. Since woman's greatest misfortune has been that she was looked upon as either angel or devil, her true salvation lies in being placed on earth; namely, in being considered human, and therefore subject to all human follies and mistakes. Are we, then, to believe that two wrongs will make one right? Are we to assume that the poison already inherent in politics will be decreased, if women were to enter the political arena? The most ardent suffragists would hardly maintain such a folly.

59. The author of the passage is primarily concerned with

    A. discussing the possible implications of a change
    B. arguing that a particular change will not have the desired effect
    C. exploring definitions of a concept
    D. comparing the advantages of a particular change with its disadvantages
    E. clarifying an ambiguous term

60. What can be inferred from the lines *'her true salvation lies in being placed on earth'*?

A. The author does not believe that giving women the right to vote would solve the problems that the political system faces
B. The author is against adopting an extreme view of women in general
C. The author does not believe that two wrongs will make one right
D. The author believes that a woman does not have supernatural powers
E. The author believes women should suffer as much as men, no more and no less

For the following question, consider each of the choices separately and select all that apply.

61. Which of the following options is suggested by the passage?

A. Most ardent suffragists believe that women can succeed where men have failed and that women can cleanse the political system
B. Most ardent suffragists believe that giving women the right to vote will not resolve the problems that beset the political system
C. The author is overall in favour of woman suffrage

Passage 28

Aesthetics has for its object the vast realm of the beautiful, and it may be most adequately defined as the philosophy of art or of the fine arts. To some this definition may seem arbitrary, as excluding the beautiful in nature, but it will cease to appear so if it is remarked that the beauty which is the work of art is higher than natural beauty because it is the offspring of the mind. Moreover, if, in conformity with a certain school of modern philosophy, the mind be viewed as the true being, including all in itself, it must be admitted that beauty is only truly beautiful when it shares in the nature of mind, and is mind's offspring. Viewed in this light, the beauty of nature is only a reflection of the beauty of the mind, only an imperfect beauty, which as to its essence is included in that of the mind.

62. According to the passage, why is natural beauty considered inferior to man-made beauty?

A. It is not clearly understood by man
B. It is an imperfect beauty
C. It is not a creation of the human mind
D. It is too uncertain
E. It does not have a tangible form

For the following question, consider each of the choices separately and select all that apply.

63. Which of the following can be inferred from the information in the passage?

A. Aesthetics is in some way related to beauty
B. An object is not truly beautiful if it is not a creation of the mind
C. Some people have disputed the non-inclusion of natural beauty in Aesthetics

Passage 29

One of the commonest forms of madness is the desire to be noticed, the pleasure derived from being noticed. Perhaps it is not merely common, but universal. In its mildest form it doubtless is universal. Every child is pleased at being noticed; many intolerable children put in their whole time in distressing and idiotic effort to attract the attention of visitors; boys are always "showing off"; apparently all men and women are glad and grateful when they find that they have done a thing which has lifted them for a moment out of obscurity and caused wondering talk. This common madness can develop, by nurture, into a hunger for notoriety in one, for fame in another.

It is this madness for being noticed and talked about which has invented kingship and the thousand other dignities, and tricked them out with pretty and showy fineries; it has made kings pick one another's pockets, scramble for one another's crowns and estates, slaughter one another's subjects; it has raised up prize-fighters, and poets, and village mayors, and little and big politicians, and big and little charity-founders, and bicycle champions, and bandit chiefs, and frontier desperadoes, and Napoleons. Anything to get notoriety; anything to set the village, or the township, or the city, or the State, or the nation, or the planet shouting, "Look—there he goes—that is the man!"

64. What is the passage primarily concerned with?

A. Providing conflicting definitions of a phrase
B. Discussing a human desire and its impact
C. Analyzing the positive and negative aspects of a phenomenon
D. Arguing that all famous men have one thing in common
E. Concluding that people will do anything to get noticed

For the following question, consider each of the choices separately and select all that apply.

65. Which of the following can be concluded from the information in the passage?

    A. The desire to be noticed does not only have a negative impact
    B. In the past, kings have tricked their subjects using the desire to get noticed
    C. At least some people would prefer to be noticed for the wrong reason than not be noticed at all

66. Which of the following would the author most likely agree with, based on the information in the second paragraph?

    A. Charities are not always founded out of purely altruistic motives
    B. The desire to be noticed can be a motivator for children as well
    C. Bicycle champions want to become notorious
    D. There would be no wars if people did not want to become famous
    E. The desire to be noticed can be characterized as madness

Passage 30

Metaphysics, or the attempt to conceive the world as a whole by means of thought, has been developed, from the first, by the union and conflict of two very different human impulses - one urging men towards mysticism, and the other urging them towards science. Some men have achieved greatness through one of these impulses: in Hume, for example, the scientific impulse reigns quite unchecked, while in Blake a strong hostility to science co-exists with a profound mystic insight. But the greatest men who have been philosophers have felt the need both of science and of mysticism: the attempt to harmonize the two was what made their life, and what always must, for all its arduous uncertainty, make philosophy, to some minds, a greater thing than either science or religion.

Before attempting an explicit characterization of the scientific and the mystical impulses, I will provide examples of two philosophers whose greatness lies in the very intimate blending of science and mysticism which they achieved. The two philosophers I mean are Heraclitus and Plato. Heraclitus, as everyone knows, was a believer in universal flux: time builds and destroys all things. From the few fragments that remain, it is not easy to discover how he arrived at his opinions, but there are some sayings that strongly suggest scientific observation as the source. In Plato, the same twofold impulse exists, though the mystic impulse is distinctly the stronger of the two and secures ultimate victory whenever the conflict is sharp.

67. According to the information in the passage, which of the following can be concluded about Plato?

A. For Plato, both the scientific and the mystical impulses were equally important
B. Plato and Heraclitus had opposing philosophies
C. Plato relied on the mystical impulse when in doubt
D. Plato did not believe in the concept of universal flux
E. When in conflict, Plato used his knowledge of both the mystical and the scientific impulses to resolve the same

68. What is the overall purpose of the passage?

A. To assert that the greatest philosophers are those who have achieved the perfect blend of the mystical and scientific impulses
B. To discuss the history of metaphysics
C. To explain why philosophy is superior to science or religion
D. To provide examples of philosophers who have achieved greatness either through only mystic or scientific impulses or through an amalgam of both
E. To praise philosophers who have achieved a perfect blend of science and mysticism

For the following question, consider each of the choices separately and select all that apply.

69. Which of the following can be inferred from the passage?

A. Blake and Hume were both inclined more towards mysticism than towards science
B. There is no real literary proof of how Heraclitus arrived at his opinions
C. Plato and Heraclitus were similar in some aspects

70. Select the sentence in the passage that explains why Philosophy may be superior to other sciences.

Passage 31

Science, to the ordinary reader of newspapers, is represented by a varying selection of sensational triumphs, such as wireless telegraphy and airplanes, radio-activity, and the marvels of modern alchemy. It is not this aspect of science that I wish to speak of. Science, in this aspect, consists of detached up-to-date fragments, interesting only until they are replaced by something newer and more up-to-date, displaying nothing of the systems of patiently constructed knowledge out of which, almost as a casual incident, have come the practically useful results which interest the man in the street. The increased command over the forces of nature which is derived from science is undoubtedly an amply sufficient reason for encouraging scientific research, but this reason has been so often urged and is so easily appreciated that other reasons, to my mind quite as important, are apt to be overlooked. It is with these other reasons, especially with the intrinsic value of a scientific habit of mind in forming our outlook on the world that I shall be concerned in what follows.

71. What is the main purpose of the passage?

    A. To discuss the several definitions of science
    B. To argue that an ordinary person's view of science is actually incorrect
    C. To propose increased investment the field of scientific research
    D. To state that science has several aspects beyond the one that average people take into consideration
    E. To explain certain lesser known aspects of science

72. According to the passage, which of the following could be true of an ordinary reader of newspapers?

    A. He is aware that science has more than one aspect to it
    B. He is ignorant of scientific developments taking place every day
    C. He would regard a dam as a scientific accomplishment
    D. He has a sensationalist view of science
    E. His scientific beliefs lead him to have a narrow outlook of the world

73. Which of the following would the author of the passage most likely NOT agree with?

    A. The knowledge of science is as valuable, if not more valuable, than its end results
    B. To an ordinary person the end results of science are what matter most
    C. The final tangible results of scientific knowledge are everlasting
    D. One important aspect of science is its ability to help us form our outlook of the world
    E. There are several equally important reasons why scientific research should be encouraged

Passage 32

I remember the astonishment I felt when I first read Shakespeare. I expected to receive a powerful aesthetic pleasure, but having read, one after the other, works regarded as his best: "King Lear," "Romeo and Juliet," "Hamlet" and "Macbeth," not only did I feel no delight, but I also felt an irresistible repulsion and tedium, and doubted as to whether I was senseless in feeling works regarded as the summit of perfection by the whole of the civilized world to be trivial and positively bad, or whether the significance which this civilized world attributes to the works of Shakespeare was itself senseless. My consternation was increased by the fact that I always keenly felt the beauties of poetry in every form; then why should artistic works recognized by the whole world as those of a genius not just fail to please me, but in fact be disagreeable to me?

74. Select the sentence in the passage that highlights how people in general perceived Shakespeare.

75. In context of the passage, what does the line - *'artistic works recognized by the whole world as those of a genius'* - refer to?

    A. The poetry that was read and appreciated by the author
    B. Those few works of Shakespeare that the author actually liked
    C. The translations of Shakespeare's popular works
    D. The writings of the author of the passage
    E. The majority of Shakespeare's works

76. What is the meaning of the word 'consternation' in context of the passage?

    A. Unhappiness
    B. Sorrow
    C. Disappointment
    D. Confusion
    E. Dejection

For the following question, consider each of the choices separately and select all that apply.

77. Which of the following would the author of the passage most likely agree with?

    A. People haven't been entirely honest in their praise of Shakespeare and his works
    B. The civilized world can at times behave in a rather senseless manner
    C. The author was filled with self doubt about his ability to appreciate beauty in writing, on reading the works of Shakespeare

Passage 33

Pope's life as a writer falls into three periods, answering fairly enough to the three reigns in which he worked. Under Queen Anne he was an original poet but made little money by his verses. Under George I he was chiefly a translator, and made much money by satisfying the French-classical taste with versions of the "Iliad" and "Odyssey." Under George I he also edited Shakespeare, but with little profit to himself for Shakespeare was but a Philistine in the eyes of the French-classical critics. But as the eighteenth century grew slowly to its work, signs of a deepening interest in the real issues of life distracted men's attention from the culture of the snuff-box and the fan. As Pope's genius ripened, the best part of the world in which he worked was pressing forward, as a mariner who will no longer hug the coast but crowds all sail to cross the storms of a wide unknown sea. Pope's poetry thus deepened with the course of time, and the third period of his life, which fell within the reign of George II, was that in which he produced the "Essay on Man," the "Moral Essays," and the "Satires." These deal wholly with aspects of human life and the great questions they raise, according throughout with the doctrine of the poet, and of the reasoning world about him in his latter day, that "the proper study of mankind is Man."

For the following question, consider each of the choices separately and select all that apply.

78. According to the information in the passage, which of the following CANNOT be inferred with reference to the first two periods of Pope's writings?

    A. The public in general appreciated Pope's original works
    B. Pope finally made money by copying other people's works
    C. Pope decided to stop writing original poetry and began translating other people's works in order to make money

For the following question, consider each of the choices separately and select all that apply.

79. Which of the following does the passage imply about Pope?

    A. His most famous works primarily deal with different aspects of human life
    B. He made the most money under the reign of George 1
    C. The public was not impressed with his original woks

80. In context of the passage, what do these lines imply - '*as a mariner who will no longer hug the coast but crowds all sail to cross the storms of a wide unknown sea*'?

A. Pope stopped translating other people's works and began creating original works
B. The public started taking more interest in the real issues of life
C. Pope started writing about the various aspects of human life
D. Pope worked as a sailor on a ship which changed his outlook of the world and was responsible for his subsequent writings
E. Pope decided to venture away from the tried and tested style of writing and attempt new writing styles and subjects

Passage 34

Water perfectly pure is scarcely ever met with in nature. The effects produced by the foreign matters which water may contain, are more considerable, and of greater importance, than might at first be imagined. It cannot be denied, that such waters as are *hard*, or loaded with earthy matter, have a decided effect upon some important functions of the human body. They increase the distressing symptoms under which those persons labour who are afflicted with what is commonly called gravel complaints, and many other ailments might be named that are always aggravated by the use of waters abounding in saline and earthy substances.

The purity of the waters employed in some of the arts and manufactures, is an object of not less consequence. In the process of brewing malt liquors, soft water is preferable to hard. Every brewer knows that the largest possible quantity of the extractive matter of the malt is obtained in the least possible time, and at the smallest cost, by means of soft water.

In the art of the dyer, hard water not only opposes the solution of several dye stuffs, but it also alters the natural tints of some delicate colours, whilst in others again it precipitates the earthy and saline matters with which it is impregnated into the delicate fibers of the stuff, and thus impedes the softness and brilliancy of the dye. To the manufacturer of painters' colours, water as pure as possible is absolutely essential for the successful preparation of several delicate pigments. Carmine, madder lake, ultramarine, and Indian yellow cannot be prepared without perfectly pure water.

In the culinary art, the effects of water more or less pure are likewise obvious. Good and pure water softens the fibers of animal and vegetable matters more readily than such as is called *hard*. Every cook knows that dry or ripe peas, and other farinaceous seeds, cannot *readily* be boiled soft in hard water because the farina of the seed is not perfectly soluble in water loaded with earthy salts.

81. Select the sentence in the passage that most accurately states the primary concern of the passage.

82. Which of the following would the author of the passage most likely agree with?

A. Pure water can never be found in nature
B. Spring water is better than saline water
C. At times the effects of impure water tend to be underestimated
D. The purity of water employed in the arts is of less consequence than the purity of water that humans drink
E. Hard water can cause colours to bleed

For the following question, consider each of the choices separately and select all that apply.

83. From the information in the passage, which of the following can be concluded?

A. It is not suitable for boiling vegetables
B. It increases the extractive matter obtained from malt
C. It can make colours look dull

Passage 35

In reading Nietzsche's two essays on Wagner, we are apt to be deceived by their virulent and forcible tone into believing that the whole matter is a mere cover for hidden fire, a mere blind of aesthetic discussion concealing a deep and implacable personal feud which demands and will have vengeance. In spite of all that has been said to the contrary, many people still hold this view of the two little works before us and, as the actual facts are not accessible to everyone, and as rumours are more easily believed than verified, the error of supposing that these pamphlets were dictated by personal animosity, and even by Nietzsche's envy of Wagner in his glory, seems to be a pretty common one.

Another very general error is to suppose that the point at issue here is not one concerning music at all, but concerning religion. It is taken for granted that the aspirations, the particular quality, the influence, and the method of an art like music, are matters quite distinct from the values and the conditions prevailing in the culture with which it is in harmony, and that however many Christian elements may be discovered in Wagnerian texts, Nietzsche had no right to raise aesthetic objections because he happened to entertain the extraordinary view that these Christian elements had also found their way into Wagnerian music.

To both of these views there is but one reply—they are absolutely false.

84. From the passage it can be inferred that the author viewed Nietzsche as:

A. A revengeful person
B. A deceitful individual
C. A misunderstood person
D. A literary genius
E. An envious person

85. Why do some people continue to have a negative perception of Nietzsche with regards to his works mentioned in the passage?

A. They feel his language is very rude and demeaning
B. They have chosen to believe rumours rather than verify the facts for themselves
C. They have become biased by the personal animosity between Nietzsche and Wagner
D. They are against the mixing of music with religion
E. They found Nietzsche's comments blasphemous

Passage 36

It is safe to say that no class of women in the civilized world is subjected to such incessant trials of temper, and such temptations to be fretful, as the American housekeeper. The reasons for this state of things are legion and, if in the beginning we take ground from which the whole field may be clearly surveyed, we may be able to secure a better understanding of what housekeeping means, and to guard against some of the dangers accompanying it.

One difficulty associated with housekeeping lies in taking for granted that successful housekeeping is as much an instinct as that which leads the young bird to nest-building, and that no specific training is required. The man who undertakes a business, passes always through some form of apprenticeship, and must know every detail involved in the management, but to a large proportion of women, housekeeping is a combination of accidental forces from whose working it is hoped breakfasts and dinners and suppers will be evolved at regular periods, other necessities finding place where they can. The new home, prettily furnished, seems a lovely toy, and is surrounded by a halo, which, as facts assert themselves, quickly fades away. Moth and rust and dust invade the most secret recesses. Breakage and general disaster attend the progress of Bridget or Chloe. The kitchen seems the headquarters of extraordinary smells, and the stove an abyss in its consumption of coal or wood. Food is wasted by bad cooking, or ignorance as to needed amounts, or methods of using left-over portions, and, as bills pile up, a hopeless discouragement often settles upon both wife and husband, and reproaches and bitterness and alienation are guests in the home, to which they need never have come had a little knowledge barred them out.

86. What is the relation between the highlighted sentences in the passage?

   A. The first is a proposal put forward by the author and the second provides evidence undermining that proposal
   B. The first is the argument of the author and the second is a counterargument
   C. The first is the intermediate conclusion of the passage and the second is the final conclusion
   D. The first is the conclusion of the author and the second provides evidence strengthening the conclusion
   E. The first is the conclusion of the author and the second is his assumption

87. What is implied by the lines - *'if in the beginning we take ground from which the whole field may be clearly surveyed'* in the passage?

   A. The American housekeeper's job is one of the most difficult jobs in the world
   B. A survey should be conducted of American housekeepers to identify the more difficult areas of their job
   C. It might be a good idea to have a broad understanding of a housekeeper's job before taking it on
   D. The job of a housekeeper in America should generally be avoided
   E. An American housekeeper's job might have several dangers associated with it

Passage 37

The manor was the sphere of operations of a manor court. On every manor the tenants gathered at frequent periods for a great amount of petty judicial and regulative work. The most usual period for the meeting of the manor court was once every three weeks, though in some manors no trace of a meeting is found more frequently than three times, or even twice, a year. In these cases, however, it is quite probable that less formal meetings occurred of which no regular record was kept.

Different kinds of gatherings of the tenants are usually distinguished according to the authority under which they were held, or the class of tenants of which they were made up. If the court was held by the lord simply because of his feudal rights as a landholder, and was busied only with matters of the inheritance, transfer, or grant of lands, the fining of tenants for the breach of manorial custom, or failure to perform their duties to the lord of the manor, the election of tenants to petty offices on the manor, and such matters, it was described in legal language as a court baron. If a court so occupied was made up of villain tenants only, it was called a customary court. If, on the other hand, the court also punished general offences, petty crimes, breaches of contract, breaches of the assize, that is to say, the established standard of amount, price, or quality of bread or beer, the lord of the manor drawing his authority to hold such a court either actually or supposedly from a grant from the king, such a court was called a court leet. With the court leet was usually connected the so-called view of frank pledge.

Frank pledge was an ancient system, according to which all men were obliged to be enrolled in groups, so that if any one committed an offence, the other members of the group would be obliged to produce him for trial. View of frank pledge was the right to punish by fine all who failed to so enrol themselves. In the court baron and the customary court it was said by lawyers that the body of attendants were the judges, and the steward, representing the lord of the manor, only a presiding official, while in the court leet the steward was the actual judge of the tenants. In practice, however, it is probable that not much was made of these distinctions and that the periodic gatherings were made to do duty for all business of any kind that needed attention, while the procedure was that which had become customary on that special manor, irrespective of the particular form of authority for the court.

88. Which of the following can be inferred from the information in the passage?

    A. The concept of frank pledge was created to promote solidarity within groups of people
    B. The duration between successive meetings of a manor court was not fixed
    C. A court baron had more powers than a customary court
    D. The manor court was the highest legal authority during the period mentioned in the passage
    E. The manor court did not always have a presiding official

89. Each of the following is mentioned in the passage as a power of the court baron EXCEPT:

    A. To judge matters related to inheritance
    B. To resolve disputes related to grants of land
    C. To punish tenants for negligence of duties
    D. To elect tenants to offices on the manor
    E. To fine petty criminals

90. According to the information in the first paragraph, the fact that *'in some manors no trace of a meeting is found more frequently than three times, or even twice, a year'* does NOT necessarily suggest that:

   A. more meetings were actually not held during that period
   B. meetings were not necessarily held every three weeks
   C. informal meetings may have been held during this period
   D. manor courts probably did not keep a record of all their meetings
   E. some courts met fewer times than the others

Critical Reasoning Questions

91. Arguments to restrict immigration on the grounds that immigrants will take domestic jobs ignore the fact that immigrants, once employed, will earn and spend money on goods and services, creating new jobs that will more than make up for the old ones they took.

Which of the following is an assumption on which the argument depends?

A. The immigrants will not send most of the money that they earn back to their hometowns

B. Studies show that large scale inflow of immigrants invariably leads to an increase in the incidence of crime in that city

C. The immigrants will not subsequently get their families to also join them in the new city

D. Immigrants generally tend to save most of the money that they earn

E. Opponents of immigration are not opposed to immigration for reasons other than loss of jobs

92. Recently the city council conducted a survey of 1000 car owners whose cars had recently met with an accident. Half of these car owners had got their cars repaired at authorized service stations and the other half got their cars repaired at local unauthorized service stations. The average repair cost of those who got their cars serviced at unauthorized service stations was $500 whereas the average repair cost of those who got their cars repaired at authorized service stations was $900. The city council concluded from this survey that authorized service stations in general charge more than do unauthorized service stations.

Which of the following, if true, most seriously weakens the city council's conclusion above?

A. All the car owners whose cars had faced severe damage chose to get their cars repaired at authorized service stations.

B. Many automobile companies discourage their buyers from going to unauthorized service stations.

C. Unauthorized service stations on an average take less time to repair cars than do authorized service stations.

D. All the 1000 car owners who were surveyed faced similar damage to their cars

E. Experienced car mechanics recommend unauthorized service stations over authorized ones.

93. A stain-removing agent currently available in city X can remove the most stubborn of stains from clothes but is not very popular because it leaves behind a foul smell in the clothes. It takes around ten days for the smell to completely go away from the clothes. Another stain-removing agent has just been launched in city X which is as effective at cleaning stains as the older one. An advantage of the new stain-removing agent is that its smell starts to go away from the clothes in two days itself. Thus this new agent should easily be able to outsell the older one.

Which of the following pieces of information would be most helpful in evaluating the argument above?

A. the rate of growth or decline in sales of stain-removing agents in city X
B. the total number of stain removing agents sold last year in city X
C. the per capita income of people residing in city X
D. the amount of time it takes for the smell of the new stain-removing agent to completely go away from the clothes.
E. a comparison of the smell of the new stain removing agent with that of similar agents available in other cities

94. Ever since the new Marketing Head joined Crackwell Corporation, its profits have increased steadily. In fact, over the past three years that the Marketing Head has been with Crackwell, the company's profits have grown by almost 35% every year, a figure that used to hover around the 10% mark earlier. Pleased by this fact, the Board of Crackwell Corporation has decided to reward the Marketing Head with stock options in the company.

Which of the following, if true, casts the most serious doubts on the decision taken by the Board of Crackwell Corporation?

A. The Marketing Head is disliked by his team members because of his habit of criticising them in public
B. Over the past three years, the profits of Crackwell's closest competitor have grown by 42% every year
C. The CFO of Crackwell Corporation has taken several cost cutting measures over the last three years, including retrenchment of unproductive employees and renegotiation of prices with vendors.
D. A strategy consulting firm, known to have turned around several poorly performing companies, has been recently hired by Crackwell Corporation
E. Several new marketing campaigns, which gave a lot of international exposure to the company's products, have been successfully conducted by Crackwell Corporation over the past three years

95. The Georgetown Public School recommends that all its students take an active interest in playing chess. This is because, according to a recent medical study, those students who played chess on an average performed better in tests of general intelligence than those who did not play chess. Thus the school contends that playing chess will boost up the intelligence of its students.

Which of the following raise the most serious doubt about the conclusion above?

A. Some students who perform well in tests of general intelligence do not play chess
B. Intelligent students are the only ones who take an interest in playing chess
C. A similar correlation has not been observed with regards to other sports such as baseball
D. Some of the students who play chess perform poorly in subjects such as History
E. There can be other ways in which a student could develop intelligence

96. According to a recent nationwide study by the Education Department, those students who played baseball performed much better academically than those who did not. Thus it can be concluded that students should be encouraged to participate in sporting activities, because this will have a direct bearing on their academic performance.

Which of the following provide most support to the argument above?

A. Playing baseball stimulates their brains and increases the rate of grey cell growth in the brain
B. Students who participated in sports other than baseball also showed a marked improvement in their academic performance
C. The Education Department study is representative of students nationwide
D. Non-sporting activities such as painting and writing do not have a similar positive effect on a student's academic performance
E. The number of students who play baseball in the country has been increasing at a frenetic pace over the last few years

97. The Ford Model E is the bestselling car model in country Z. Recently a leading newspaper in country Z published a report highlighting the safety flaws present in the Ford Model E. The report concludes that by driving this particular car, drivers are endangering their lives. Despite this report the public has stated that it will continue to buy Ford Model Es. However in the 2 month period following the publishing of this report, the sales of the Model E fell by more than 70%.

Which of the following best explains the discrepancy in the argument above?

A. Because country Z has very few car manufacturers, the customers don't have too much choice
B. In the period following the publishing of the report, Ford offered a heft discount on the Model E
C. After the report was published, Ford decided to voluntarily withdraw model Es from its showrooms so as to modify them to make them safer for drivers
D. Other cars available in the market are as unsafe as the Ford Model E
E. The report was publishes by a reputed newspaper known for its objective and unbiased reporting

98. The sales of jogging shoes have tripled over the last one year in Renoma city. Thus it can be safely concluded that the citizens of Renoma city have started giving a lot of importance to physical fitness activities such as jogging.

Which of the following is an assumption in the argument above?

A. The sale of jogging shoes in other cities has not gone up at the same rate as it has in Renoma city
B. In the last one year several gymnasiums and sport centres have set shop in Renoma city
C. Jogging is a physical fitness activity
D. The jogging shoes that have been sold are actually being used for jogging and not for other purposes
E. As a physical fitness activity, jogging is more beneficial than walking

99. It is interesting to note that, of the ten different brands of digital cameras available in the market, the one that sells the most is the second most expensive of the lot. This camera also offers the best picture quality of all the digital cameras available in the market. Clearly the price of the camera plays no role in the customer purchase decision; it is the picture quality of the camera that matters to them.

Which of the following, if true, would most seriously weaken the argument above?

A. Between two similarly equipped digital cameras, most customers will prefer the lower priced one
B. There is a direct correlation between the price of a camera and its picture quality
C. Some customers only purchase the cheapest available digital camera, irrespective of its picture quality
D. The second largest selling brand of digital camera, which is also the third most expensive in the market, offers poor picture quality
E. Digital cameras are usually purchased by affluent customers for whom the price of the camera isn't a big consideration

100) The Langova National park is a breeding ground for several migratory birds. The Spot-breasted Laughing Thrush, an extremely rare species of bird, has been sighted only in the Langova National park of late. The people who have sighted this bird in the park have claimed that it is possible to sight this bird only through the use of binoculars. Barry is visiting the Langova National Park next week and he will be carrying an extremely powerful pair of binoculars with him. Therefore it is safe to conclude that, as long as Barry has his binoculars on him, he will most definitely manage to sight the Spot-breasted Laughing Thrush.

Which of the following indicates a flaw in the reasoning above?

A. It fails to take into account the possibility of sighting the Spot-breasted Laughing Thrush at places other than the Langova National Park
B. It mistakes a necessary condition for a sufficient condition
C. It is based on a series of assumptions, rather than on facts
D. It does not take into account the possibility that Barry could lose or damage his binoculars on way to the park
E. It does not take into account the possibility that Barry may sight some other equally rare species of bird

Reading Comprehension - Answers & Explanations

Passage 1

Because the livelihood of many citizens is linked to the management of national parks, local politicians often encourage state involvement in federal planning. But, state legislatures have not always addressed the fundamental policy issues of whether states should protect park wildlife. Timber harvesting, ranching and energy exploration compete with wildlife within the local ecosystem. Priorities among different land uses are not generally established by current legislation. Additionally, often no mechanism exists to coordinate planning by the state environmental regulatory agencies. These factors limit the impact of legislation aimed at protecting park wildlife and the larger park ecosystem. Even if these deficiencies can be overcome, state participation must be consistent with existing federal legislation. States lack jurisdiction within national parks themselves, and therefore state solutions cannot reach activities inside the parks, thus limiting state action to the land adjacent to the national parks.

1) The passage provides support for which of the following assertions?

A. Timber harvesting and ranching are the main activities that are responsible for the decline of national parks.
B. The federal government has been selling national park land to state governments in order to raise money for wildlife conservation.
C. The actions of state governments have often failed to promote the interests of national park wildlife.
D. Local politicians want the federal government to turn control of national parks over to state governments.
E. States have the authority to control the harmful activities being carried out inside national parks

Answer

The entire passage is concerned with how states have been unable or unwilling to protect national parks. In fact the 2nd sentence of the passage specifically suggests that states have often failed to address the issue of whether they are responsible for the protection of park wildlife. Thus they have definitely failed to promote the interests of national park wildlife i.e. **(C) should be the best answer**

2) Select the sentence in the passage which highlights some of the activities that are harming national parks

Answer

Timber harvesting, ranching and energy exploration compete with wildlife within the local ecosystem

The question is asking us about specific activities which are only mentioned in the above sentence

Passage 2

In the third decade of the nineteenth century, Americans began to define their character in light of the railroads that had just been introduced. They liked the idea that it took special people to foresee and capitalize on the promise of science. Railroad promoters, using the steam engine as a metaphor for what they thought Americans were and what they thought Americans were becoming, frequently discussed parallels between the locomotive and national character, pointing out that both possessed youth, power, speed, single-mindedness, and bright prospects.

However, these metaphors also had their dark side. A locomotive was quite unlike anything Americans had ever seen. It was large, mysterious and dangerous; many thought that it was a monster waiting to devour the unwary. There was a suspicion that a country founded upon Jeffersonian agrarian principles had bought a ticket and boarded a train pulled by some iron monster into the dark recesses of an unknown future.

To ease such public apprehensions, promoters, poets, editors, and writers alike adopted the notion that locomotives were really only iron horses, an early metaphor that lingered because it made steam technology ordinary and understandable. Iron horse metaphors assuaged fears about inherent defects in the national character, prompting images of a more secure future, and made an alien technology less frightening, and even comforting and congenial.

3) From the information in the passage, which of the following can be inferred about the railroads?

A. Some Americans viewed the introduction of the railroads with scepticism
B. The railroads proved extremely beneficial for Americans in general
C. Many prominent people of that time supported the introduction of railroads

Answer

The 2nd para clearly states that some people were suspicious about railroads, which is the same thing as being sceptical, hence A can be inferred.

The passage never talks about the beneficial impact of railroads so B is not supported by the passage

The opening lines of the 3rd para state that people such as writers, editors, etc. (who would definitely be considered prominent) tried to assuage people's fears with regards to the railroads so it can be safely concluded that they were in support of the railroads. Hence C is also supported by the passage.

Thus the answer is (A) and (C)

4) Which of the following assertions is not consistent with the information in the passage?

A. Railroads created trepidation in the minds of a lot of Americans
B. Americans viewed the inventors of the railroad with respect
C. Parallels were drawn between the railroads and the character of the American people to project the railroads in a positive light
D. The railroads helped to remove the inherent defects in the national character
E. The railroads were introduced in America the nineteenth century

Answer

The 3rd para states that railroads helped assuage fears about inherent defects in the national character but these were just fears and there actually was no defect in the national character. **Thus (D) is not consistent** with the information in the passage and should be the correct answer.

A – Can be concluded from the 2nd para
B – Can be inferred from the second sentence of the 1st para
C – This is again mentioned in the 1st para
E – The opening lines of the passage state this

5) Select the sentence in the passage that mentions one of the things that was done to allay the fears of people with regards to railroads.

Answer

To ease such public apprehensions, promoters, poets, editors, and writers alike adopted the notion that locomotives were really only iron horses, an early metaphor that lingered because it made steam technology ordinary and understandable.

The passage clearly mentions that, to ease the fears of the people, promoters, poets, etc. started projecting railroads as iron horses.

Passage 3

While leaks are generally defended by media officials on the grounds of the public's right to know, in reality they are part of the Washington political power game, as well as part of the policy process. The "leaker" may be currying favour with the media, or may be planting information to influence policy. In the first case, he is helping himself by enhancing the prestige of a journalist; in the second, he is using the media as a stage for his preferred policies. In either instance, it closes the circle: the leak begins with a political motive, is advanced by a politicized media, and continues because of politics. Although some of the journalists think *they* are doing the work, they are more often than not instruments of the process, not prime movers. The media must be held accountable for their activities, just like every other significant institution in our society, and the media must be forced to earn the public's trust.

6) Which of the following can be inferred from the information in the passage?

A. Media leaks are a part of the American government's policy
B. The primary purpose of media leaks is to influence public policy
C. There needs to be accountability among media with regards to its actions

Answer

The passage never states that media leaks are part of the American government's policy but rather that there are implications of the leak on the policy process. So A cannot be inferred

The passage mentions two rationales behind the leaks – to curry favour with the media or to influence policy. There is no way of determining which of these is the primary purpose of the leaks. So B goes out as well

C can be clearly inferred from the last sentence of the passage.

Hence (C) is the correct answer

7) What does the passage state about journalists who believe that they are the prime movers behind media leaks?

A. Their belief is correct because media leaks can make or break governments
B. Their belief is correct because they are the link between the public and the government
C. Their belief is incorrect because more often than not they are just being used to serve somebody else's larger purpose
D. Their belief is incorrect because at times the public may not chose to believe them
E. Their belief is incorrect because they are as accountable to the people as any other institution in the society

Answer

Towards the end the passage clearly states that these journalists, who think that they are the prime movers, are actually just instruments of the process and hence are being used by someone else. They are merely messengers. **(C) states this best** and is the correct answer

A. The passage clearly states that their belief is incorrect
B. Same as A
D. The passage never mentions whether the public believes the information in media leaks or not
E. While accountability is mentioned in the passage, it is in no way connected to the belief of the journalists with reference to this particular question

Passage 4

In the decades following World War II, American business had undisputed control of the world economy, producing goods of such high quality and low cost that foreign corporations were unable to compete. But in the mid-1960s the United States began to lose its advantage and by the 1980s American corporations lagged behind the competition in many industries. In the computer chip industry, for example, American corporations had lost most of both domestic and foreign markets by the early 1980s.

The first analysts to examine the decline of American business blamed the U.S. government. Still later analysts blamed the American workforce, citing labour demands and poor productivity as the reasons American corporations have been unable to compete with Japanese and European firms. Finally, a few analysts even censured American consumers for their unpatriotic purchases of foreign goods. **The blame actually lies with corporate management, which has made serious errors based on misconceptions about what it takes to be successful in the marketplace**. These missteps involve labour costs, production choices, and growth strategies.

8) What is the relation between the highlighted parts of the passage?

A. The first is a premise of the author and the second is the main conclusion of the author
B. The first is an intermediate conclusion made by the author and the second provides evidence to justify this conclusion
C. The first provides the opinion of one particular group and the second provides the contrasting conclusion of the author
D. The first provides evidence that undermines the author's conclusion and the second strengthens the author's conclusion
E. The first is a strategy adopted that failed and the second is a strategy adopted that succeeded

<u>Answer</u>

For such questions it is best to paraphrase an answer before looking at the options. In this case, the first sentence is a claim made by people other than the author (and which the author disagrees with) and the second is the author's contradictory conclusion. **(C) states this best** and should be the correct answer.

A. While the second part is definitely the main conclusion of the author, the first is in no way a premise on which this conclusion is based. In fact the author contradicts this view
B. The first is not a conclusion of the author in the first place so there is no way that the second can justify the same
D. The first does not provide evidence; rather it is a conclusion in itself. Moreover, the second doesn't strengthen the author's conclusion; rather it is the author's conclusion
E. The passage does not talk about strategies anywhere

9) Which of the following can be concluded from the information in the passage?

A. American consumers are partly responsible for the decline in the global standing of American corporates
B. American businesses functioned extremely efficiently in the period following World War II
C. Poor production choices made by the leaders of American companies are partly to be blamed for the decline in the stature of these companies

Answer

(A) cannot be inferred from the passage. The author states this only to offer an alternative perspective subsequently.

(B) can be inferred from the opening lines of the passage

(C) can be inferred from the last lines of the passage

Hence the correct answer is (B) and (C)

10) What is the main purpose of the passage?

A. To blame American corporate leaders for making poor growth strategies
B. To provide an alternative explanation for an event
C. To justify the taking place of an event
D. To repudiate the claim that the corporate management was responsible for the decline in American industry during the 80s
E. To analyze several interpretations of an event and to support one of them

Answer

Again paraphrasing always helps on a global question such as this one. The author starts by stating that the standing of American companies globally has gone down. He then goes on to state some explanations for this event provided by other people before providing his own alternative explanation. **(B) comes the closest** to this and should be the correct answer

A. This is just a specific detail from the passage and cannot be the answer to a 'main purpose' question. For that matter the author also blames these leaders for labour costs and production choices, so these can also be the answer
C. The author not justify anything in the passage
D. The author actually makes this claim rather than repudiate it

E. 'Interpretations' is the wrong word because the author is more concerned with 'explanations' of an event and not its interpretations. Again the use of analyze is inappropriate since the author just states these explanations rather than analyze them

Passage 5

Though he left us with numerous great works and, to be sure, is widely regarded as America's first internationally renowned author, Washington Irving's sometimes enigmatic tendencies and techniques have left literary critiques and academics to ponder his motives more than 140 years after his death. One such trait that raises the proverbial eyebrow of the community of readers and critiques is Irving's repeated, and varied, use of pseudonyms throughout his career.

11) Which of the following can be inferred from the information in the passage?

A. Irving never wrote under his own name
B. All great authors have some eccentricities related to them
C. Several centuries have passed since Irving died
D. Irving was criticized by people of his time for writing under different pseudonyms
E. There are aspects of Irving's personality that remain unexplained

<u>**Answer**</u>

The passage suggests that Irving's reasons for writing under pseudonyms remain an enigma or mystery to this day. **(E) can be most reasonably inferred** from this and should be the correct answer

A. The passage never mentions that Irving *never* wrote under his own name, just that he used several pseudonyms
B. The passage only talks about Irving so we can't generalize for all great authors
C. 140 years does not connote *several* centuries but just one century
D. People could not find the rationale for this act of Irving but this does not mean that he was criticized for the same

Passage 6

The 1960s and 1970s witnessed a new boomtown era in the West. The typical contemporary boomtown is fuelled by a quest for energy in the form of a fossil-fuelled electric generating plant, a hydroelectric dam or a new mine. The energy project is typically located near a small community or is forced to start a community from scratch. Often, the boomtown is poorly planned and under-financed. Long-time residents find their community changed for the worse and newcomers find the town an undesirable place to live.

The boomtown is characterized by inadequate public services, undesirable labour conditions, confusion in community structure, and deterioration of the quality of life arising from rapid population growth due to a major economic stimulus. Accelerated growth is the most distinguishing characteristic of a boomtown.

12) Select the sentence in the passage that explains what can accelerate the process of setting up of boomtowns?

Answer

The typical contemporary boomtown is fuelled by a quest for energy in the form of a fossil-fuelled electric generating plant, a hydroelectric dam or a new mine.

The above lines clearly state the factors that fuel or accelerate boomtown growth.

13) According to the passage, which of the following can be a characteristic of a boomtown?

A. Poor planning and infrastructure
B. Sluggish economy and a low growth rate
C. Lack of finances

Answer

While A and C are clearly mentioned in the passage, the last sentence of the passage actually states that accelerated growth is a distinguishing feature of a boomtown. Hence B can definitely not be inferred.

(A) and (C) is the correct answer

Passage 7

In a now-famous study, Stephen Kosslyn asked subjects to imagine an animal, such as a rabbit, next to either an elephant or a fly. When the image was formed, Kosslyn would ask whether or not the target animal had a particular attribute. For example, Kosslyn might say, "elephant, rabbit," and then "leg." He found that it took subjects longer to answer when the target animal was next to the large animal than when it was next to the small animal. Kosslyn interpreted this to mean that subjects had to zoom in on the image to detect the particular feature. Just as one has difficulty seeing details on small objects, so the subjects could not simply mentally "see" details on the smaller object in their mental image.

14) If the experiment discussed in the passage were to be recreated then, as per the information in the passage, in which of the following situations would a person take the least time to answer?

A. If the target were next to an object of the same size
B. If the target were next to a larger object
C. If the target had a unique distinguishing mark
D. If the target was of a different shape than the other objects
E. If the target was next to a smaller object

Answer

According to the passage, people answered the fastest when the target animal was next to a small animal. **Hence (E) should be the best answer**.

A – The passage does not state or suggest this
B – The passage states that in this case people took longer to answer
C and D – The passage only talks about the size of the object and makes no mention of any distinguishing mark or shape

15) Select the sentence in the passage that leads to Kosslyn's interpretation that subjects have to zoom in on an image.

Answer

He found that it took subjects longer to answer when the target animal was next to the large animal than when it was next to the small animal.

Be careful, the question asks you to select the line that leads to Kosslyn's interpretation and not Kosslyn's interpretation itself. Hence the answer should be the above lines from which Kosslyn made his interpretation.

Passage 8

Artistic movies are composed of a multitude of 'shots' or discrete scenes usually lasting only 6 to 20 seconds; together the hundreds of individual scenes combine to make up the movie. For each shot the director has many options on how to film the same. For example, imagine that the movie's script calls for two actors to speak a fixed dialogue in a specified location. Even while the director stays true to the script, he has considerable leeway in how to film the scene. He may film an 'extreme long shot', with the camera far away. This tends to show the setting in a panorama, emphasizing the background while underplaying the actors, and is used primarily in outdoor scenes where the backdrop is particularly impressive. Or, he may employ the 'long shot', which brings the camera close enough to capture the actor's entire bodies, together with some of the setting. And finally there is the 'close-up', where the camera is brought in close enough to focus on the actors' heads and faces and has the effect of spotlighting a particular actor while hiding the setting and other actors.

16) The passage discussion most clearly suggests that the most important aspect of filmmaking is

A. figuring out what moviegoers are going to love
B. deciding how to make a movie artistic
C. using a good director
D. signing a top actor for the lead role
E. using a great cameraman

<u>Answer</u>

The passage clearly tells us that it is the director who decides what shot to take. This makes hiring a good 'director' the most important aspect of filmmaking. **(C) sums it up very well** and is the correct answer.

A. The passage speaks about what moviegoers love
B. While the passage does mention 'artistic movies', the person who makes a movie artistic is again the director only
D. Out of scope

E. The passage clearly states that it is the director and not the cameraman who decides what shot to take

17) Which of the following can be inferred from the information in the passage?

A. For a scene in which it is important to highlight the facial expression of an actor, it is best to use the close up shot
B. A director shooting a movie in Zurich for its beautiful locales should use a lot of extreme long shots
C. A fight scene between two actors in a nondescript setting should be best filmed in a long shot

Answer

The passage clearly states that to emphasize the expressions of the actors, a director should use close up. Hence A can be inferred

Again the passage states that to capture the scenery of a place, extreme long shot should be used. So B can also be inferred

In a fight scene the idea should be to show the entire bodies of the two actors so the close up goes out. Again since the setting is nondescript, we do not need the extreme long shot, which will anyways take the emphasis away from the actors' bodies. The best shot should then be a long shot. Hence C can also be inferred.

Thus the correct answer is (A), (B), and (C)

Passage 9

In spite of the conventional interpretation, a survey of source material reveals that the image of the plains as Desert was restricted in 1825 to certain portions of the country and to certain segments of the population. Analysis of newspapers and periodical literature indicates that the Desert image was strongest in the rural areas of the Northeast and weakest in the rural areas of the South and trans-Appalachian West. Acceptance of the Desert concept was more likely among the well-educated elite, particularly in the Northeast, and acceptance of a "Garden" notion was greater among the rural populations, particularly in the South and West.

American historians have argued that the myth of the Great American Desert dominated the pre-Civil War view of the Great Plains. It was this conception of the plains as Desert, according to the traditional interpretation, that caused the American folk migration westward to leap over the region during the 1840's and the 1850's. This conventional understanding is neither completely invalid nor necessarily incorrect; but it is too simplistic to be fully satisfying. To claim the universal acceptance of stereotyped images of the Great Plains is to ignore the presence of a considerable array of data to the contrary.

18) Which of the following can most likely be inferred from the passage?

A. The conventional view holds that the Great Plains were in fact largely a desert
B. People in the South west were much less likely to think of the Great Plains as a desert
C. During the American migration mentioned in the passage, people moved from the Great Plains to more urban areas

<u>**Answer**</u>

The opening lines of the passage suggest that, according to the conventional view, the Great Plains were in fact a desert. So A can be inferred

B can also be inferred from the information in the 1st para

The passage never suggests that, during the migration, people moved from the Great Plains. It just suggests that during this migration the people leaped over or skipped the Great Plains altogether. Hence C cannot be inferred from the passage.

Thus the **correct answer is (A) and (B)**

19) Select the sentence in the passage that provides the reason why migrants did not settle down in the Great Plains.

<u>**Answer**</u>

It was this conception of the plains as Desert, according to the traditional interpretation, that caused the American folk migration westward to leap over the region during the 1840's and the 1850's.

The above lines clearly state that it is because of the conception of plains as desert that migrants decided to skip over this area.

20) Which of the following would the author of the passage most likely agree with?

A. Educated and well-off people were more likely to believe in the concept of the Desert than the rural people
B. The myth of the Great American Desert dominated the pre Civil War view of the Plains
C. The conventional view of the of the Plains as a Desert is not entirely incorrect

Answer

A and C can be clearly inferred from the 1st and the 2nd paras respectively. However B is a trap answer. It is American Historians who have argued that the myth of the Great American Desert dominated the pre-Civil War view of the Great Plains. We have no idea whether the author would agree with their views. Hence B cannot be inferred.

Thus the correct answer is **(A) and (C)**

21) Which of the following can be inferred from the last sentence of the passage – *"To claim the universal acceptance of stereotyped images of the Great Plains is to ignore the presence of a considerable array of data to the contrary."*

A. The Great Plains was in fact not a desert
B. There is considerable data available that could prove that the Great Plains was much more than what stereotyped images make it out to be
C. It is almost universally accepted that the Great Plains were in fact a Desert
D. The reason migrants decided to skip over the Great Plains is because they thought of this area as a desert
E. Not everyone in America believed in the notion that the Great Plains was a Desert

Answer

It can easily be inferred from this sentence that there is data available that shows that the Great Plains was not just a desert. **(B) almost states this verbatim** and is the correct answer.

A – While this is partly correct, the last sentence does much more than just convey this fact
C – In fact this sentence doubts this fact that the stereotyped images of the Great Plains are universally accepted
According to the question, the inference has to be made only from the last sentence of the passage. Hence D and E can be eliminated because they are not connected to the last sentence.

Passage 10

Scientists study reef fishes not only because of the diverse sampling of species but also because of the range of behaviours and relationships between species and other animals that is available for analysis. Intense competition and predation have caused fishes to carve out special niches. Mimicry and camouflage offer just two ways for species to blend in with their surroundings. Symbiotic relationships between fish and other organisms also occur with frequency on coral reefs. The anemonefish share their habitat with sea anemones in a symbiotic relationship that scientists have yet to unravel completely. The defensive nematocysts of the anemone are used to stun prey, but the anemonefish are resistant to these stinging cells. Researchers believe that the fish secrets a mucous coating that mimics that of the anemone allowing for chemical signals to prohibit the firing of the cells. One theory holds that the fish obtain these chemicals by rubbing against the sea anemone's tentacles. The benefits, if any, to the anemone for having these fish live with them are not clear.

22) Which of the following options provides the rationale behind why scientists study reef fishes?

A. Scientists want to study the anemoneship, which is only found in reefs
B. The reefs provide scientists with a wide variety of fish species in one place
C. The reefs provide scientists with several examples of interdependence between different species

Answer

The opening sentence of the passage explains the reason why scientists study reef fishes. B and C can be easily inferred from these lines.

The passage just provides us with an example of anemonefish to illustrate the symbiotic relationship between species. Nowhere is it stated that scientists actually study reef fishes because they want to study this particular fish. Hence A cannot be inferred.

Thus the correct answer is **(B) and (C)**

23) Select the sentence in the passage that explains how species in coral reefs can blend in with their environment.

Answer

Mimicry and camouflage offer just two ways for species to blend in with their surroundings.

These lines clearly state that species can blend in with their environment by using either mimicry or camouflage

Passage 11

Because we have so deeply interiorized writing, we find it difficult to consider writing to be an alien technology, as we commonly assume printing and the computer to be. **Most people are surprised to learn that essentially the same objections commonly urged today against computers were urged by Plato in the *Phaedrus*, against writing.** Writing, Plato has Socrates say, is inhuman, pretending to establish outside the mind what in reality can be only in the mind. Secondly, Plato's Socrates urges, writing destroys memory. Those who use writing will become forgetful, relying on external resource for what they lack in internal resources. Thirdly, **a written text is basically unresponsive, whereas real speech and thought always exist essentially in a context of give-and-take between real persons**.

24) Which of the following would the author of the passage most likely agree with?

A. Writing can at times appear as inhuman
B. A negative aspect of writing is that it could destroy memory
C. Writing can at times fail to provide the right context
D. Writing is more important than other cognitive skills
E. There have been people in the past who have opposed the technology of writing

Answer

Be careful to make note of the person from whose point of view the question has been asked. In this question we have been asked from the point of view of the author. A, B, and C are all mentioned in the passage but as comments ascribed to Plato. D is never mentioned in the passage at all. It is only E that can be ascribed to the author based on the opening lines of the passage. **Hence the correct answer is (E)**

25) What is the relation between the highlighted lines in the passage?

A. The first is the main thesis of the author and the second provides explanation for the main thesis
B. The first is the primary conclusion of the passage and the second provides an alternate contradictory conclusion
C. The first is a rebuttal of Platos's argument and the second is Plato's main argument
D. The first is the main thesis of the author and the second contradicts the main thesis of the author
E. The first is a point made in opposition of the advocacy of a truth and the second is that truth

<u>**Answer**</u>

Remember to paraphrase on such questions. The first is clearly the point that the author is trying to convey through the passage - that there was a time when people criticized writing - and the second provides an example of such criticism, so it obviously supports the first highlighted part. **Thus (A) should be the best answer**

B. The second is not a conclusion but one of Plato's three criticisms of writing
C. The second is not Plato's main argument
D. As explained above, the second does not contradict but rather support the main thesis of the author
E. The first is just a general statement and is not opposing or advocating anything. In fact the entire passage does not advocate or oppose anything

Passage 12

Arguments abound over whether marijuana should be legalized. Medical research has repeatedly provided evidence that marijuana use causes permanent physical, psychological, and thus emotional damage to those who regularly use it. Studies at the University of Maryland and UCLA indicated that the regular smoking of only two marijuana cigarettes a day would tend to promote toe fungus and thrush. But over the years, much stronger claims have surfaced: heavy marijuana users perform poorly at work or school, are more likely to be delinquent and develop psychiatric problems, or have abnormal brain waves. *Repeatedly, however, such studies encounter the same objection: are the problems caused by smoking marijuana, or is it just that people with problems are more likely to end up using marijuana heavily?*

26) Which of the following questions is most similar in structure to the one contained in the highlighted lines in the passage?

A. Recently several bridges have collapsed in Tycho city for which the architects' poor design has been blamed. But couldn't the bridges have collapsed because of some other reason beyond the control of the architects, such as use of poor quality construction material?
B. Students who get scholarships tend to perform better than students who don't. However is it because of the scholarships that the students perform better or is it that the students were good students because of which they got the scholarship in the first place?
C. It has been noticed that children who play basketball are much taller than other children, so parents should encourage their children to play basketball if they want them to become tall. However is it that the children are tall because they play basketball or is it that they play basketball because they are tall?

Answer

This is an interesting question. We need to start by paraphrasing the content in the highlighted lines. Basically these lines are suggesting the possibility of a reversal of a cause and effect relationship. Is marijuana the cause and the problems the effect or are the problems the cause and marijuana the effect.

(A) starts off by stating that architects' designs are the cause and the collapse of bridges is the effect. However the second part of the argument does not reverse this cause and effect relationship. Instead it introduces a new cause (poor construction material) for the same effect. Hence A can be eliminated

(B) starts off by stating that the cause is scholarships and the effect is students performing well. The second part reverses this relation by questioning whether scholarships are the cause of the good performance or whether good performance was the cause of the scholarships. Hence B can be inferred

(C) starts off by stating that basketball is the cause and children growing tall is the effect. Again the second part reverses this logic by questioning whether basketball leads to height or whether height leads to basketball. Hence C can also be inferred.

Thus the **correct answer is (B) and (C)**

27) Which of the following options best summarizes the passage as a whole?

A. According to experts, there are several harmful effects of using marijuana
B. There are people who believe that the use of marijuana should be legalized
C. Poor performance at work and psychiatric problems could be the result of marijuana use
D. At the moment there is no consensus on whether marijuana's benefits outweigh its harmful effects or vice versa
E. Marijuana use should not be legalized as it can have serious deleterious effects

Answer

The opening sentence of the passage states that legalizing of marijuana use is an argumentative issue. The passage then mentions some harmful effects of marijuana but the last lines again question whether marijuana is the cause of these problems or the effect. Hence the passage basically introduces us to both points of view without taking any sides or arriving at any conclusion about marijuana use. **(D) summarizes this best** and should be the correct answer

A, B, and C – While the passage does state all of these, these options do not encompass the passage as a whole

E – The passage never arrives at such a conclusion

Passage 13

The simple statement that the universe had a beginning in time is by now so obvious to astrophysicists that few give it a second thought. Yet it is a statement that has profound implications. Most civilizations embrace one of two opposite concepts of time. Linear time has a beginning, a duration, and an end; cyclical time, as its name suggests, continues around and around forever. In a universe that functions through cyclical time, the question of creation never arises; the universe always was and always will be. The minute you switch to linear time you immediately confront the vexing question not only of creation, but also of the Creator. Although there is no logical reason for the assumption, many people believe that if something comes into existence, it must do so in response to the actions of some rational being. Because of that belief, astronomers, even though they resist becoming involved in theological discussion, find themselves in one when they posit the Big Bang universe. It puts them squarely in the middle of an age-old debate.

28) Each of the following is suggested by the passage EXCEPT:

A. Astronomers in general support the Big Bang model
B. Linear time and cyclical time are contradictory in nature
C. The belief that the universe had a beginning in time can lead to some difficult to answer questions
D. The Big Bang model is not based on sound logical reasoning
E. Astronomers typically avoid getting into debates about the existence of god

Answer

The passage states that *the belief of people that everything that comes into existence does so because of the actions of some rational being* is not based on sound logic. However the passage does not necessarily state this for the Big Bang model. So **(D) should be the correct answer**

A. This can be inferred from the last three sentences of the passage
B. This can be easily inferred from the passage

C. This belief is the same as believing in linear time which, the passage clearly states, can lead to vexing questions
E. This can be inferred from the last lines of the passage

Passage 14

The value of old maps as documents useful for historicity depends necessarily on to what degree they depict and on how accurately. For virtually all periods of pre-modern history some maps have survived to serve as historiography, depicting, however imperfectly, certain features of past geography. The work of Claudius Ptolemy—who lived in the 2nd century A.D.—for centuries provided the basis for maps of the known world and its major regions. Although many were drawn on the scientific basis which he provided, they nevertheless embodied many errors—of location, distance, and the shape of areas of land and sea. The medieval Portolan charts of the Mediterranean Sea and the later charts which provided sailing directions, produced in Holland, were accurate enough to be useful in practical navigation. However, few of the early maps approach modern standards, which require accurate representation of distances and of heights above mean sea-level and the use of carefully distinguished symbols. This is because it was not until the 18th century that cartography, as an exact science, was born.

29) The author of the passage would most likely agree with which of the following?

A. Ancient maps are almost as accurate as modern maps
B. It is not necessary that a map be completely error free to be useful
C. Claudius Ptolemy's was the most famous map maker of his era
D. Cartography is a modern field of study
E. Information provided by ancient maps is most often incorrect

Answer

The author states several times in the passage that even though ancient maps were not completely accurate, they provided useful information about the geographical features of that time. **Hence (B) should be the correct answer.**

A. The passage states the opposite
C. Extreme option. The passage never states that Ptolemy was the *most* famous map maker of his time
D. According to the last line of the passage, cartography began in the 18th century so it can hardly be called modern
E. The information can sometimes be inaccurate but it is extreme to assume that it is most often incorrect

Passage 15

As formal organizations, business corporations are distinguished by their particular goals, which include maximization of profits, growth, and survival. Providing goods and services is a means to this end. If, for example, a number of individuals (outsiders or even insiders) believe that a company's aggressive marketing of infant formula in third world countries is morally wrong, the company is unlikely to be moved by arguments based on ethos alone as long as what it is doing remains profitable. But if those opposed to the company's practice organize a highly effective boycott of the company's products, their moral views will soon enter into the company's deliberations indirectly as limiting operating conditions. They can, at this point, no more be ignored than a prohibitive increase in the costs of certain raw materials.

30) According to the information in the passage, which of the following business corporations is achieving its primary goal?

A. A business corporation that takes every possible step to ensure that its customers are satisfied
B. A business corporation that spends a lot of money in hiring external consultants to devise growth strategies for the business
C. A business corporation that gives top-most priority to profitability

Answer

B and C can easily be inferred from the first sentence of the passage (growth strategies and maximization of profits)

Customer satisfaction is not mentioned anywhere in the passage, Thus A cannot be inferred.

Hence the **correct answer is (B) and (C)**

31) Suppose a company is indulging in some unethical practice. Then, according to the information in the passage, under which of the following conditions is the company most likely to correct this practice?

A. If a group of consumers were to file a court case against the company
B. If a newspaper ran a campaign encouraging citizens not to purchase the products of the company
C. If the actions of the company were to lead to it being criticized in the international media

Answer

According to the passage, a company is likely to be moved to take action only if something affects its primary purpose – profits, survival, and growth.

A court case does not make a difference to any of these three things so (A) cannot be the answer

If people were to stop purchasing the products of the company then its profitability would definitely be affected. So (B) can be inferred

Criticism in the international media does not directly affect the primary goals of the company. It could actually benefit the company by providing it international publicity for free. Hence (C) also cannot be inferred.

Thus the **correct answer is (B) only**

Passage 16

What is the biggest lesson from the Great Depression? In my view, it is that monetary policy and the financial sector play a crucial role in economic development. One important component of the monetary policy is the financial market, more specifically the banking sector.

Why are financial markets and the banking sector so important? Banks fulfil a very important role in the economy by matching borrowers and lenders. When we deposit $100 in a bank, the bank keeps, at most, two to three dollars in its vaults (some of this is actually kept with the central bank), the remaining $98 or so are lent to a borrower.

Most businesses require loans for their normal operations. When the banking sector does not work properly, businesses cannot get loans and they have to curtail their production and lay off workers. As they curtail production, they demand fewer products from their suppliers and therefore their suppliers have to reduce their output and fire workers. If manufacturers cannot sell their goods because the firm downstream does not need as many products as before, they cannot generate enough revenue to repay their earlier loans. Businesses go bankrupt and banks experience further problems as their balance sheet deteriorates due to non-performing loans. At this point, banks want to lend even less because of the uncertainty generated from bankruptcies. As they lend less, the vicious circle continues – with producers cutting production and firing workers. On top of this, depositors start worrying about their deposits because the non-performing loans have made some banks go belly up – your bank has lent out your money to borrowers who cannot return it. Depositors start withdrawing their cash and banks have even fewer possibilities for lending as they have to hoard cash in case there is a run on the bank. If the financial sector does not work, the real economy can go into a deadly spiral and shrink by 30 per cent as during the Great Depression.

One would have thought that this fact would be obvious to all the policy makers. However all the lessons from the Great Depression seem to have been lost within three-quarters of a century. It seems, to paraphrase Marc Bard, that politics (especially of the petty and partisan variety) eats policy for lunch seven days a week.

32) What is the main purpose of the author in writing the passage?

A. To explain how banks and other financial institutions function
B. To discuss the lessons learnt from the Great Depression
C. To argue that banks and manufacturing businesses are interdependent
D. To criticize a group of people for not learning from the lessons of the Great Depression
E. To conclude that people give preference to politics over policies

Answer

The author starts off by describing how monetary policy works and the interdependence among its different players. He then goes on to conclude that policymakers have failed to learn from the lessons of the past as far as monetary policy is concerned. From this **(D) follows as the best answer**

A. The author is doing much more than just this. This option fails to take into account the last paragraph
B. Again the purpose is not just to describe the lessons but also to assert that policymakers haven't learnt from these lessons
C. Same as above, the purpose is broader than this.
E. This is true specifically for the policymakers but not for people in general

33) According to the information in the passage, which of the following can be inferred?

A. Banks are short of cash most of the time
B. Banks do not like to keep money with the central bank.
C. Banks do not like to keep large amounts of money in their vaults.

D. Banks usually keep some money with the central bank.
E. Banks actually fool the customers

Answer

A. Incorrect as it is not mentioned nor can it be inferred from the paragraph
B. Incorrect as the author doesn't mention anything about whether banks like this or not
C. A tricky one. While it is true from the 2nd paragraph that banks do not like to keep a large *proportion* of their funds within their vaults, the *amount* of money (in absolute terms) in their vaults could still be fairly *large*.
D. Is correct from the lines within brackets in the 2nd Para
E. Is false as no such inference can be drawn from the passage

34) In the last paragraph, the tone of the author is:

A. Adulatory
B. Optimistic
C. Critical
D. Analytical
E. Ridiculing

Answer

A. Is incorrect as the author is not adulating or praising anyone in the last para
B. Is incorrect as the author is critical of the policy makers, so he is in fact closer to being pessimistic
C. Is the correct answer because the author is clearly criticizing the policy makers for not having learnt from the lessons of the Great Depression
D. Is incorrect as the author is *opinionated* and not *analytical* in the last para
E. Is incorrect as 'ridiculing' is a very strong term and the author doesn't really ridicule or make fun of the policymakers

35) Which of these could be a result of the banking system not functioning properly?

A. The economy can go into a depression.
B. Workers of manufacturing companies can be fired.
C. Businesses can find it difficult to get loans.

Answer

All the three statements are either directly mentioned or can be inferred from the 3rd paragraph of the passage

Hence the **correct answer is (A), (B), and (C)**

Passage 17

During the late 1990s, HP, the second largest computer manufacturer in the world, faced major challenges in an increasingly competitive market. In 1998, while HP's revenues grew by just 3%, competitor Dell's rose by 38%. Also HP's share price remained more or less stagnant, while competitor IBM's share price increased by 65% during 1998. Analysts said HP's culture, which emphasized teamwork and respect for co-workers, had over the years translated into a consensus-style culture that was proving to be a sharp disadvantage in the fast-growing Internet business era. Analysts felt that instead of Lewis Platt, HP needed a new leader to cope with rapidly changing industry trends. Responding to these concerns, in July 1999, the HP board appointed Carleton S. Fiorina (Fiorina) as the company's CEO.

Fiorina implemented several cost-cutting measures to streamline the company's operations. Some of the measures included forced five-day vacation for workers and postponement of wage hikes for three months in December 2000. Even though the employees protested vociferously against such measures, Fiorina did not relent in implementing the same.

The steps taken by Fiorina surprised analysts. They said that these steps were a major departure from HP's organizational culture - 'The HP Way' of promising lifelong employment and employee satisfaction. According to the company insiders, though change was necessary, employees' morale had suffered badly.

36) According to the passage, the consensus-style culture of HP was

A. The most important factor responsible for the fall in HPs revenues
B. A Cost saver
C. Passive towards changing market conditions
D. Out of sync with the competitor's strategies
E. A Quality booster

Answer

From the information in the passage, the "consensus-style culture" definitely had a *negative* impact on HP, so options (B), and (E) go out because they talk about *positive* effects. (A) is an extreme option because the passage never suggests that this was the *most* important factor responsible for the fall in HPs revenues. Between (C) and (D), the passage doesn't really tell us anything about the competitor's strategies but just that HP wasn't able to respond quickly or effectively enough to the changing market environment. **Thus (C) should be the correct answer.**

37) Which of the following can be inferred from the passage?

A. Dell had a much stronger brand image as compared to HP.
B. Share price of a company can be an indicator of its success.
C. Fiorina favoured cost cutting even at the cost of employee morale.

Answer

The passage only talks about Dell's revenues; from this we cannot infer anything about its brand image as compared to that of HP. Hence A cannot be inferred.

In the opening lines of the passage, share price is mentioned in the context of challenges that HP was facing from competitors and is used as a measure of its lack of success vis-a-vis its competitors. Hence B can be inferred

Again C can also be inferred from the 2nd and 3rd paragraphs because Fiorina did not pay heed to the employees' protests so she clearly favoured cost cutting to improving employee morale.

Thus the **correct answer is (B) and (C)**

Passage 18

To account for the conformation of the Alps, two hypotheses have been advanced, which may be respectively named the hypothesis of fracture and the hypothesis of erosion. The former assumes that the forces by which the mountains were elevated produced fissures in the earth's crust, and that the valleys of the Alps are the tracks of these fissures; the latter maintains that the valleys have been cut out by the action of ice and water, the mountains themselves being the residual forms of this grand sculpture.

I had heard the Via Mala cited as a conspicuous illustration of the fissure theory — the profound chasm thus named, and through which the Hinter-Rhein now flows, could, it was alleged, be nothing else than a crack in the earth's crust. To the Via Mala I therefore went in 1864 to instruct myself upon the point in question. The gorge commences about a quarter of an hour above Tusis and, on entering it, the first impression certainly is that it must be a fissure. This conclusion, in my case, was modified as I advanced because the signs I saw thereupon left no doubt in my mind that this gorge was created due to river action.

38) What is the function of the first sentence of the second paragraph - *'The gorge commences......it must be a fissure'*?

A. It is a hypothesis that the author later disagrees with
B. It is a hypothesis that the author goes on to prove right
C. It is a neutral observation made by the author
D. It confirms the author's initial belief
E. It is the first step in the author's experiment

Answer

In this line the author states that the initial signs suggested that the theory of fracture was correct but in the next line itself he states that he modified this theory as he advanced further. **Thus (A) should be the answer**

B. Opposite. The author actually goes on to agree with the theory of erosion
C. As explained above this is definitely not a neutral observation made by the author
D. The author didn't really have any initial belief. He had heard that the theory of fracture was correct and had gone to the site to verify the same
E. The author is not conducting any experiment in the passage

39) Which of the following can be inferred from the information provided in the passage?

A. It is now absolutely clear what led to the formation of the Alps
B. According to the hypothesis of erosion, the valleys in the Alps have been created by the action of ice and water
C. The Via Mala is the name of a river that flows through the Alps

Answer

The passage doesn't state anywhere that it is now absolutely clear how the Alps were formed. For all we know, some new evidence could always come up that could challenge the theory of erosion. Also note the extreme tone of the option. So A cannot be inferred

B is absolutely correct, as stated in the first paragraph of the passage

According to the opening sentence of the 2nd paragraph, Via Mala was the name of the chasm; the name of the river was Hinter-Rheine. So C also cannot be inferred.

Thus the **correct answer is (B) only**.

Passage 19

Among the men and women prominent in the public life of America there are but few whose names are mentioned as often as that of Emma Goldman. Yet the real Emma Goldman is almost quite unknown. The sensational press has surrounded her name with so much misrepresentation and slander, it would seem almost a miracle that, in spite of this web of calumny, the truth breaks through and a better appreciation of this much maligned idealist begins to manifest itself. There is but little consolation in the fact that almost every representative of a new idea has had to struggle and suffer under similar difficulties. Is it of any avail that a former president of a republic pays homage at Osawatomie to the memory of John Brown? Or that the president of another republic participates in the unveiling of a statue in honour of Pierre Proudhon, and holds up his life to the French nation as a model worthy of enthusiastic emulation? Of what avail is all this when, at the same time, the LIVING John Browns and Proudhons are being crucified? The honour and glory of a Mary Wollstonecraft or of a Louise Michel are not enhanced by the City Fathers of London or Paris naming a street after them—the living generation should be concerned with doing justice to the LIVING Mary Wollstonecrafts and Louise Michels. Posterity assigns to men like Wendel Phillips and Lloyd Garrison the proper niche of honour in the temple of human emancipation, but it is the duty of their contemporaries to bring them due recognition and appreciation while they live.

40) Select the sentence in the passage that most accurately describes the primary concern of the author in writing the passage.

Answer

Posterity assigns to men like Wendel Phillips and Lloyd Garrison the proper niche of honour in the temple of human emancipation, but it is the duty of their contemporaries to bring them due recognition and appreciation while they live.

The author, by means of this passage, is mainly trying to convey the point that people should be given credit for their achievements when they are alive and not after they are dead. The above sentence identifies this best.

41) Why does the author mention *'the President of another country'* in the passage?

A. To assert that every proponent of a new idea has had to face difficulties in the past
B. To state that Pierre Proudhon had been unfairly treated by his contemporaries when he was alive
C. To demonstrate that a situation discussed earlier in the passage is prevalent in all countries
D. To provide an example of an incident in which the good work of a person was appreciated only after his death
E. To demand that Pierre Proudhon be given some compensation for the unjust treatment meted out to him when he was alive

Answer

The author mentions the President of another country to give an example of a situation in which the work of a person was appreciated after his death. **Hence (D) is the best answer.**

A - The use of 'every' makes this extreme

B and E - The author is not specifically concerned with the case of Pierre Proudhon. He is stating a more general observation

C - The passage makes no claim about 'all' countries

42) With which of the following statements would the author most likely agree?

A. The press is primarily responsible for the negative reception that new ideas are greeted with
B. Emma Goldman's contemporaries are partly to be blamed for the way she was treated when she was alive
C. Nobody knows the real Emma Goldman

Answer

The press is definitely responsible but there is nothing in the passage to suggest that the press is 'primarily' responsible. So the author will not agree with A

From the last sentence of the passage, it can definitely be inferred that a person's contemporaries are to be blamed, at least partially, for not highlighting his or her achievements during the person's lifetime. This applies to Emma Goldman's contemporaries as well, at least partly. Hence the author will agree with B

The first part of the passage clearly states that people do have an understanding of the real Emma Goldman despite all that was written about her in the media. So the author will not agree with C.

Thus **the correct answer is (B) only**

Passage 20

Although the Great Plains country of the West was the natural home of the American Bison, where it flourished most abundantly, it also wandered south across Texas to the burning plains of North-eastern Mexico, westward across the Rocky Mountains into New Mexico, Utah, and Idaho, and northward across a vast treeless waste to the bleak and inhospitable shores of the Great Slave Lake itself. It is more than probable that had the bison remained unmolested by man and uninfluenced by him, he would eventually have crossed the Sierra Nevadas and the Coast Range and taken up his abode in the fertile valleys of the Pacific slope. It is also very likely that, had the bison remained for a few more centuries in undisturbed possession of his range and with liberty to roam at will over the North American continent, several distinctly recognizable varieties would have been produced. The individuals inhabiting the extreme north, in the vicinity of Great Slave Lake, for example, would have developed still longer hair, and taken on more of the dense hairiness of the musk ox.

43) The passage mentions each of the following as a negative impact of man's activities on the American bison EXCEPT:

A. The bison could not inhabit the valleys of the Pacific slope
B. Certain new varieties of the bison could not be produced
C. The bison could not cross the Sierra Nevada
D. There was a drastic fall in the bison population
E. The bison's ability to roam at will was curtailed

Answer

It is not stated anywhere in the passage that the bison population fell drastically at any time. **Hence (D) is the correct answer**

Options A, B, C, and E are all mentioned in the passage

44) Which of the following can be inferred from the information provided in the passage?

A. The American bison is a long-haired animal
B. The American bison has now become extinct
C. The Rocky Mountains was not the natural habitat of the American bison

Answer

The lines in the last paragraph *'would have developed still longer hair'* imply that the bison was already a long-haired animal, so A can be inferred

Nowhere does the passage state that the Bison has become extinct, so B cannot be inferred

The passage starts off by stating that the Great Plains was the natural habitat of the Bison and that it wandered to other areas such as the Rocky Mountains. Hence C can be inferred.
Thus the **correct answer is (A) and (C)**

45) Select the sentence in the passage that points out one physical characteristic of the American Bison.

Answer

The individuals inhabiting the extreme north, in the vicinity of Great Slave Lake, for example, would have developed still longer hair, and taken on more of the dense hairiness of the musk ox.

This sentence clearly implies that the American Bison was a long haired animal which is a physical characteristic of the animal.

Passage 21

A relic I still have in my possession amongst my naval memorabilia is a black, mourning armband issued to us when King George VI died on February 6, 1952. It was dispatched by Messrs Gieves of Old Bond Street in London, the naval tailors 'By appointment to the King'. I recall listening to the last Christmas day broadcast of King George VI, with his consort by his side, while having dinner with a friend in Surrey. Then a few weeks later we were to receive news of his death while we were at sea on board our training cruiser HMS Devonshire headed for the Caribbean. As we proceeded to drop anchor in Barbados harbour, we were struck first, by the magnificent sight of flying fish which kept darting across the placid blue waters, and then, by the great alacrity with which mourning bands were delivered to us for the funeral ceremonies. Inevitably, we were billed by 'Messrs Thieves' for five shillings, a princely sum then, because our pay was four shillings a day.

46) At the end of the passage, the author refers to 'Messrs Gieves of Old Bond Street' as 'Messrs Thieves'. This most likely suggests that the author

A. did not appreciate being charged a high price for the black armbands that he did not order for voluntarily
B. believed that 'Messrs Gieves' had shown a lot of alacrity in delivering the armbands on time
C. thought that he was underpaid for his work in the army
D. was miserly by nature
E. was not in favour of elaborate funeral ceremonies

<u>**Answer**</u>

From the overall text of the passage, it is obvious that the author considered it improper to be forcibly charged for a ceremonial armband. He was further unhappy at the price of the armband, which was more than his daily pay at that time. **Thus (A) should be the best answer**.

B: While this fact is mentioned in the previous line in the passage, this is not the reason why the author addresses Messrs Gieves as thieves.

C: The author is implying that the armbands were expensive and not that he was underpaid

D: There is nothing in the passage to suggest that the author was miserly

E: This may or may not be true but is definitely not the reason why the author addresses Messrs Gieves as thieves

47) Select the sentence in the passage that identifies the author's location when King George VI died.

Then a few weeks later we were to receive news of his death while we were at sea on board our training cruiser HMS Devonshire headed for the Caribbean

The above lines clearly state that when King George VI died, the author was on board a ship headed for the Caribbean

Passage 22

It is one of the disadvantages of reading books about natural scenic wonders that they fill the mind with pictures, often exaggerated, often distorted, often blurred, and, even when well drawn, injurious to the freshness of first impressions. Such has been the fate of most of us with regard to the Falls of Niagara. There was little accuracy in the estimates of the first observers of the cataract. Startled by an exhibition of power so novel and so grand, emotion leaped beyond the control of the judgment, and gave currency to notions which have often led to disappointment.

48) Which of the following would the author of the passage most likely agree with?

A. One should never read books about natural scenic wonders
B. Reading books about natural scenic wonders can prevent a person from having an unbiased viewing of that wonder
C. The Niagara Falls have been described incorrectly in books
D. The Niagara Falls are actually not grand and novel
E. Emotional descriptions of natural wonders are always exaggerated

Answer

The passage clearly suggests that if one reads books about natural wonders before visiting such a wonder, then one could get a distorted picture of that wonder in one's mind. So when a person actually views the wonder, he would be biased by the picture that he already has in his mind i.e. he won't be able to view the wonder with an unbiased mind. (B) states the same and should be the correct answer

A. 'Never' makes this option extreme. One should ideally avoid reading books about natural wonders only if one has not yet visited that wonder
C. While this could be true for some books, we cannot make a general statement for all books
D. The passage in fact suggests that the Niagara Falls are grand and novel which is why the people got carried away in their descriptions of the same

E. Again the use of 'always' makes this option an extreme one. Some emotional descriptions may not be exaggerated, for all that we know

Passage 23

The purpose of mechanics is to describe how bodies change their position in space with time. I should load my conscience with grave sins against the sacred spirit of lucidity were I to formulate the aims of mechanics in this way, without serious reflection and detailed explanations. Let us proceed to disclose these sins.

It is not clear what is to be understood here by "position" and "space." I stand at the window of a railway carriage which is travelling uniformly, and drop a stone on the embankment, without throwing it. Then, disregarding the influence of the air resistance, I see the stone descend in a straight line. A pedestrian who observes the misdeed from the footpath notices that the stone falls to earth in a parabolic curve. I now ask: Do the "positions" traversed by the stone lie "in reality" on a straight line or on a parabola? Moreover, what is meant here by motion "in space" ? From the considerations of the previous section the answer is self-evident. In the first place we entirely shun the vague word "space," of which, we must honestly acknowledge, we cannot form the slightest conception, and we replace it by "motion relative to a practically rigid body of reference." The positions relative to the body of reference (railway carriage or embankment) have already been defined in detail in the preceding section. If instead of "body of reference " we insert " system of co-ordinates," which is a useful idea for mathematical description, we are in a position to say: The stone traverses a straight line relative to a system of co-ordinates rigidly attached to the carriage, but relative to a system of co-ordinates rigidly attached to the ground (embankment) it describes a parabola. With the aid of this example it is clearly seen that there is no such thing as an independently existing trajectory, but only a trajectory relative to a particular body of reference.

49) What can be inferred about the author from the first paragraph of this passage?

A. The author agrees with the definition of a term as mentioned in the first line of the passage
B. The author wants to reflect on the definition of a term as mentioned in the first line of the passage
C. The author believes that concepts such as 'space' cannot be defined in absolute terms
D. The author does not completely agree with the definition of a term as mentioned in the first line of the passage
E. The author is a physics expert

Answer

The 1st para clearly suggests that the author considers it a sin to define 'mechanics' the way it has been defined in the first line of the paragraph. **Hence (D) should be the answer**

A. Opposite as explained above
B. The author isn't limiting himself to merely reflecting; he clearly has a negative view of the definition
C. This only comes up in the second paragraph
E. This may or may not be the case. The author could very well be an inquisitive Physics student

50) If a stone were to be dropped on a platform 20 feet below, from the window of a moving vehicle, which of the following must be true, according to the information in the passage?

A. To a person sitting in the vehicle the stone would appear to fall in the shape of a parabola
B. To a person sitting in another vehicle 500 metres behind, the stone would appear to fall in a straight line
C. To a person standing on the platform the stone would appear to fall in a straight line
D. To a person standing on the platform the stone would appear to fall either in a straight line or in the shape of a parabola
E. To a person standing on the platform the stone would appear to fall in the shape of a parabola

Answer

The experiment described in the question is very similar to the one described in the passage so look for the option that matches the conclusion of the experiment in the passage. **(E) clearly follows from this as the answer**

A. Opposite. According to the experiment in the passage, to a person in the vehicle the stone should appear to fall in a straight line
B. The passage does not suggest anything about how an object should appear to a person sitting in another vehicle
C. Opposite. To this person the stone should appear to fall in the shape of a parabola
D. Such an outcome is not supported by the information in the passage

51) The passage implies that scientists should refrain from doing which of the following?

A. Coming up with theoretical definitions without judging the practical veracity of the same
B. Considering concepts in the field of physics in absolute terms
C. Attempting to define terms from the realm of Physics in the relative sense rather in absolute terms

Answer

(A) - Sounds logical but not supported by the passage.

(B) - The entire gist of the passage is that certain concepts in physics are relative ones and cannot be described in absolute terms. (B) clearly follows from this

(C) - Opposite. The passage suggests that scientists should actually do this and not 'refrain' from doing this

Hence the **correct answer is (B) only**

52) The author conducts an experiment in the passage. Select the sentence in the passage that highlights one qualifier that the author gives in his experiment.

Answer

Then, disregarding the influence of the air resistance, I see the stone descend in a straight line.

To answer this question correctly, it is very important to understand the meaning of the term 'qualifier'. In the context of an experiment, a qualifier is a restricting or a limiting factor without which the experiment's finding cannot be justified. In the above sentence the author clearly states that the influence of air resistance needs to be disregarded so this becomes a qualifier because if the air resistance were to be taken into consideration then the findings of the experiment may get distorted.

Passage 24

The Cyclopses, according to mythology, were a race of bad-tempered and rather stupid one-eyed giants. Not, perhaps, a great portend for a new generation of robots. But Andrew Davison, a computer scientist at Imperial College, London, thinks one eye is enough for a robot, provided its brain can think fast enough. For a robot to work autonomously, it has to understand its environment. Stereoscopic vision, integrating the images from two "eyes" looking at the same thing from different angles, is one approach to achieve this, but it involves a lot of complicated computer processing. The preferred method these days, therefore, is SLAM (Simultaneous Localization and Mapping), which uses sensors such as laser-based range finders that "see" by bouncing beams of light off their surroundings and timing the return.

53) Which of the following assertions can be made from the information in the passage?

A. A Robots with two eyes is most likely making use of stereoscopic vision
B. Cyclopses were mythical beings with one eye and small stature
C. SLAM is probably simpler than Stereoscopic vision

Answer

(A) can be inferred from the information in the passage, especially because of the use of the words 'most likely'. Had it said 'always' instead of 'most likely,' then A would have been out as an extreme option

(B) is partially correct in that Cyclopses are indeed mythical creatures with one eye but the passage refers to them as giants so 'small stature' doesn't make sense. Hence B cannot be inferred

(C) can be inferred because the passage faults stereoscopic vision for being too complicated. Then, if SLAM is preferred to stereoscopic vision, it most probably is simpler of the two

Thus the **correct answer is (A) and (C)**

Passage 25

The sole use and sole object of existence is enjoyment or pleasure, which two words will here be treated as synonymous; happiness, also, though not quite identical in meaning, being occasionally substituted for them. Enjoyment, it must be observed, is of various kinds, measures, and degrees. It may be sensual, or emotional, or imaginative, or intellectual, or moral. It may be momentary or eternal; intoxicating delight or sober satisfaction. It may be unmixed and undisturbed, in which case, however short of duration or coarse in quality, it may in strictness be called happiness; or it may be troubled and alloyed, although of a flavour which would be exquisite if pure, and if there were nothing to interfere with the perception of it. Understood, however, in a sufficiently comprehensive sense, enjoyment or pleasure may be clearly perceived to be the sole object of existence. The whole value of life plainly consists of the enjoyment, present or future, which life affords, or is capable of affording or securing. Now, the excellence of all rules depends on their conduciveness to the object they have in view. The excellence of all rules of life must, therefore, depend on their conduciveness to the sole object which life has in view, viz., enjoyment. But the excellence of rules of life, or of conduct or modes of acting, would seem to be but another name for their morality, and the morality of actions obviously depends on their conformity to moral rules. Whence, if so much be admitted, it necessarily follows that the test of the morality of actions is their conduciveness to enjoyment.

54) What is the main purpose of the author in writing the passage?

A. To define a term by giving examples
B. To put forward a point of view and explain its implication
C. To describe several interpretations of a belief
D. To present an unusual interpretation of a well known fact
E. To evaluate two competing beliefs

Answer

Elimination might be a good way to answer this question. **(B) looks good** because the first line of the passage gives the author's point of view and the last line gives its implication with respect to morality of actions.

A. is out because the author does not define any term, nor does he give any examples of the same.
C. the passage does not talk about a belief or its several interpretations
D. There is nothing to suggest that there is anything *unusual* in the passage
E. No such competing beliefs are mentioned in the passage

55) The author of the passage would agree with each of the following EXCEPT:

A. Pleasure always leads to happiness
B. Pleasure can be of different types
C. Enjoyment is no different from pleasure

D. Unmixed enjoyment cannot strictly be called enjoyment
E. The sole purpose of life is the quest for happiness

Answer

The first line of the passage clearly states that pleasure and enjoyment are the same but that these two terms are not the same as 'happiness'. Also nowhere does the passage suggest that pleasure and happiness are linked. Hence the author will not agree with **(A) which is the correct answer**

B. The passage describes several types of pleasure such as sensual, emotional, imaginative, etc.
C. The opening line of the passage states that enjoyment and pleasure are the same
D. The line *'It may be unmixed and undisturbed, in which case, however short of duration or coarse in quality, it may in strictness be called happiness'* clearly implies that this is true
E. This is the main purpose of the passage

56) The passage provides information in support of which of the following assertions?

A. An act of crime cannot be considered an immoral act if a person derives enjoyment from that act
B. The morality of actions cannot solely be judged by their perceived enjoyment
C. The excellence of all rules of life depends on their morality

Answer

A. The last line of the passage states that the morality of actions can be judged by whether they give one pleasure or not so if an act gives one pleasure, it cannot be considered immoral. Hence A can be inferred

B. The last line of the passage states the opposite, so B cannot be inferred

C. According to the passage, the excellence of all rules of life depends on whether they can provide enjoyment (and not morality) or not

Thus the **correct answer is (A) only**

Passage 26

Progress became a theme in European thought in about 1750. The thinkers of the Enlightenment wanted to replace the Biblical account of time (Genesis, Creation, Fall, Redemption) with a myth which put Man, not God, at the centre of the story. The narrative of human progress was understood to be both a material and a moral process; not just changing our technologies, but altering our instincts, and for the better.

We now live in ironic, anti-heroic times. Do we still believe in the story of progress? It sits in the attic of our minds like a glorious Victorian antique, as magnificent as a stuffed moose head and just as useless. Perhaps worse than useless. Modern political correctness has lodged a suspicion in our mind about the Ascent of Man. What do you mean, Man? What about Woman? And which Man? Surely not the European conquerors? And Ascent? Surely you're not implying that western civilization is superior to everything that's gone before? And so on. The Ascent of Man may be an idea we had better do without.

57) The author mentions the thinkers of the Enlightenment in order to:

A. assert that the Bible was an impediment in the way of progress.
B. demonstrate that Man is superior to God
C. affirm that human progress is akin to mastery over the world.
D. illustrate the transformation in man's approach towards the concept of 'progress'
E. conclude that the Ascent of Man is an obsolete idea.

<u>Answer</u>

The author mentions in the first few lines that the thinkers wanted to include the narrative of human progress as supreme. It was understood to be both a material and a moral process; not just changing our technologies but altering our instincts, and for the better. **This makes Option (D) correct.**

A. The author never states or implies this
B. Extreme. While 'man' was given more importance, there is nothing in the passage to suggest that he was considered superior to god
C. The author never talks about 'mastery over the world'
E. This thought doesn't come until much later in the passage

58) Select the sentence in the passage that highlights the primary difference between the Modern and the Biblical accounts of time/

Answer

The thinkers of the Enlightenment wanted to replace the Biblical account of time (Genesis, Creation, Fall, Redemption) with a myth which put Man, not God, at the centre of the story

The above lines clearly highlight the major point of difference between the two accounts of time – one put God at the centre of the story while the other put Man at the centre of the story

Passage 27

Woman's demand for equal suffrage is based largely on the contention that a woman must have equal rights in all affairs of society. Needless to say, I am not opposed to woman suffrage on the conventional ground that she is not equal to it. I see no physical, psychological, or mental reasons why a woman should not have the equal right to vote with man. But that cannot possibly blind me to the absurd notion that a woman will accomplish that wherein man has failed. If she would not make things worse, she certainly could not make them better. To assume, therefore, that she would succeed in purifying something which is not susceptible of purification, is to credit her with supernatural powers. Since woman's greatest misfortune has been that she was looked upon as either angel or devil, her true salvation lies in being placed on earth; namely, in being considered human, and therefore subject to all human follies and mistakes. Are we, then, to believe that two wrongs will make one right? Are we to assume that the poison already inherent in politics will be decreased, if women were to enter the political arena? The most ardent suffragists would hardly maintain such a folly.

59) The author of the passage is primarily concerned with

A. discussing the possible implications of a change
B. arguing that a particular change will not have the desired effect
C. exploring definitions of a concept
D. comparing the advantages of a particular change with its disadvantages
E. clarifying an ambiguous term

Answer

The author is stating that giving women the right to vote will not lead to a purification of the political system. **(B) states this best and is the correct answer**

A. The author is not just discussing the implications of a change but actually arguing that one of the implications will not take place
C. The author is not *exploring* any definitions in the passage

D. The author does not make any comparisons in the passage
E. The author doesn't *clarify* any ambiguity in the passage

60) What can be inferred from the lines *'her true salvation lies in being placed on earth'*?

A. The author does not believe that giving women the right to vote would solve the problems that the political system faces
B. The author is against adopting an extreme view of women in general
C. The author does not believe that two wrongs will make one right
D. The author believes that a woman does not have supernatural powers
E. The author believes women should suffer as much as men, no more and no less

Answer

This line follows from the author's statement that most people view a woman as either an angel or a devil whereas he just wants a woman to be treated as a human. **(B) states this best.**

(A) - Though this is true for the overall passage, this is not implied by the quoted lines
(C) - Again true for the passage but not for the quoted lines
(D) & (E) - Not suggested by the passage

61) Which of the following options is suggested by the passage?

A. Most ardent suffragists believe that women can succeed where men have failed and that women can cleanse the political system
B. Most ardent suffragists believe that giving women the right to vote will not resolve the problems that beset the political system
C. The author is overall in favour of woman suffrage

Answer

A. Opposite as explained below
B. The last line of the passage states that *'most ardent suffragists would hardly maintain such a folly'*. The folly here refers to the notion that giving women the right to vote would solve all the problems that the political system faces. So if most ardent suffragists do not agree with this notion, then B can definitely be inferred

C. Opposite, the author is in fact against woman suffrage because of the reason highlighted in the passage

So the **correct answer is (B) only**

Passage 28

Aesthetics has for its object the vast realm of the beautiful, and it may be most adequately defined as the philosophy of art or of the fine arts. To some this definition may seem arbitrary, as excluding the beautiful in nature, but it will cease to appear so if it is remarked that the beauty which is the work of art is higher than natural beauty because it is the offspring of the mind. Moreover, if, in conformity with a certain school of modern philosophy, the mind be viewed as the true being, including all in itself, it must be admitted that beauty is only truly beautiful when it shares in the nature of mind, and is mind's offspring. Viewed in this light, the beauty of nature is only a reflection of the beauty of the mind, only an imperfect beauty, which as to its essence is included in that of the mind.

62) According to the passage, why is natural beauty considered inferior to man-made beauty?

A. It is not clearly understood by man
B. It is an imperfect beauty
C. It is not a creation of the human mind
D. It is too uncertain
E. It does not have a tangible form

Answer

The passage states that man-made art is superior to natural art because it is a creation of the human mind. **Hence (C) should be the answer.**

A. The passage never states this
B. True but this is so because it is not a creation of the human mind
D. The passage never states this
E. The passage never states this

63) Which of the following can be inferred from the information in the passage?

A. Aesthetics is in some way related to beauty
B. An object is not truly beautiful if it is not a creation of the mind
C. Some people have disputed the non-inclusion of natural beauty in Aesthetics

Answer

A. This can be easily inferred from the passage
B. The passage again states this as well
C. The passage states that some people find the non–inclusion of natural beauty in aesthetics arbitrary. So C can also be inferred

Thus the correct answer is **(A), (B), and (C)**

Passage 29

One of the commonest forms of madness is the desire to be noticed, the pleasure derived from being noticed. Perhaps it is not merely common, but universal. In its mildest form it doubtless is universal. Every child is pleased at being noticed; many intolerable children put in their whole time in distressing and idiotic effort to attract the attention of visitors; boys are always "showing off"; apparently all men and women are glad and grateful when they find that they have done a thing which has lifted them for a moment out of obscurity and caused wondering talk. This common madness can develop, by nurture, into a hunger for notoriety in one, for fame in another.

It is this madness for being noticed and talked about which has invented kingship and the thousand other dignities, and tricked them out with pretty and showy fineries; it has made kings pick one another's pockets, scramble for one another's crowns and estates, slaughter one another's subjects; it has raised up prize-fighters, and poets, and village mayors, and little and big politicians, and big and little charity-founders, and bicycle champions, and bandit chiefs, and frontier desperadoes, and Napoleons. Anything to get notoriety; anything to set the village, or the township, or the city, or the State, or the nation, or the planet shouting, "Look—there he goes—that is the man!"

64) What is the passage primarily concerned with?

A. Providing conflicting definitions of a phrase
B. Discussing a human desire and its impact
C. Analysing the positive and negative aspects of a phenomenon
D. Arguing that all famous men have one thing in common
E. Concluding that people will do anything to get noticed

Answer

The passage mainly discusses the desire amongst humans to be noticed and the impact of this, which could be both good and bad, with several examples. **(B) states this best** and should be the correct answer.

A. The passage does not contain any conflicting definitions
C. 'Phenomenon' is the wrong term to refer to a human desire, and the passage does not contain any analysis either
D. The passage never states that the desire to be noticed is common among 'all' famous men
E. Extreme option, not supported by the passage

65) Which of the following can be concluded from the information in the passage?

A. The desire to be noticed does not only have a negative impact
B. In the past, kings have tricked their subjects using the desire to get noticed
C. At least some people would prefer to be noticed for the wrong reason than not be noticed at all

Answer

A. The passage clearly states that the desire to be noticed can have both positive and negative effects. So A can be concluded
B. The passage never states that kings tricked their subjects. The first sentence of the second para actually states that it was the kings who were tricked by others using the desire to get noticed. Hence B cannot be concluded
C. This can also be concluded from the information in the passage because there definitely are people who would do something wrong just to get noticed rather than do no wrong and be not noticed at all

Hence the **correct answer is (A) and (C)**

66) Which of the following would the author most likely agree with, based on the information in the second paragraph?

A. Charities are not always founded out of purely altruistic motives
B. The desire to be noticed can be a motivator for children as well
C. Bicycle champions want to become notorious
D. There would be no wars if people did not want to become famous
E. The desire to be noticed can be characterized as madness

Answer

Note that the question is only asking about the second para so options related to the first para can be immediately eliminated. The author concludes in the second para that, amongst other things, the desire to get noticed gives rise to charity founders so he is concluding that these charities could not have been founded for any other reason such as altruistic ones. Hence **(A) is the correct answer**.

B. This is mentioned in the 1st para and not in the 2nd

C. The 2nd para does not state or imply this. The bicycle champion becomes a champion because of his desire to be noticed

D. The 2nd para does not state what causes or leads to wars.

E. This is mentioned in the 1st para and not in the 2nd

Passage 30

Metaphysics, or the attempt to conceive the world as a whole by means of thought, has been developed, from the first, by the union and conflict of two very different human impulses - one urging men towards mysticism, and the other urging them towards science. Some men have achieved greatness through one of these impulses: in Hume, for example, the scientific impulse reigns quite unchecked, while in Blake a strong hostility to science co-exists with a profound mystic insight. But the greatest men who have been philosophers have felt the need both of science and of mysticism: the attempt to harmonise the two was what made their life, and what always must, for all its arduous uncertainty, make philosophy, to some minds, a greater thing than either science or religion.

Before attempting an explicit characterisation of the scientific and the mystical impulses, I will provide examples of two philosophers whose greatness lies in the very intimate blending of science and mysticism which they achieved. The two philosophers I mean are Heraclitus and Plato. Heraclitus, as everyone knows, was a believer in universal flux: time builds and destroys all things. From the few fragments that remain, it is not easy to discover how he arrived at his opinions, but there are some sayings that strongly suggest scientific observation as the source. In Plato, the same twofold impulse exists, though the mystic impulse is distinctly the stronger of the two and secures ultimate victory whenever the conflict is sharp.

67) According to the information in the passage, which of the following can be concluded about Plato?

A. For Plato, both the scientific and the mystical impulses were equally important
B. Plato and Heraclitus had opposing philosophies
C. Plato relied on the mystical impulse when in doubt
D. Plato did not believe in the concept of universal flux
E. When in conflict, Plato used his knowledge of both the mystical and the scientific impulses to resolve the same

Answer

The last line of the passage states that the mystical impulse was the stronger impulse in Plato and whenever Plato was in conflict or doubt, the mystical impulse won. **(C) states this best** and is the correct answer.

A. Opposite. The passage clearly states that in Plato the mystical impulse was stronger
B. Out of Scope. The passage never states this. In fact the author provides the example of these two philosophers to show a point of similarity – their near perfect blending of the scientific and mystical impulses
D. Out of Scope. Just because Heraclitus believed in this does not mean that Plato did not
E. Opposite as explained above in A

68) What is the overall purpose of the passage?

A. To assert that the greatest philosophers are those who have achieved the perfect blend of the mystical and scientific impulses
B. To discuss the history of metaphysics
C. To explain why philosophy is superior to science or religion
D. To provide examples of philosophers who have achieved greatness either through only mystic or scientific impulses or through an amalgam of both
E. To praise philosophers who have achieved a perfect blend of science and mysticism

Answer

The passage primarily talks about the combination of science and mysticism as the ideal combination that makes philosophy superior to science or religion. It then goes on to provide examples of two philosophers who have managed to achieve a near-perfect blend of these two impulses. **(A) follows best from this** as the correct answer.

B. Apart from the opening lines, the passage does not really even discuss metaphysics as such
C. While this fact is mentioned in the passage, this is too specific to be the main purpose
D. The main purpose of the passage is more than to just provide examples.
E. While the passage does mention two such philosophers, the entire passage was not written to just praise them but to highlight the underlying theme of their achievement - the amalgam of science and mysticism

69) Which of the following can be inferred from the passage?

A. Blake and Hume were both inclined more towards mysticism than towards science
B. There is no real literary proof of how Heraclitus arrived at his opinions
C. Plato and Heraclitus were similar in some aspects

Answer

A. The first para states that it was just Blake who was inclined towards mysticism; Hume was in fact a supporter of the scientific impulse. Hence we cannot infer (A)
B. The 2nd para clearly states that this belief is actually based on 'sayings'. So (B) can be inferred
C. The author wrote the 2nd para to highlight this similarity - both of them achieved a perfect blend of science and mysticism. Hence (C) can be inferred

Thus the **correct answer is (B) and (C)**

70) Select the sentence in the passage that explains why Philosophy may be superior to other sciences

Answer

But the greatest men who have been philosophers have felt the need both of science and of mysticism: the attempt to harmonize the two was what made their life, and what always must, for all its arduous uncertainty, make philosophy, to some minds, a greater thing than either science or religion.

The lines clearly states what makes Philosophy a greater thing than either science or religion

Passage 31

Science, to the ordinary reader of newspapers, is represented by a varying selection of sensational triumphs, such as wireless telegraphy and airplanes, radio-activity, and the marvels of modern alchemy. It is not this aspect of science that I wish to speak of. Science, in this aspect, consists of detached up-to-date fragments, interesting only until they are replaced by something newer and more up-to-date, displaying nothing of the systems of patiently constructed knowledge out of which, almost as a casual incident, have come the practically useful results which interest the man in the street. The increased command over the forces of nature which is derived from science is undoubtedly an amply sufficient reason for encouraging scientific research, but this reason has been so often urged and is so easily appreciated that other reasons, to my mind quite as important, are apt to be overlooked. It is with these other reasons, especially with the intrinsic value of a scientific habit of mind in forming our outlook on the world that I shall be concerned in what follows.

71) What is the main purpose of the passage?

A. To discuss the several definitions of science
B. To argue that an ordinary person's view of science is actually incorrect
C. To propose increased investment the field of scientific research
D. To state that science has several aspects beyond the one that average people take into consideration
E. To explain certain lesser known aspects of science

Answer

The author never states that people think of science incorrectly. He merely states that there are several other aspects of science which are equally important and that these would be the subject of his discussion. Thus **(D) is the best answer**

A. The passage doesn't provide *several* definitions of science

B. The author never states that this view is incorrect but that this may be just one aspect of science

C. The author never mentions investment in scientific research

E. The author merely states that he would like to discuss these; he never actually explains these aspects in the passage

72) According to the passage, which of the following could be true of an ordinary reader of newspapers?

A. He is aware that science has more than one aspect to it
B. He is ignorant of scientific developments taking place every day
C. He would regard a dam as a scientific accomplishment
D. He has a sensationalist view of science
E. His scientific beliefs lead him to have a narrow outlook of the world

Answer

The passage states that an ordinary reader of newspapers is more concerned with the end results of science. The passage also mentions that anything that provides man control over the forces of nature is considered a scientific accomplishment. **(C) follows best from here**.

A. Opposite. The passage states that he is unaware of this

B. He is ignorant of other aspects of science but that does not mean he is ignorant of scientific developments

D. The passage mentions 'sensational triumphs' but this does not necessarily translate into a sensationalist view of science

E. The passage never mentions his outlook of the world

73) Which of the following would the author of the passage most likely NOT agree with?

A. The knowledge of science is as valuable, if not more valuable, than its end results
B. To an ordinary person the end results of science are what matter most
C. The final tangible results of scientific knowledge are everlasting
D. One important aspect of science is its ability to help us form our outlook of the world
E. There are several equally important reasons why scientific research should be encouraged

Answer

In the middle of the passage the author states that the end results of science are fleeting in nature and will be eventually be replaced with newer results; it is actually the scientific knowledge on which these results are based that is everlasting. So the author would never agree with **(C), the correct answer**.

A. The author would agree with this since this is the main thesis of the passage
B. The author states this in the passage
D. The last line of the passage states this
E. The author states this in the passage as well

Passage 32

I remember the astonishment I felt when I first read Shakespeare. I expected to receive a powerful aesthetic pleasure, but having read, one after the other, works regarded as his best: "King Lear," "Romeo and Juliet," "Hamlet" and "Macbeth," not only did I feel no delight, but I also felt an irresistible repulsion and tedium, and doubted as to whether I was senseless in feeling works regarded as the summit of perfection by the whole of the civilized world to be trivial and positively bad, or whether the significance which this civilized world attributes to the works of Shakespeare was itself senseless. My consternation was increased by the fact that I always keenly felt the beauties of poetry in every form; then why should artistic works recognized by the whole world as those of a genius not just fail to please me, but in fact be disagreeable to me?

74) Select the sentence in the passage that highlights how people in general perceived Shakespeare.

Answer

My consternation was increased by the fact that I always keenly felt the beauties of poetry in every form; then why should artistic works recognized by the whole world as those of a genius not just fail to please me, but in fact be disagreeable to me?

The above lines clearly indicate that people, in general, considered Shakespeare a genius. In case you are confused about the line - *'feeling works regarded as the summit of perfection by the whole of the civilized world'* – remember that these lines praise Shakespeare's work but don't really state anything about Shakespeare himself and so cannot be the answer.

75) In context of the passage, what does the line - *'artistic works recognized by the whole world as those of a genius'* - refer to?

A. The poetry that was read and appreciated by the author
B. Those few works of Shakespeare that the author actually liked
C. The translations of Shakespeare's popular works
D. The writings of the author of the passage
E. The majority of Shakespeare's works

Answer

The quoted phrase clearly refers to the works of Shakespeare in general that the author found repulsive. Hence **(E) should be the best answer**.

A. The lines are clearly referring to Shakespeare's works and not to the poetry mentioned in the passage

B. The author states that he did not like any of Shakespeare's works

C. The passage makes no mention of translations

D. The passage never mentions the writings of the author of the passage or that the author is actually a writer.

76) What is the meaning of the word 'consternation' in context of the passage?

A. Unhappiness
B. Sorrow
C. Disappointment
D. Confusion
E. Dejection

Answer

In earlier lines in the 1st para, the author states that he was not sure whether the people who consider Shakespeare were wrong in their judgment or whether he was wrong in his. He further goes on to say that this *doubt* was further aggravated by the fact that he was normally easily able to appreciate the beauty in every type of writing, so he was confused as to why couldn't he find the same in Shakespeare's works. **(D) follows best from this** as the correct answer.

A. Unhappy isn't the correct word, as explained above

B. The author never really feels sorrowful anywhere in the passage

C. Same as A

E. The author never feels dejected or heartbroken anywhere in the passage

77) Which of the following would the author of the passage most likely agree with?

A. People haven't been entirely honest in their praise of Shakespeare and his works
B. The civilized world can at times behave in a rather senseless manner
C. The author was filled with self doubt about his ability to appreciate beauty in writing, on reading the works of Shakespeare

Answer

A. The author never states or implies that people have been dishonest in their praise, just that he does not agree with them. So (A) cannot be inferred

B. The author wonders about this fact but we don't know whether he eventually agrees or disagrees with it. So (B) cannot be inferred

C. The author clearly states this fact throughout the passage, including the last sentence. Hence (C) can be inferred

Thus the **correct answer is (C) only**

Passage 33

Pope's life as a writer falls into three periods, answering fairly enough to the three reigns in which he worked. Under Queen Anne he was an original poet but made little money by his verses. Under George I he was chiefly a translator, and made much money by satisfying the French-classical taste with versions of the "Iliad" and "Odyssey." Under George I he also edited Shakespeare, but with little profit to himself for Shakespeare was but a Philistine in the eyes of the French-classical critics. But as the eighteenth century grew slowly to its work, signs of a deepening interest in the real issues of life distracted men's attention from the culture of the snuff-box and the fan. As Pope's genius ripened, the best part of the world in which he worked was pressing forward, as a mariner who will no longer hug the coast but crowds all sail to cross the storms of a wide unknown sea. Pope's poetry thus deepened with the course of time, and the third period of his life, which fell within the reign of George II, was that in which he produced the "Essay on Man," the "Moral Essays," and the "Satires." These deal wholly with aspects of human life and the great questions they raise, according throughout with the doctrine of the poet, and of the reasoning world about him in his latter day, that "the proper study of mankind is Man."

78) According to the information in the passage, which of the following CANNOT be inferred with reference to the first two periods of Pope's writings?

A. The public in general appreciated Pope's original works
B. Pope finally made money by copying other people's works
C. Pope decided to stop writing original poetry and began translating other people's works in order to make money

Answer

A. Opposite. Pope made little money when he wrote original poetry so most likely the public did not appreciate his original works. So (A) cannot be inferred
B. Distortion. 'Translating' is not the same as 'copying'. So (B) cannot be inferred
C. The passage never clarifies why Pope made this decision. So (C) cannot be inferred

Remember that the question asks us for the options that *cannot* be inferred from the passage. Hence the **correct answer is (A), (B), and (C)**

79) Which of the following does the passage imply about Pope?

A. His most famous works primarily deal with different aspects of human life
B. He made the most money under the reign of George 1
C. The public was not impressed with his original woks

Answer

A. The last part of the passage states this, so (A) can be inferred
B. The passage only states that Pope made more money under George 1 than he did under Queen Anne. This does not mean that he did not go on to make even more money in the 3rd phase of his life. Hence (B) cannot be inferred

C. This is a trap option. Just because the public was not impressed with Pope's works under Queen Anne (and the passage never states this) does not mean that in general the public was not impressed with his original works. The latter part of the passage describes several such works with which the public was very impressed. So (C) cannot be inferred

So the **correct answer is (A) only**

80) In context of the passage, what do these lines imply - *'as a mariner who will no longer hug the coast but crowds all sail to cross the storms of a wide unknown sea'*?

A. Pope stopped translating other people's works and began creating original works
B. The public started taking more interest in the real issues of life
C. Pope started writing about the various aspects of human life
D. Pope worked as a sailor on a ship which changed his outlook of the world and was responsible for his subsequent writings
E. Pope decided to venture away from the tried and tested style of writing and attempt new writing styles and subjects

<u>**Answer**</u>

The quoted lines provide an analogy to Pope's actions at that time. To hug the coast means to stick to the safe zone and not take risks so this mariner is not sticking to the safe zone but rather he is crowding his sails and taking the unknown sea head on. **(E) follows best as the answer.**

A. This is true but has no connection with the meaning of the quoted lines
B. Same as A
C. Same as A
D. Out of Scope. The passage mentions no such thing.

Passage 34

Water perfectly pure is scarcely ever met with in nature. The effects produced by the foreign matters which water may contain, are more considerable, and of greater importance, than might at first be imagined. It cannot be denied, that such waters as are *hard*, or loaded with earthy matter, have a decided effect upon some important functions of the human body. They increase the distressing symptoms under which those persons labour who are afflicted with what is commonly called gravel complaints, and many other ailments might be named that are always aggravated by the use of waters abounding in saline and earthy substances.

The purity of the waters employed in some of the arts and manufactures, is an object of not less consequence. In the process of brewing malt liquors, soft water is preferable to hard. Every brewer knows that the largest possible quantity of the extractive matter of the malt is obtained in the least possible time, and at the smallest cost, by means of soft water.

In the art of the dyer, hard water not only opposes the solution of several dye stuffs, but it also alters the natural tints of some delicate colours, whilst in others again it precipitates the earthy and saline matters with which it is impregnated into the delicate fibers of the stuff, and thus impedes the softness and brilliancy of the dye. To the manufacturer of painters' colours, water as pure as possible is absolutely essential for the successful preparation of several delicate pigments. Carmine, madder lake, ultramarine, and Indian yellow cannot be prepared without perfectly pure water.

In the culinary art, the effects of water more or less pure are likewise obvious. Good and pure water softens the fibers of animal and vegetable matters more readily than such as is called *hard*. Every cook knows that dry or ripe peas, and other farinaceous seeds, cannot *readily* be boiled soft in hard water because the farina of the seed is not perfectly soluble in water loaded with earthy salts.

81) Select the sentence in the passage that most accurately states the primary concern of the passage.

Answer

The effects produced by the foreign matters which water may contain, are more considerable, and of greater importance, than might at first be imagined.

The primary concern of the passage is to highlight the fact that impurities in water can have a deleterious effect on a wide range of activities. The above lines summarize this best.

82) Which of the following would the author of the passage most likely agree with?

A. Pure water can never be found in nature
B. Spring water is better than saline water
C. At times the effects of impure water tend to be underestimated
D. The purity of water employed in the arts is of less consequence than the purity of water that humans drink

E. Hard water can cause colours to bleed

Answer

The second sentence of the passage states that the effects of impure water are much more considerable than what might have been imagined. From this it can be inferred that at times these effects are underestimated i.e. **(C) should be the correct answer**.

A. Extreme option. The first sentence of the passage states that perfectly pure water is scarcely ever met but 'scarcely' does not mean 'never'
B. The passage makes no mention of spring water and we cannot use our knowledge of the same to answer questions
D. The first line of the 2nd para implies that this is not the case
E. The passage never states this

83) From the information in the passage, which of the following can be concluded?

A. It is not suitable for boiling vegetables
B. It increases the extractive matter obtained from malt
C. It can make colours look dull

Answer

A. This can be inferred from the last para
B. The last line of the 2nd para states that soft water increases the quantity of extractive matter obtained from malt, so (B) cannot be inferred
C. The 3rd para states that hard water can reduce the brilliancy of the dye i.e. make colours look dull. So (C) can be inferred

Thus the **correct answer is (A) and (C)**

Passage 35

In reading Nietzsche's two essays on Wagner, we are apt to be deceived by their virulent and forcible tone into believing that the whole matter is a mere cover for hidden fire, a mere blind of aesthetic discussion concealing a deep and implacable personal feud which demands and will have vengeance. In spite of all that has been said to the contrary, many people still hold this view of the two little works before us and, as the actual facts are not accessible to everyone, and as rumours are more easily believed than verified, the error of supposing that these pamphlets were dictated by personal animosity, and even by Nietzsche's envy of Wagner in his glory, seems to be a pretty common one.

Another very general error is to suppose that the point at issue here is not one concerning music at all, but concerning religion. It is taken for granted that the aspirations, the particular quality, the influence, and the method of an art like music, are matters quite distinct from the values and the conditions prevailing in the culture with which it is in harmony, and that however many Christian elements may be discovered in Wagnerian texts, Nietzsche had no right to raise aesthetic objections because he happened to entertain the extraordinary view that these Christian elements had also found their way into Wagnerian music.

To both of these views there is but one reply—they are absolutely false.

84) From the passage it can be inferred that the author viewed Nietzsche as:

A. A revengeful person
B. A deceitful individual
C. A misunderstood person
D. A literary genius
E. An envious person

Answer

From the last line of the passage it is clear that the author believes that people's negative view of Nietzsche's two works is incorrect, yet a lot of people seem to have this view. **(C) follows best from this** as the correct answer.

A. The author actually disagrees with this
B. Not stated by the author
D. The passage never mentions anything about Nietzsche's genius
E. Again this is the view of some people that the author does not agree with

85) Why do some people continue to have a negative perception of Nietzsche with regards to his works mentioned in the passage?

A. They feel his language is very rude and demeaning
B. They have chosen to believe rumours rather than verify the facts for themselves
C. They have become biased by the personal animosity between Nietzsche and Wagner

D. They are against the mixing of music with religion
E. They found Nietzsche's comments blasphemous

Answer

The author clearly states in the 1st para that despite enough having been said to the contrary, some people have chosen to believe the rumours about Nietzsche's dislike towards Wagner. **(B) follows best as the correct answer** from this.

A. The passage never implies that Nietzsche's language was demeaning
C. The passage never states that there was personal animosity between Nietzsche and Wagner, the people assumed this
D. The passage never mentions people's views on religion
E. Same as D

Passage 36

It is safe to say that no class of women in the civilized world is subjected to such incessant trials of temper, and such temptations to be fretful, as the American housekeeper. The reasons for this state of things are legion and, if in the beginning we take ground from which the whole field may be clearly surveyed, we may be able to secure a better understanding of what housekeeping means, and to guard against some of the dangers accompanying it.

One difficulty associated with housekeeping lies in taking for granted that successful housekeeping is as much an instinct as that which leads the young bird to nest-building, and that no specific training is required. The man who undertakes a business, passes always through some form of apprenticeship, and must know every detail involved in the management, but to a large proportion of women, housekeeping is a combination of accidental forces from whose working it is hoped breakfasts and dinners and suppers will be evolved at regular periods, other necessities finding place where they can. The new home, prettily furnished, seems a lovely toy, and is surrounded by a halo, which, as facts assert themselves, quickly fades away. Moth and rust and dust invade the most secret recesses. Breakage and general disaster attend the progress of Bridget or Chloe. The kitchen seems the headquarters of extraordinary smells, and the stove an abyss in its consumption of coal or wood. Food is wasted by bad cooking, or ignorance as to needed amounts, or methods of using left-over portions, and, as bills pile up, a hopeless discouragement often settles upon both wife and husband, and reproaches and bitterness and alienation are guests in the home, to which they need never have come had a little knowledge barred them out.

86) What is the relation between the highlighted sentences in the passage?

A. The first is a proposal put forward by the author and the second provides evidence undermining that proposal
B. The first is the argument of the author and the second is a counterargument
C. The first is the intermediate conclusion of the passage and the second is the final conclusion
D. The first is the conclusion of the author and the second provides evidence strengthening the conclusion
E. The first is the conclusion of the author and the second is his assumption

Answer

Clearly the main idea of the passage is to elaborate on the difficulties faced by an American housekeeper. The first sentence highlights this fact and so should be the conclusion of the author/passage. The second describes one of the difficulties so it obviously strengthens the conclusion. Hence **(D) should be the correct answer**

A. The author never puts forward any proposal in the first sentence and the second sentence doesn't undermine the first sentence either
B. The first is more of a conclusion and the second does not counter this in any way
C. The second is not the conclusion of the passage, it just provides support for the conclusion
E. Remember the assumption can never be written in the passage, it is always assumed. So there is no way that the second sentence can be an assumption since it is explicitly stated in the passage

87) What is implied by the lines - '*if in the beginning we take ground from which the whole field may be clearly surveyed*' in the passage?

A. The American housekeeper's job is one of the most difficult jobs in the world
B. A survey should be conducted of American housekeepers to identify the more difficult areas of their job
C. It might be a good idea to have a broad understanding of a housekeeper's job before taking it on
D. The job of a housekeeper in America should generally be avoided
E. An American housekeeper's job might have several dangers associated with it

Answer

In context of the passage, the purpose of the quoted lines is to state that one could avoid the dangers associated with a housekeeper's job if one has a good understanding of the same beforehand. **(C) states this best** and should be the correct answer.

Passage 37

The manor was the sphere of operations of a manor court. On every manor the tenants gathered at frequent periods for a great amount of petty judicial and regulative work. The most usual period for the meeting of the manor court was once every three weeks, though in some manors no trace of a meeting is found more frequently than three times, or even twice, a year. In these cases, however, it is quite probable that less formal meetings occurred of which no regular record was kept.

Different kinds of gatherings of the tenants are usually distinguished according to the authority under which they were held, or the class of tenants of which they were made up. If the court was held by the lord simply because of his feudal rights as a landholder, and was busied only with matters of the inheritance, transfer, or grant of lands, the fining of tenants for the breach of manorial custom, or failure to perform their duties to the lord of the manor, the election of tenants to petty offices on the manor, and such matters, it was described in legal language as a court baron. If a court so occupied was made up of villain tenants only, it was called a customary court. If, on the other hand, the court also punished general offences, petty crimes, breaches of contract, breaches of the assize, that is to say, the established standard of amount, price, or quality of bread or beer, the lord of the manor drawing his authority to hold such a court either actually or supposedly from a grant from the king, such a court was called a court leet. With the court leet was usually connected the so-called view of frank pledge.

Frank pledge was an ancient system, according to which all men were obliged to be enrolled in groups, so that if any one committed an offence, the other members of the group would be obliged to produce him for trial. View of frank pledge was the right to punish by fine all who failed to so enrol themselves. In the court baron and the customary court it was said by lawyers that the body of attendants were the judges, and the steward, representing the lord of the manor, only a presiding official, while in the court leet the steward was the actual judge of the tenants. In practice, however, it is probable that not much was made of these distinctions and that the periodic gatherings were made to do duty for all business of any kind that needed attention, while the procedure was that which had become customary on that special manor, irrespective of the particular form of authority for the court.

88) Which of the following can be inferred from the information in the passage?

A. The concept of frank pledge was created to promote solidarity within groups of people
B. The duration between successive meetings of a manor court was not fixed
C. A court baron had more powers than a customary court
D. The manor court was the highest legal authority during the period mentioned in the passage
E. The manor court did not always have a presiding official

Answer

The 1st para states that successive meetings of a manor court were usually held every 3 weeks but this does not mean that they were compulsorily held every 3 weeks. Hence **(B) can be inferred from the passage** and is the correct answer.

A. According to para 3, frank pledge was actually intended to deter people from committing dishonest acts
C. The passage does not provide any such comparison
D. Extreme option. There might have been higher legal authorities at that time
E. The passage never states this. In fact from the passage it appears that the manor court always had a presiding official

89) Each of the following is mentioned in the passage as a power of the court baron EXCEPT:

A. To judge matters related to inheritance
B. To resolve disputes related to grants of land
C. To punish tenants for negligence of duties
D. To elect tenants to offices on the manor
E. To fine petty criminals

Answer

According to the 2nd para, a court leet could judge and punish petty crimes. **Hence (E) is the correct answer.**

A. Mentioned in the 2nd para
B. Mentioned in the 2nd para
C. Mentioned in the 2nd para *('fining of tenants.........')*
D. Mentioned in the 2nd para

90) According to the information in the first para, the fact that *'in some manors no trace of a meeting is found more frequently than three times, or even twice, a year'* does NOT necessarily suggest that:

A. more meetings were actually not held during that period
B. meetings were not necessarily held every three weeks
C. informal meetings may have been held during this period
D. manor courts probably did not keep a record of all their meetings
E. some courts met fewer times than the others

Answer

The last line of the 1st para states that just because in some manors meetings were held twice or thrice a year does not necessarily mean that in these manors more informal meetings were not held during that period. Hence the information in the quoted line does not suggest that more meetings were actually not held during that period i.e. **(A) is the correct answer.**

B. Opposite. This information actually does suggest that meetings were not always held every three weeks
C. Opposite. This information could suggest that informal meetings may have been held during that period
D. Again if unrecorded informal meeting are a possibility then the quoted lines do suggest that manor courts probably did not keep a record of all their meetings
E. Opposite. This information clearly suggests that some courts met fewer times than the others

Critical Reasoning Questions

91) Arguments to restrict immigration on the grounds that immigrants will take domestic jobs ignore the fact that immigrants, once employed, will earn and spend money on goods and services, creating new jobs that will more than make up for the old ones they took.

Which of the following is an assumption on which the argument depends?

A. The immigrants will not send most of the money that they earn back to their hometowns

B. Studies show that large scale inflow of immigrants invariably leads to an increase in the incidence of crime in that city

C. The immigrants will not subsequently get their families to also join them in the new city

D. Immigrants generally tend to save most of the money that they earn

E. Opponents of immigration are not opposed to immigration for reasons other than loss of jobs

Answer

The argument assumes that the immigrants will spend money in their city of immigration thereby helping create jobs in the city, but what if the immigrants did not do so? The argument obviously assumes that this will not be the case. A states this and is the assumption in the argument.

A. The correct answer
B. This is extra information and not an assumption
C. If the immigrants do so it will be a good thing because they will spend even more money in the new city
D. This would actually make the argument fall apart. The assumption has to be the opposite of this
E. The motives of the opponents of immigration are outside the scope of the argument

92) Recently the city council conducted a survey of 1000 car owners whose cars had recently met with an accident. Half of these car owners had got their cars repaired at authorized service stations and the other half got their cars repaired at local unauthorized service stations. The average repair cost of those who got their cars serviced at unauthorized service stations was $500 whereas the average repair cost of those who got their cars repaired at authorized service stations was $900. The city council concluded from this survey that authorized service stations in general charge more than do unauthorized service stations.

Which of the following, if true, most seriously weakens the city council's conclusion above?

A. All the car owners whose cars had faced severe damage chose to get their cars repaired at authorized service stations.
B. Many automobile companies discourage their buyers from going to unauthorized service stations.
C. Unauthorized service stations on an average take less time to repair cars than do authorized service stations.
D. All the 1000 car owners who were surveyed faced similar damage to their cars
E. Experienced car mechanics recommend unauthorized service stations over authorized ones.

Answer

In this argument the city council is assuming that all the cars had faced similar damages and so their repair costs should be the same. What if the cars that were taken to authorized service stations had suffered substantially more damages? **(A) addresses this issue and should be the correct answer**.

B. The views of automobile companies have no bearing on the argument
C. Time is outside the scope of the argument; we are only concerned with the cost aspect
D. As explained above, this is the assumption of the argument and hence will strengthen (and not weaken) the argument
E. The views of car mechanics have no bearing on the argument

93) A stain-removing agent currently available in city X can remove the most stubborn of stains from clothes but is not very popular because it leaves behind a foul smell in the clothes. It takes around ten days for the smell to completely go away from the clothes. Another stain-removing agent has just been launched in city X which is as effective at cleaning stains as the older one. An advantage of the new stain-removing agent is that its smell starts to go away from the clothes in two days itself. Thus this new agent should easily be able to outsell the older one.

Which of the following pieces of information would be most helpful in evaluating the argument above?

A. the rate of growth or decline in sales of stain-removing agents in city X
B. the total number of stain removing agents sold last year in city X
C. the per capita income of people residing in city X
D. the amount of time it takes for the smell of the new stain-removing agent to completely go away from the clothes.
E. a comparison of the smell of the new stain removing agent with that of similar agents available in other cities

Answer

The author suggests that the new stain-removing agent will outsell the older one, but takes no account of the fact that there's a disparity in the information given. The smell of the new agent starts to wear off in two days, but we need to know how long it takes for the smell to wear off completely. Only then would we be able to compare the new and the old agents. **(D) provides this information and is therefore the correct answer.**

(A), (B), and (C) present irrelevant issues. Neither of these pieces of information helps us to differentiate between the two stain-removing agents.

(E) We are just comparing the two agents available in city X. A comparison with cleaning agents available in other cities has no bearing on the argument.

94) Ever since the new Marketing Head joined Crackwell Corporation, its profits have increased steadily. In fact, over the past three years that the Marketing Head has been with Crackwell, the company's profits have grown by almost 35% every year, a figure that used to hover around the 10% mark earlier. Pleased by this fact, the Board of Crackwell Corporation has decided to reward the Marketing Head with stock options in the company.

Which of the following, if true, casts the most serious doubts on the decision taken by the Board of Crackwell Corporation?

A. The Marketing Head is disliked by his team members because of his habit of criticising them in public
B. Over the past three years, the profits of Crackwell's closest competitor have grown by 42% every year

C. The CFO of Crackwell Corporation has taken several cost cutting measures over the last three years, including retrenchment of unproductive employees and renegotiation of prices with vendors.
D. A strategy consulting firm, known to have turned around several poorly performing companies, has been recently hired by Crackwell Corporation
E. Several new marketing campaigns, which gave a lot of international exposure to the company's products, have been successfully conducted by Crackwell Corporation over the past three years

Answer

The argument suggests that the marketing head is the cause of the increase in profits over the last three years. To weaken this argument, we need to find an option that could provide an alternate explanation for this fact. C does this best by suggesting that the profits may have been increased because of the actions taken by the CFO and not the marketing head.

A. This doesn't take away from the fact that the marketing head could be still responsible for the increase in sales
B. The fact that Crackwell's competitor has performed better does not take away from the fact that Crackwell's profits have increased from 10% to 35%
C. The correct answer
D. The strategy consulting firm has only been hired recently whereas the profits of Crackwell have been increasing over the past three years
E. The credit for the successful marketing campaigns should obviously go to the marketing head, so this actually strengthens the argument.

95) The Georgetown Public School recommends that all its students take an active interest in playing chess. This is because, according to a recent medical study, those students who played chess on an average performed better in tests of general intelligence than those who did not play chess. Thus the school contends that playing chess will boost up the intelligence of its students.

Which of the following raise the most serious doubt about the conclusion above?

A. Some students who perform well in tests of general intelligence do not play chess
B. Intelligent students are the only ones who take an interest in playing chess
C. A similar correlation has not been observed with regards to other sports such as baseball
D. Some of the students who play chess perform poorly in subjects such as History
E. There can be other ways in which a student could develop intelligence

Answer

This is a classic case of correlation being confused with causation. Just because those students who play chess perform better in tests of intelligence does not necessarily imply that it is because of chess that these students have become intelligent. It could very well be that since these students are intelligent, they like to play chess i.e. the causality could actually be the other way around. **(B) points this out and is the correct answer.**

A. The argument does not contend that playing chess is the only way to boost intelligence. There could be other ways as well. All the argument contends is that if a student plays chess then he or she will definitely become intelligent

C. Other sports are outside the scope of the argument

D. The argument restricts itself to tests of intelligence; there is nothing in the argument to suggest that all intelligent students will perform well in all subjects.

E. Other ways of developing intelligence are again outside the scope of the argument

96) According to the constitution of Country X, the national flag of country X can be flown only on top of government establishments and any business establishment found flying the national flag is to be fined for the same. Such a regulation however is completely wrong since constitutional technicalities should not restrict a business establishment from expressing its patriotism.

Which of the following, if true, most seriously weakens the argument?

A. The overseas customers of a business establishment are usually unable to understand the significance of the national flag
B. A business establishment needs to hire dedicated staff to raise and lower the flags during the day and night respectively
C. The constitution of the country was written several decades ago and may not be practical in modern times
D. Most business establishments fly the national flag mainly to attract customers
E. If businesses are allowed to fly the national flag then it will arouse the spirit of patriotism among the general masses

Answer

The argument contends that businesses should be allowed to fly the national flag because they are doing so to express their patriotism. If we can somehow show that the businesses are flying the flag not to show their patriotism but because they have some other agenda, then the argument is immediately weakened. (D) does this by pointing out that businesses are actually flying the flag to attract customers. **Hence (D) should be the correct answer**

A. Whether overseas customers are able to understand the significance of the flag or not is outside the scope of the argument

B. A business might be willing to hire such a staff but this is no reason for the business to be fined

C. The application of the constitution to modern times is not the issue in the argument

E. Again the spirit of patriotism among the general masses is outside the scope of the argument

97) According to a recent nationwide study by the Education Department, those students who played baseball performed much better academically than those who did not. Thus it can be concluded that students should be encouraged to participate in sporting activities, because this will have a direct bearing on their academic performance.

Which of the following provide most support to the argument above?

A. Playing baseball stimulates their brains and increases the rate of grey cell growth in the brain
B. Students who participated in sports other than baseball also showed a marked improvement in their academic performance
C. The Education Department study is representative of students nationwide
D. Non-sporting activities such as painting and writing do not have a similar positive effect on a student's academic performance
E. The number of students who play baseball in the country has been increasing at a frenetic pace over the last few years

Answer

This argument is a classic case of scope shift. The evidence i.e. the study only talks of baseball but the conclusion generalizes it for all sporting activities. Obviously the argument assumes that what is true for baseball will also be true for other sporting activities. **(B) states this and should be the correct answer** because the assumption will always strengthen the argument

A. This evidence is only for baseball so how can we generalize for all sporting activities based on this

C. Agreed but the study was only done for students who played baseball so how can we conclude for all sports

D. Non-sporting activities are outside the scope of the argument

E. The number of students who play baseball has no bearing on the argument

98) The Ford Model E is the bestselling car model in country Z. Recently a leading newspaper in country Z published a report highlighting the safety flaws present in the Ford Model E. The report concludes that by driving this particular car, drivers are endangering their lives. Despite this report the public has stated that it will continue to buy Ford Model Es. However in the 2 month period following the publishing of this report, the sales of the Model E fell by more than 70%.

Which of the following best explains the discrepancy in the argument above?

A. Because country Z has very few car manufacturers, the customers don't have too much choice
B. In the period following the publishing of the report, Ford offered a heft discount on the Model E
C. After the report was published, Ford decided to voluntarily withdraw model Es from its showrooms so as to modify them to make them safer for drivers
D. Other cars available in the market are as unsafe as the Ford Model E
E. The report was publishes by a reputed newspaper known for its objective and unbiased reporting

Answer

What we need to explain in the argument is the fact that even when the customers said that they would continue to buy Ford Model Es, how did the sale of the car fall in the two month period following the publishing of the report. Since there is no problem from the demand side (customers are ready to buy the car) there must be a problem from the supply side. C points out that during this period Ford itself withdrew its cars to improve their safety. Since there were no cars available, the sales obviously fell down. Hence **(C) is the correct answer**

A. If the customers don't have much choice, then all the more reason for the sales of Model Es not to have fallen, so why did the sales fall?

B. Again the sales should have gone up because of the discount, especially when the customers were ready to buy the car

D. If all the cars are equally unsafe, why did the sales of Model Es fall?

E. The accuracy of the report is never at stake, the fact it that customers have stated that irrespective of the report they will continue to buy Model Es. Then why did the sales fall down?

99) It is interesting to note that, of the ten different brands of digital cameras available in the market, the one that sells the most is the second most expensive of the lot. This camera also offers the best picture quality of all the digital cameras available in the market. Clearly the price of the camera plays no role in the customer purchase decision; it is the picture quality of the camera that matters to them.

Which of the following, if true, would most seriously weaken the argument above?

A. Between two similarly equipped digital cameras, most customers will prefer the lower priced one

B. There is a direct correlation between the price of a camera and its picture quality

C. Some customers only purchase the cheapest available digital camera, irrespective of its picture quality

D. The second largest selling brand of digital camera, which is also the third most expensive in the market, offers poor picture quality

E. Digital cameras are usually purchased by affluent customers for whom the price of the camera isn't a big consideration

Answer

The argument arrives at an extreme conclusion. Just because price is not the main determinant of which digital camera to buy does not mean that price plays no role in the customer purchase decision, when it comes to digital cameras. A correctly highlights this fact by pointing out that while picture quality may be the number one consideration on customer's list of preferences, price also matters because between two similarly equipped digital cameras, most customers prefer the lower priced one.

A. The correct answer
B. This may be true but it does not weaken the argument
C. The use of *some* means that this cannot be the answer. Some customers prefer the cheapest available camera and some don't; this fact does not tell us anything about most customers

D. While this strengthens the fact that picture quality is not the only determinant of which digital camera to buy, this option does not weaken the fact that price plays no role in making this choice because this camera is still the third most expensive in the market, so customers couldn't possibly be buying it because of its low price
E. This again does not weaken the argument. It just explains why price doesn't play a big role in deciding which digital camera to purchase, but our agenda is to weaken this conclusion itself

100. The Langova National park is a breeding ground for several migratory birds. The Spot-breasted Laughing Thrush, an extremely rare species of bird, has been sighted only in the Langova National park of late. The people who have sighted this bird in the park have claimed that it is possible to sight this bird only through the use of binoculars. Barry is visiting the Langova National Park next week and he will be carrying an extremely powerful pair of binoculars with him. Therefore it is safe to conclude that, as long as Barry has his binoculars on him, he will most definitely manage to sight the Spot-breasted Laughing Thrush.

Which of the following indicates a flaw in the reasoning above?

A. It fails to take into account the possibility of sighting the Spot-breasted Laughing Thrush at places other than the Langova National Park
B. It mistakes a necessary condition for a sufficient condition
C. It is based on a series of assumptions, rather than on facts
D. It does not take into account the possibility that Barry could lose or damage his binoculars on way to the park
E. It does not take into account the possibility that Barry may sight some other equally rare species of bird

Answer

The argument states that the bird cannot be sighted without the use of binoculars so the use of binoculars is a necessary condition for sighting the bird. However this does not mean that just because one has a pair of binoculars, he will be able to spot the bird. The argument never states that everyone with binoculars spots this bird but that everyone who spots the bird has binoculars. B states this point and is the correct answer.

A. The argument is only concerned with the chances of spotting the bird inside the Langova National Park
B. The correct answer

C. The argument is in fact based on facts – it is a fact that people have spotted the bird using binoculars
D. The argument clearly states that as long as *Barry has his binoculars on him* he will be able to spot the bird. If he loses or damages his binoculars, then it's outside the scope of the argument.
E. Other species of birds are outside the scope of the argument

SECTION 5

The GRE Vocabulary

Vocabulary

As stated earlier in this book, vocabulary will comprise roughly 50% of the questions on the verbal reasoning section of the Revised GRE Test. Does that mean students need to cram thousands of words? Absolutely not!

We have spent considerable time and effort debriefing students who have taken the revised GRE Test over the past 10 months or so and there is a set of words that seem to be tested regularly on the GRE. Accordingly we have made a compilation of these words and added some more based on our understanding and experience to arrive at a list of 1000 high frequency words i.e. words that are more likely to appear on the test. Of course this is not a foolproof list and you will, almost certainly, see words from outside this list on the test but as a first step it is a good idea to start with this list. Once you complete these words and, assuming you still have time on your hands, you can easily do more words beyond these 1000.

Remember that 'consistency' is the most important thing when it comes to taking in words. We regularly see students start out very enthusiastically, doing 100 or 200 hundreds words in a day or two but then they get tired or bored and do nothing for the next 10 days. As a result they end up forgetting even those words that they had done earlier. We suggest that you start with a small number of words every day – say 20 words a day – and then gradually take this number up. Even if progress at the rate of 20 words a day, you would have completed all 1000 words in just 50 days!

A

Abase	lower; degrade; humiliate
Abash	to make ashamed or uneasy
Abate	to reduce in amount, degree, or intensity; lessen
Abdicate	to relinquish (power or responsibility) formally
Abet	assist usually in doing something wrong; encourage
Abhorrent	one that is hated, disgusting, loathsome, or repellent
Abjure	to renounce, repudiate, retract, or give up usually under oath

Abnegation	renunciation; self-sacrifice
Abominable	detestable; extremely unpleasant
Abortive	unsuccessful; fruitless
Abridge	condense or shorten
Absolve	pardon (an offense)
Abstemious	exercising moderation and self-restraint in appetite and behaviour
Abstruse	difficult to understand; recondite
Abut	to touch at one end or side; lie adjacent
Abyss	an immeasurably deep chasm, depth, or void
Accolade	an expression of approval; praise
Acerbic	sour or bitter tasting; acidic
Acme	the highest point, as of achievement or development
Acquiesce	assent; agree passively; comply without protest
Acumen	shrewdness shown by keen insight
Acquit	free from a charge or accusation
Acrimony	bitter ill-natured animosity in speech or behaviour
Adage	wise saying; proverb
Admonish	take to task; to criticize for a fault
Advocate	support or push for something
Aegis	protection; endorsement; guidance
Aesthetic	concerning or characterized by an appreciation of beauty or good taste
Affectation	a deliberate pretense or exaggerated display
Aggress	take the initiative and go on the offensive
Alacrity	liveliness and eagerness

Alleviate	to lessen the pain; to make something better
Altruism	the quality of unselfish concern for the welfare of others
Ambiguous	open to two or more interpretations; or of uncertain nature or significance
Ambrosial	worthy of the gods; highly pleasing to the senses-especially that of taste
Ameliorate	to make better
Amenable	disposed or willing to comply
Amnesty	a general pardon granted by a government, especially for political offenses
Anachronism	from an incorrect time period
Anarchy	a state of lawlessness and disorder
Anathema	a damnation or a curse
Animadversion	harsh criticism or disapproval
Antediluvian	old; ancient; before the great flood
Antipathy	deep-seated hatred; extreme hostility and dislike
Apathy	lack of interest or concern; indifference
Aphorism	a short pithy instructive saying; an adage
Apocalyptic	prophetic of devastation or ultimate doom
Apogee	a final climactic stage; the highest/farthest point
Appall	fill with apprehension or alarm; cause to be unpleasantly surprised
Appellation	a name, title, or designation
Apposite	being of striking appropriateness and pertinence
Approbation	official recognition or approval
Arduous	difficult to accomplish; demanding considerable mental effort and skill
Arrogate	seize and take control without authority and possibly with force
Articulate	able to express oneself easily in clear and effective language

Artless	having or displaying no guile, cunning, or deceit; innocent
Assiduous	perseverance in carrying out an action; diligent
Assuage	to satisfy or appease; to calm or to pacify
Attenuate	to make slender, fine, or small; to lessen the density of; rarefy
Audacious	fearlessly, often recklessly daring; bold
Austere	severe or stern in disposition or appearance; sombre and grave; bare
Autonomous	independent in mind or judgment; self-directed
Avarice	immoderate desire for wealth; cupidity
Aver	to assert formally as a fact; to justify or prove

B

Badger	annoy persistently
Baffle	frustrate; perplex
Bait	food or other lure used to catch fish or trap animals
Balk	hesitate; recoil
Balmy	mild and pleasant; soothing
Banal	repeated too often; familiar through overuse; boring
Bane	something causing misery or death
Baleful	deadly or sinister
Base	contemptible; morally bad; inferior in value or quality
Bask	derive or receive pleasure from; get enjoyment from; take pleasure in
Bawl	cry loudly
Bedlam	a state of extreme confusion and disorder

Bedraggle	make wet and dirty, as from rain
Befuddle	confuse thoroughly
Begrudge	envy; give or allow unwillingly
Beguile	attract; cause to be enamoured
Behemoth	huge creature; something of monstrous size or power
Belittle	lessen the authority, dignity, or reputation of; express a negative opinion
Bellicose	having or showing a ready disposition to fight
Belie	represent falsely
Belligerent	someone who fights or is aggressive
Bellow	shout loudly and without restraint
Bemused	confused; lost in thought; preoccupied
Benediction	the act of praying for divine protection
Benevolent	showing kindness; generous
Benign	kindly; favourable; not malignant
Bequeath	leave or give by will after one's death
Berate	censure severely or angrily
Besmirch	charge falsely; attack the good name and reputation of someone
Blandish	praise somewhat dishonestly
Blasphemy	the act of depriving something of its sacred character
Boisterous	noisy and lacking in restraint or discipline
Bombastic	ostentatiously lofty in style
Boorish	ill-mannered and coarse; contemptible in behaviour or appearance
Brackish	slightly salty
Braggart	a very boastful and talkative person

Brusque	abrupt and curt in manner or speech
Bucolic	descriptive of rural or pastoral life
Burgeon	grow and flourish
Buttress	a support, usually of stone or brick

C

Cache	hiding place
Cacophony	a loud harsh or strident noise
Cajole	persuade by praise or false promise; coax; wheedle
Callous	hardened; unfeeling; without sympathy for the sufferings of others
Camaraderie	goodwill and light-hearted rapport between or among friends
Canard	unfounded false rumour; exaggerated false report
Candid	free from prejudice; impartial; frank
Capitulate	to surrender under specified conditions; come to terms
Capricious	characterized by or subject to whims; impulsive and unpredictable
Cardinal	of foremost importance; paramount
Caricature	a representation of a person that is exaggerated for comic effect
Carnage	the savage and excessive killing of many people
Castigation	punishment; chastisement; reproof
Cataclysm	an event resulting in great loss and misfortune; a great flood
Catholic	relating to the Church; comprehensive or universal
Cavalier	casual and offhand; arrogant

Cede	surrender formally
Celerity	speed; rapidity
Censure	harsh criticism or disapproval
Certitude	certainty
Charlatan	a person who makes fraudulent, and often voluble claims to skill or knowledge
Chasm	a deep opening in the earth's surface; a difference of ideas, beliefs, or opinions.
Chagrin	strong feelings of embarrassment
Chicanery	deception by trickery or sophistry.
Choleric	characterized by anger
Circumlocution	an indirect way of expressing something
Citadel	a stronghold into which people could go for shelter during a battle; fortress
Clairvoyant	a person who can look into the future
Coercion	using force to cause something to occur
Cogent	powerfully persuasive
Cognizant	marked by comprehension and perception: fully informed & aware
Collusion	secret agreement or conspiracy
Colossus	a person of exceptional importance and reputation
Comeliness	the quality of being good looking and attractive
Commensurate	corresponding in size, degree or extent; proportional
Commiserate	to feel or express sympathy or compassion
Compendium	a concise but comprehensive summary of a larger work
Complacent	contented to a fault; self-satisfied and unconcerned
Complaisant	showing a cheerful willingness to do favours for others
Concurrent	occurring or operating at the same time

Condone	excuse, overlook, or make allowances for; be lenient with
Congeal	to thicken or to solidify
Connoisseur	an expert in some field, especially in the fine arts
Consecrate	render holy by means of religious rites
Consequential	having great significance
Contentious	argumentative; quarrelsome; controversial
Conundrum	a difficult problem; a puzzling situation
Convene	call together
Convivial	fun loving; fond of good company
Convoluted	having numerous overlapping coils or folds
Copious	affording an abundant supply
Cornucopia	the property of being extremely abundant
Corporal	of or relating to the body
Corpulent	excessively fat
Covert	covered over; sheltered; secret
Cower	show submission or fear
Craven	an abject coward
Credulous	believe too readily; gullible
Crestfallen	brought low in spirit; dejected
Cryptic	secret; obscure in meaning
Culmination	a concluding action
Culpable	deserving blame or censure as being wrong or evil
Cursory	hasty and without attention to detail; not thorough
Cynicism	feeling of distrust

D

Dabble	work in an amateurish manner
Dainty	delicate; delicately beautiful
Dandy	a man who is much concerned with his dress and appearance
Dapper	neat in appearance and quick in movements
Dauntless	having or showing courage
Dawdle	loiter; hang around; waste time doing nothing
Deadpan	impassive; with no show of feeling; with an expressionless face
Dearth	a scarce supply; a lack
Debacle	a complete failure
Debase	degrade; reduce in quality or value; degenerate
Debauchery	extreme indulgence in sensual pleasures; immoral self-indulgence
Debilitate	weaken (through heat, hunger, illness); enfeeble
Decadence	the state of being degenerate in mental or moral qualities
Decapitate	to cut off the head; behead
Decipher	decode
Decorum	appropriate behaviour; good manners
Decrepit	weak and in bad condition (from old age)
Decry	to condemn openly
Defection	withdrawing support or help despite allegiance

Deference	high degree of respect or courtesy
Defunct	no longer in use, force, or operation
Delectable	greatly pleasing, normally associated with food
Deleterious	having a harmful effect; injurious
Deluge	a great flood or a heavy downpour
Demur	to voice opposition; object
Demure	shy
Denigrate	to defame or belittle
Depravity	moral corruption or degradation
Derelict	deserted by an owner or keeper; abandoned; run-down; dilapidated
Derision	the act of deriding or treating with contempt
Descry	to discover by careful observation or scrutiny; detect
Despondent	the condition of being depressed
Detrimental	causing damage or harm; injurious
Diatribe	a bitter, abusive denunciation
Dictum	an authoritative statement
Diffident	lacking self-confidence
Digress	turn aside especially from the main subject of attention
Dilapidation	a state of deterioration due to old age or long use
Dilatory	wasting time
Dilemma	a confusing situation; a difficult choice
Dilettante	lacking the required professional skill
Dirge	a funeral hymn or lament
Disabuse	free somebody (from an erroneous belief)

Discern	detect with the senses
Disconsolate	sad beyond comforting; incapable of being consoled
Disgruntled	in a state of sulky dissatisfaction
Disparage	to speak of in a slighting or disrespectful way; belittle
Disquietude	feelings of anxiety that make you tense and irritable
Dissemble	to disguise or conceal behind a false appearance
Disseminate	to scatter widely, as in sowing seed
Dissidence	disagreement, especially disagreement with the government
Dissuasion	the act or an instance of dissuading
Divulge	reveal a secret
Dogmatic	relating to, characteristic of, or resulting from dogma
Dolorous	showing sorrow
Dregs	the sediment in a liquid; the basest or least desirable portion; residue
Droll	arousing laughter
Dulcet	pleasing to the ear

E

Ebb	recede; lessen; diminish
Ebullience	zestful enthusiasm
Eclectic	combining elements from a variety of sources
Ecstasy	rapture; very strong feeling of joy and happiness
Edifice	building (of imposing size)

Effeminate	having womanish traits or qualities; characterized by weakness and excessive refinement.
Effervescence	enthusiasm; vivacity; the process of bubbling as gas escapes
Effete	exhausted, infertile, or no longer effective; no longer possessing a unique quality
Efficacy	power or capacity to produce a desired effect; effectiveness
Effulgence	brilliant radiance; bright and sending out rays of light
Egregious	bad or offensive; strong and offensive in odour or flavour
Egress	a path or opening for going out; an exit
Elated	filled with excited joy and pride; overjoyed
Elegy	a poem or song composed especially as a lament for a deceased person.
Elicit	to bring or draw out
Eloquent	persuasive, powerful discourse
Elucidate	explain; make clear; clarify; enlighten
Elusive	evasive; not frank; baffling; hard to grasp, catch, or understand
Emaciation	extreme thinness and wasting, caused by disease or under nutrition
Emanate	issue forth; come out
Emancipate	action or process of setting free, especially from legal, social, or political restrictions
Embroil	involve in dispute; complicate
Eminent	rising above others; high; lofty; distinguished
Emolument	salary; payment for an office; compensation
Emulate	imitate; rival; try to equal or excel
Encomium	warm, glowing praise

Endemic	prevalent in or peculiar to a particular locality, region, or people
Endorse	approve; support
Enervate	to weaken or destroy the strength or vitality
Engender	to procreate; propagate; give rise to
Engross	occupy fully; absorb
Enigmatic	difficult to explain or understand
Enjoin	to give orders to
Ennui	the feeling of being bored by something tedious
Enthrall	hold spellbound
Entice	lure; persuade to do (something wrong); attract; tempt
Entrench	fix firmly or securely
Epiphany	a revelatory manifestation of a divine being.
Equanimity	the quality of being calm and even-tempered; maintaining composure
Equivocal	deliberately ambiguous or vague
Erratic	lacking consistency, regularity, or uniformity
Erudite	extremely learned
Eschew	to keep away from or to avoid
Esoteric	known by a restricted number of people; understood by few
Eulogy	high praise or commendation
Euphemism	substituting a mild, indirect, or vague term for one considered harsh, blunt, or offensive
Euphoria	a feeling of great happiness or well-being
Exacerbate	to increase the severity; to aggravate further
Exasperate	to provoke or annoy to an extreme degree

Exhume	to remove from a grave; to dig out of the earth something that has been buried
Exigent	requiring immediate action or remedy; demanding; exacting
Exodus	a departure of a large number of people
Exonerate	to free from blame.
Expatriate	to give up residence in one's homeland; to send into exile
Expiate	to make amends; atone
Expurgate	remove parts considered harmful or improper for publication
Extirpate	to destroy totally; exterminate
Extol	to pay tribute or homage to; to honour
Exuberant	full of unrestrained enthusiasm or joy

F

Fabrication	a deliberately false or improbable account
Fallacy	a misconception resulting from incorrect reasoning
Fluke	a stroke of luck
Fledgling	any new participant in some activity; young and inexperienced
Flabbergasted	as if struck dumb with astonishment and surprise
Flag	become less intense; lessen
Farce	broad comedy; mockery; humorous play full of silly things happening
Fickle	changeable (in affections or friendship); faithless

Fervent	characterized by intense emotion; extremely hot
Fathom	comprehend
Flagrant	conspicuously and outrageously bad or reprehensible
Finesse	delicate skill
Fatuous	devoid of intelligence
Fractious	difficult in operation; likely to be troublesome or easily irritated or annoyed
Fastidious	giving careful attention to detail; hard to please; excessively concerned with cleanliness
Fetid	having a foul smell
Falter	hesitate; weaken in purpose or action; walk or move unsteadily through weakness
Frustrate	hinder or prevent (the efforts, plans, or desires of)
Formidable	inspiring fear or extremely impressive in strength or excellence
Fructify	make productive or fruitful
Feral	not domestic; wild
Factitious	not produced by natural forces
Fortuitous	occurring by chance (positive) having no apparent cause
Felicity	pleasing and appropriate manner or style; contentment; joy
Feign	pretend
Frugality	prudence in avoiding waste
Furtive	Secretive; sly; done with caution and stealth
Facile	superficial; not deep
Forage	the act of searching for food and provisions
Façade	the face or front of a building OR a showy misrepresentation intended to conceal something unpleasant
Fidelity	the quality of being faithful

Flustered	thrown into a state of agitated confusion
Flout	treat with contemptuous disregard
Fawn	try to gain favour by cringing or flattering

G

Gullible	easily tricked because of being too trusting
Grandiloquence	high-flown style; excessive use of verbal ornamentation
Gait	a person's manner of walking
Gauche	clumsy (in social behaviour); coarse and uncouth
Grouse	complain
Giddy	dizzy; causing dizziness
Gamut	entire range
Gist	essence; main point; substance
Gloat	express evil satisfaction; look at or think about with evil satisfaction
Garrulous	full of trivial conversation ; talkative
Gambol	gay or light-hearted recreational activity for diversion or amusement
Gluttonous	given to excess in consumption of especially food or drink
Gregarious	instinctively or temperamentally seeking and enjoying the company of others
Gaunt	lean and angular; thin and bony; emaciated

Gibe	mock; make jeering remarks
Gesticulate	motion; gesture
Garbled	not orderly or coherent; lacking continuity
Gargantuan	of great mass; huge and bulky
Gape	open the mouth wide; stare wonderingly with the mouth open
Garish	overbright in colour; unpleasantly bright; gaudy
Germane	relevant and appropriate
Ghastly	shockingly repellent; inspiring horror
Grovel	show submission or fear
Gainsay	to deny, dispute, or contradict OR to speak or act against
Galvanize	to stimulate to action
Gingerly	very carefully

H

Harangue	a loud bombastic declamation expressed with strong emotion
Harrowing	agonizing; distressing; traumatic
Hiatus	an interruption in the intensity or amount of something
Hallowed	blessed; consecrated
Heterodox	characterized by departure from accepted beliefs or standards
Hoodwink	conceal one's true motives by pretending to have good intentions so as to gain an end
Hail	frozen rain

Hale	healthy
Herald	messenger; sign of something to come; announce; proclaim
Hubris	overbearing pride or presumption
Heed	pay attention to
Haughty	proud and arrogant
Hackneyed	repeated too often; overfamiliar through overuse
Harbinger	something that precedes and indicates the approach of something or someone
Hone	to sharpen; make perfect or complete
Husband	use cautiously and frugally
Heckle	verbally harass, as with gibes
Headstrong	wilful; stubborn; unyielding

I

Iconoclast	someone who attacks cherished ideas or traditional institutions
Idiosyncrasy	a characteristic, habit, mannerism, or the like, that is peculiar to an individual.
Ignominy	a state of dishonour
Illicit	illegal
Illusory	illusive; deceptive; not real
Imminent	close in time; about to occur
Immutable	unchanging

Impair	make worse or less effective or imperfect
Impassioned	filled with passion; fervent
Impassive	having or revealing little emotion or sensibility; not easily aroused or excited
Impeccable	faultless; perfect
Impecunious	not having enough money to pay for necessities
Impede	block or obstruct
Impending	nearing; approaching; about to happen
Impenitent	not penitent or remorseful
Imperious	having or showing arrogant superiority to and disdain of those one views as unworthy
Impertinence	the trait of being rude and inappropriate; inclined to take liberties
Impervious	not admitting of passage or capable of being affected
Impetuous	characterized by undue haste and lack of thought or deliberation
Impetus	incentive; stimulus; momentum
Impiety	without respect for God or religious values
Implacable	incapable of being consoled/calmed
Implausible	highly imaginative but unlikely
Implicate	incriminate; involve incriminatingly; show to be involved (in a crime)
Implicit	understood but not stated; implied
Implore	ask or beg earnestly; beseech
Imponderable	difficult or impossible to evaluate with precision
Impoverish	make poor
Impuissance	powerlessness revealed by an inability to act
Impunity	exemption from punishment or loss

Inadvertent	happening by chance or unexpectedly or unintentionally
Inane	silly; senseless
Incapacitate	permanently injure or in any way make unable to perform an action
Incarcerate	imprison
Incessant	uninterrupted; unceasing
Incinerate	reduced to ashes and burned out completely
Incontrovertible	impossible to deny or disprove
Incorrigible	impossible to correct or reform
Incumbent	currently holding an office
Indiscreet	lacking good judgment; thoughtless
Indolent	disinclined to work or exertion; lazy
Inebriate	become drunk or drink excessively
Inexorable	not to be moved by persuasion; unyielding
Infallible	incapable of failure or error
Infringe	advance beyond the usual limit
Ingenious	showing inventiveness and skill
Ingenuous	inability to mask your feelings, lacking in sophistication or worldliness
Inherent	in the nature of something though not readily apparent
Inimical	not friendly
Innocuous	not injurious to physical or mental health; incapable of causing harm
Inordinate	beyond normal limits
Insidious	working or spreading in a hidden and usually injurious way

Insipid	lacking interest or significance or impact; without flavour or taste
Insular	narrowly restricted in outlook or scope; suggestive of the isolated life of an island
Intangible	incapable of being perceived by the senses, especially the sense of touch
Interment	the ritual placing of a corpse in a grave
Interminable	tiresomely long; seemingly without end
Intractable	difficult to manage or mould or change
Intransigent	impervious to pleas, persuasion, requests, or reason
Intrepid	without fear or cannot be intimidated
Intuition	a keen and quick insight; the ability to perceive the truth in something
Inundate	fill or cover completely or beyond normal capacity, usually with water
Inured	made tough and immune by habitual exposure
Invective	abusive or venomous language used to express blame or bitter deep-seated ill will
Irascible	quickly aroused to anger
Irrepressible	impossible to control or suppress
Irresolute	uncertain how to act or proceed
Itinerary	a proposed route of travel

J

Jabber	chatter rapidly or unintelligibly
Jargon	a characteristic language of a particular group
Jest	activity characterized by good humour
Jibe	agree; be in harmony with
Jocose/Jocular	given to (having a tendency of) joking
Jubilant	joyful and proud, especially because of triumph or success
Juxtapose	place side by side
Jeopardize	pose a threat to; present a danger to
Jeer	showing your contempt by derision

K

Kinship	a close connection marked by community of interests or similarity in nature or character
Knave	a deceitful and unreliable scoundrel
Kudos	an expression of approval and commendation
Kindle	call forth (emotions, feelings, and responses) or cause to start burning
Kernel	central or vital part; core
Knotty	intricate; difficult; tangled
Knoll	little round hill; hillock
Kleptomaniac	someone with an irrational urge to steal in the absence of an economic motive
Knack	special talent
Knell	tolling of a bell especially to indicate a funeral, disaster, etc.

L

Labyrinth	complex system of paths or tunnels in which it is easy to get lost
Lachrymose	showing sorrow
Lackadaisical	idle or indolent especially in a dreamy way; lacking spirit or liveliness
Lacklustre	lacking lustre (shine; gloss); dull
Laconic	brief and to the point
Laggard	someone who lags behind
Lament	grieve; express sorrow
Languid	lacking spirit or liveliness
Languish	lose vigour, health, or flesh, as through grief; become feeble
Largess	liberality in bestowing gifts; extremely liberal and generous of spirit
Lassitude	weariness; listlessness
Laud	praise, glorify, or honour
Lax	careless; negligent; not paying enough attention
Lethargic	deficient in alertness or activity
Levity	a manner lacking seriousness
Libertine	a dissolute person; usually a man who is morally unrestrained
Limpid	crystal clear
Linger	be slow in leaving; delay going
Linguistic	consisting of or related to language
Lionize	treat (a person) as a celebrity

Lissome	moving and bending with ease
List	tilt to one side
Listless	lacking in spirit or energy; languid
Livid	extremely angry
Loath	reluctant; unwilling; disinclined
Loathe	find repugnant
Loquacious	full of trivial conversation
Loutish	ill-mannered and coarse and contemptible in behaviour or appearance
Lucid	transparently clear; easily understandable, transmitting light; able to be seen through with clarity
Lucrative	producing a sizeable profit
Lugubrious	excessively mournful
Luminous	softly bright or radiant
Lurid	glowing unnaturally, glaringly vivid and graphic; marked by sensationalism

M

Magnanimity	liberality in bestowing gifts; extremely liberal and generous of spirit
Maim	mutilate; injure lastingly; disable
Maladroit	not skillful
Malady	illness
Malapropism	the unintentional misuse of a word by confusion with one that sounds similar

Malediction	the act of calling down a curse that invokes evil (and usually serves as an insult)
Malevolent	having or exerting a malignant influence
Malfeasance	wrongful conduct by a public official
Malleable	adaptable; tractable; yielding
Malinger	to pretend illness, especially in order to shirk one's duty, avoid work, etc.
Malodorous	having an unpleasant smell
Manifest	evident; visible; obvious
Manipulate	control or play upon (people, forces, etc.) artfully; manoeuvre
Mar	spoil the appearance of
Martyr	one who suffers for the sake of principle
Masquerade	wear a mask or disguise; pretend
Masticate	chew (food); to bite and grind with the teeth
Maul	handle roughly; batter; injure by beating
Maverick	someone who exhibits great independence in thought and action
Maxim	proverb; truth pithily stated
Mayhem	violent disorder
Meagre	scanty; inadequate
Meander	wind or turn in its course; follow a winding or turning course; move aimlessly and idly
Meddlesome	Intrusive; interfering
Medley	mixture
Meek	submissive; patient and long-suffering
Melancholy	gloomy; morose
Melee	a noisy riotous fight

Mellifluous	sounds that are pleasing to the ear
Menace	something that is a source of danger
Mendacity	the tendency to be untruthful
Mendicant	a pauper who lives by begging
Mesmerize	hypnotize
Metamorphosis	change of form
Meticulous	marked by extreme care in treatment of details
Mettle	the courage to carry on
Misanthrope	someone who dislikes people in general
Misconstrue	interpret in the wrong way
Misdemeanour	misbehaviour; misdeed; a crime less serious than a felony
Misnomer	an incorrect or unsuitable name
Misogynist	a misanthrope who dislikes women in particular
Mitigate	make less severe or harsh
Mollify	make less rigid or softer; make more temperate, acceptable, or suitable
Mollycoddle	treat with excessive indulgence
Morose	showing a brooding ill humour
Mundane	not ideal or heavenly; found in the ordinary course of events
Munificent	very generous
Myopic	unable to see distant objects clearly; lacking foresight or scope

N

Nuance	a subtle difference in meaning or opinion or attitude
Neophyte	any new participant in some activity
Nascent	being born or beginning
Nettle	cause annoyance in; disturb
Necromancy	conjuring up the dead, especially for prophesying
Notoriety	disrepute; ill fame
Nefarious	extremely wicked
Nepotism	favouritism (to a relative)
Nausea	feeling of sickness and desire to vomit
Nonplussed	filled with bewilderment
Noisome	foul-smelling; causing or able to cause nausea
Numismatics	the collection and study of money (and coins in particular)
Noxious	injurious to physical or mental health
Nebulous	lacking definition or definite content
Nostalgia	longing for the past
Nonchalant	marked by complete lack of concern
Naive	marked by or showing unaffected simplicity and lack of guile or worldly experience
Natty	marked by up-to-dateness in dress and manners
Nugatory	of no real value
Nimble	quick in movement; agile; quick in understanding
Novice	someone new to a field or activity
Nemesis	something that brings an end to something; causing misery or death

Notoriety — the state of being known for some unfavourable act or quality

O

Obdurate — stubborn; resistant

Obeisance — the act of obeying; dutiful or submissive behaviour ; a sign of reverence or submission or shame or greeting

Obese — excessively fat

Obfuscate — make obscure or unclear

Objurgating — to reproach or denounce vehemently; upbraid harshly; berate sharply

Obliterate — destroy completely; wipe out

Oblivious — inattentive or unmindful; unaware; wholly absorbed

Obnoxious — causes disapproval or harm to something

Obscure — dark; vague; unclear; not well known

Obsequious — attentive in an ingratiating or servile manner

Obsolete — outmoded; no longer used

Obstinate — persist stubbornly

Obstreperous — boisterously and noisily aggressive or defiant

Obtuse — slow to learn or understand; lacking intellect

Obviate — prevent the occurrence of; prevent from happening

Occlude — block passage through

Odious — sincerely hated and despised

Olfactory — concerning the sense of smell

Ominous — threatening; of an evil omen

Omnipotent	having unlimited power
Omnipresent	universally present; ubiquitous
Onerous	burdensome, tiring, heavy load that makes one weary
Onus	an onerous or difficult concern
Opprobrium	a state of extreme dishonour and disgrace
Opulence	wealth as exhibited by sumptuous living
Ordain	order by virtue of superior authority; decree
Ordeal	severe trial or affliction; difficult experience
Orthodox	traditional; (of someone) conservative in belief; adhering to an established doctrine
Ossified	set in a rigidly conventional pattern of behaviour, habits, or beliefs
Ostentatious	intended to attract notice and impress others
Ostracize	avoid speaking to or dealing with; expel
Overbearing	having or showing arrogant superiority to and disdain of those one views as unworthy
Overt	open and observable; not secret or hidden

P

Pacify	soothe; make calm or quiet; subdue
Paean	a formal expression of praise
Painstaking	taking pains; showing hard work; taking great care
Palatable	agreeable; pleasing to the taste
Palate	roof of the mouth

Palette	board on which painter mixes pigments
Palindrome	a word or phrase that reads the same backward as forward
Pallid	pale; wan
Palpable	easily perceptible; obvious
Paltry	meagre
Pan	criticize harshly
Panacea	hypothetical remedy for all ills or diseases
Panache	flair; flamboyance
Pandemic	widespread; affecting the majority of people;
Pandemonium	wild noisy disorder
Panegyric	a formal expression of praise
Paradox	a statement that contradicts itself
Paragon	a perfect embodiment of a concept
Paramount	foremost in importance; supreme
Paraphernalia	equipment; odds and ends used in a particular activity
Paraphrase	restatement of text in one's own words
Parched	extremely dry; very thirsty
Pare	cut away the outer covering or skin of (with a knife); trim
Parochial	narrowly restricted in outlook or scope
Parry	dodge; circumvent
Parsimonious	excessively unwilling to spend
Partisan	one-sided; prejudiced
Passive	inactive
Patent	obvious; easily seen; open for the public to read

Pathogenic	able to cause disease
Pathos	tender sorrow; pity
Patronize	be a regular customer or client of
Paucity	scarcity; dearth
Pauper	very poor person
Peccadillo	slight offense or fault
Pecuniary	pertaining to money
Pedagogue	someone who educates young people
Pedant	a person who pays more attention to formal rules and book learning than they merit
Pedestrian	lacking wit or imagination
Pejorative	having a disparaging, derogatory, or belittling effect or force
Pellucid	transparently clear; easily understandable
Penitent	feeling or expressing remorse for misdeeds
Penurious	excessively unwilling to spend
Peremptory	not allowing contradiction or refusal
Perennial	recurring again and again
Perfidy	an act of deliberate betrayal
Perfunctory	hasty and without attention to detail; as a formality only
Pernicious	working or spreading in a hidden and usually injurious way
Peroration	the concluding section of an oration
Perspicacious	having keen mental perception and understanding; acutely insightful and wise
Peruse	examine or consider with attention and in detail
Pervasive	spreading or spread throughout

Philanthropy	donations to charity
Phlegmatic	showing little emotion
Pillage	the act of stealing valuable things from a place
Pillory	to expose to public derision, ridicule, or abuse
Pine	have a desire for something or someone
Pique	to arouse an emotion or provoke to action
Pith	the choicest or most essential or most vital part of some idea or experience
Pithy	concise and full of meaning
Pittance	an inadequate payment
Placate	to appease or pacify, especially by concessions or conciliatory gestures
Plagiarize	take without referencing from someone else's writing or speech
Plebiscite	a vote by the electorate determining public opinion on a question of national importance
Plethora	extreme or excess
Pluck	courage or resolution in the face of difficulties
Plumb	examine thoroughly and in great depth; exactly
Plummet	drop sharply
Polemic	a controversial argument, as one against some opinion, doctrine, etc.
Potion	a medicinal or magical or poisonous beverage
Pragmatic	concerned with practical matters
Prattle	idle or foolish and irrelevant talk
Precursor	something that precedes and indicates the approach of something or someone
Predilection	a predisposition in favour of something

Preen	to be exultant or proud
Preponderant	having superior power and influence
Prescience	the power to foresee the future
Presumptuous	unwarrantedly or impertinently bold
Prevaricate	be deliberately ambiguous or unclear in order to mislead or withhold information
Pristine	immaculately clean and unused
Privation	a state of extreme poverty
Probity	having strong moral principles
Proclivity	a natural inclination
Prodigal	wastefully or recklessly extravagant
Prodigious	so great in size or force or extent as to elicit awe
Profligate	shameless; dissolute; extravagant
Profound	showing intellectual penetration or emotional depth; pervasive or intense; thorough; complete
Profuse	produced or growing in extreme abundance
Proletariat	a social class comprising those who do manual labour or work for wages
Proliferate	cause to grow or increase rapidly
Prolific	productive
Prolix	tediously prolonged or tending to speak or write at great length
Promulgate	put a law into effect by formal declaration
Propound	put forward, as of an idea
Propriety	correct or appropriate behaviour
Prosaic	lacking wit or imagination
Proscribe	command against; prohibit

Proselytize	convert to another faith or religion
Prudence	discretion in practical affairs
Puerile	displaying or suggesting a lack of maturity
Pugilist	someone who fights with his fists for sport
Punctilious	marked by precise accordance with details
Pungent	strong and sharp
Pusillanimous	lacking in courage and manly strength
Putrefy	become putrid; decay with an offensive smell

Q

Quack	medically unqualified
Quaff	to swallow hurriedly or greedily
Quagmire	a soft wet area of low-lying land that sinks underfoot
Qualms	a sudden feeling of apprehensive uneasiness
Quandary	state of uncertainty or perplexity, especially as requiring a choice between equally unfavourable options
Quarantine	isolation to prevent the spread of infectious disease
Quarry	animal hunted or caught for food
Quash	put down by force or intimidation
Queasy	causing or fraught with or showing anxiety
Quench	suppress or crush completely
Querulous	habitually complaining

Quibble	argue over petty things
Quiddity	the quality that makes a thing what it is
Quiescent	being at rest; quiet; still; inactive or motionless
Quirk	a strange attitude or habit
Quisling	a person who betrays his or her own country by aiding an invading enemy
Quiver	a shaky motion
Quixotic	not sensible about practical matters; idealistic and unrealistic
Quorum	a gathering of the minimal number of members of an organization to conduct business
Quotidian	found in the ordinary course of events; usual or customary

R

Rabble	mob; noisy crowd
Rabid	marked by excessive enthusiasm for and intense devotion to a cause or idea
Racketeer	carry on illegal business activities involving crime
Raconteur	a person skilled in telling anecdotes
Raffish	marked by a carefree unconventionality or disreputableness
Raffle	lottery
Rail	criticize severely
Rake	immoral or dissolute person
Rally	come or bring together; call up or summon
Ramification	one of the results following from an action or decision

Rampant	growing or spreading uncontrollably; growing in profusion
Ramshackle	in deplorable condition
Rancid	smelling of fermentation or staleness
Rancorous	showing deep-seated resentment
Rank	offensive in odour or flavour
Rankle	irritate; fester; annoy
Ransack	search thoroughly; pillage
Rant	speak violently or excitedly; rave
Rapacious	devouring or craving food in great quantities
Rapport	close relationship; emotional closeness; harmony
Rapt	engrossed; absorbed; enchanted
Rapture	great joy and delight; ecstasy
Rarefy	make more subtle or refined; become thin
Rave	an extravagantly enthusiastic review
Recalcitrant	marked by stubborn resistance to authority
Recant	to reject or disavow a formerly held belief or opinion
Recondite	difficult to penetrate; incomprehensible to one of ordinary understanding or knowledge
Recuperate	get over an illness or shock
Redoubtable	worthy of respect or honour
Referendum	a legislative act is referred for final approval to a popular vote by the electorate
Relegate	assign to a lower position; reduce in rank
Remiss	failing in what duty requires
Remonstrate	censure severely or angrily

Renascence	a second or new birth
Rendezvous	a meeting planned at a certain time and place
Renege	fail to fulfil a promise or obligation
Repertoire	the entire range of skills or aptitudes or devices used in a particular field or occupation
Reprehensible	bringing or deserving severe rebuke or censure
Reprisal	a retaliatory action against an enemy in wartime
Repudiate	eject as untrue, unfounded, or unjust
Requiem	a song or hymn of mourning composed or performed as a memorial to a dead person
Rescind	cancel officially
Resilience	an occurrence of rebounding or springing back
Restive	being in a tense state
Reticence	hesitation; shyness
Reverent	feeling or showing profound respect or veneration
Rhetoric	study of the technique and rules for using language effectively
Ribald	someone who uses vulgar and offensive language
Risqué	suggestive of sexual impropriety
Robust	sturdy and strong in form, constitution, or construction
Rupture	burst

S

Sacerdotal	associated with the priesthood or priests
Sacrilege	blasphemous behaviour

Sacrosanct	must be kept sacred
Sagacious	acutely insightful and wise
Salubrious	promoting health; healthful
Salutary	synonym of salubrious
Salvage	rescue (goods or property) from loss
Sanctimonious	excessively or hypocritically pious
Sanction	the act of final authorization; restrictions or limitations
Sanguinary	marked by eagerness to resort to violence and bloodshed
Sanguine	a blood-red colour; confidently optimistic and cheerful
Sap	deplete
Sapid	full of flavour
Sardonic	disdainfully or ironically humorous; scornful and mocking
Satiate	fill to satisfaction
Satire	witty language used to convey insults or scorn
Saturnine	sluggish in temperament; gloomy; taciturn
Saunter	a leisurely walk
Savour	enjoy; have a distinctive flavour, smell, or quality
Scale	climb up; ascend;
Scanty	meagre
Scapegoat	someone who is punished for the errors of others
Schism	division of a group into opposing factions
Scintillate	sparkle; flash; be animated; be full of life
Scion	a descendent or heir
Scoff	laugh (at); mock; ridicule

Scorch	a discoloration caused by heat; sear
Scowl	frown angrily
Scrupulous	arising from a sense of right and wrong; principled
Scrutinize	examine closely and critically
Scurrilous	grossly or obscenely abusive
Seasoned	experienced
Secede	withdraw from an organization or communion
Seclusion	isolation; solitude
Sedate	cause to be calm or quiet as by administering a sedative to
Sedentary	requiring sitting or little activity
Sedition	incitement of discontent or rebellion against a government.
Sedulous	marked by care and persistent effort
Seedy	run-down; decrepit; disreputable
Seminal	very important; containing seeds of later development
Senescent	growing old
Sententious	given to excessive moralizing
Sepulcher	a chamber that is used as a grave
Serendipity	good luck in making unexpected and fortunate discoveries
Servitude	state of subjection to an owner or master or forced labour imposed as punishment
Sever	cut off from a whole
Shard	a broken piece of a brittle artefact
Silhouette	a drawing of the outline of an object
Simper	to smile in a silly, self-conscious way

Simulate	create a representation or model of
Sinewy	consisting of tendons or resembling a tendon; possessing physical strength and weight; rugged and powerful
Sinister	threatening or foreshadowing evil or tragic developments
Skirmish	a minor short-term fight
Sloth	a disinclination to work or exert yourself
Solicitous	anxious or concerned; eager
Somatic	affecting or characteristic of the body as opposed to the mind or spirit
Sophistry	a subtle, tricky, superficially plausible, but generally fallacious method of reasoning; a false argument
Sophomore	a second-year undergraduate
Soporific	sleep inducing
Sordid	meanly selfish; dirty; filthy
Specious	plausible but false
Spendthrift	someone who spends money prodigally
Sporadic	recurring in scattered and irregular or unpredictable intervals
Spurious	intended to deceive; fake
Squander	spend extravagantly; waste
Static	showing little if any change; angry criticism
Steep	let sit in a liquid to extract a flavour or to cleanse
Stentorian	very loud or powerful in sound
Stickler	someone who insists on something
Stoic	someone who is seemingly indifferent to emotions
Stolid	having or revealing little emotion or sensibility; not easily aroused or excited

Strut	a proud stiff pompous gait
Stultify	deprive of strength or efficiency; make useless or worthless
Stupefy	make senseless or dizzy by or as if by a blow
Stymie	hinder or prevent the progress
Sublime	lofty or grand
Succinct	expressed in few words; concise
Succulent	full of juice
Suffuse	cause to spread or flush or flood through
Sully	to soil, stain, or tarnish
Supercilious	expressive of contempt
Superfluous	more than is needed, desired, or required
Supplant	take the place or move into the position of
Supplicate	ask humbly (for something)
Surreptitious	conducted with or marked by hidden aims or methods
Swelter	suffer from intense heat
Sycophant	a person who tries to please someone in order to gain a personal advantage

T

Tacit	implied by or inferred from actions or statements
Taciturn	habitually reserved and uncommunicative

Tawdry	cheap and shoddy
Tedium	dullness owing to length or slowness
Teetotaller	one who abstains from drinking
Temerity	fearless daring
Tempestuous	characterized by violent emotions or behaviour
Tenacity	persistent determination
Tendentious	having or showing a definite tendency, bias, or purpose
Tenet	a religious doctrine that is proclaimed as true without proof
Tenuous	lacking substance or significance; thin or slender in form
Tepid	moderately warm; feeling or showing little interest or enthusiasm
Terse	brief and to the point
Tether	tie with a tether
Thrall	the state of being under the control of another person
Throes	violent pangs of suffering
Thwart	hinder or prevent
Timorous	timid by nature or revealing timidity
Tirade	a speech of violent denunciation
Titan	a person of exceptional importance and reputation
Toady	a person who tries to please someone in order to gain a personal advantage
Topography	precise detailed study of the surface features of a region
Torpid	slow and apathetic
Torpor	inactivity resulting from lethargy and lack of vigour or energy
Torque	a twisting force

Tortuous	not straightforward
Tousled	in disarray; extremely disorderly
Tractable	easily managed or controlled
Traduce	speak unfavourably about
Transgression	the action of going beyond or overstepping some boundary or limit
Transient	one who stays for only a short time
Translucent	allowing light to pass through diffusely
Transmute	change in outward structure or looks
Travesty	any grotesque or debased likeness or imitation
Trenchant	incisive or keen; vigorous; clear-cut
Truculent	defiantly aggressive
Truism	an obvious truth
Truncate	make shorter as if by cutting off
Tryst	a secret rendezvous; a date
Tumefy	expand abnormally
Turbid	cloudy; murky
Turpitude	a corrupt or depraved or degenerate act or practice
Tutelage	teaching pupils individually
Tyro	someone new to a field or activity

U

Ubiquitous	being present everywhere at once

Ulterior	being beyond what is seen or avowed; intentionally kept concealed
Umbrage	a feeling of anger caused by being offended
Unabashed	not embarrassed
Unconscionable	lacking a conscience
Unctuous	characterized by excessive piousness or moralistic fervour
Undermine	to attack by indirect, secret, or underhand means
Underscore	give extra weight to
Undulate	move in a wavy pattern or with a rising and falling motion
Unfathomable	impossible to understand
Unfeigned	not pretended; sincerely felt or expressed
Unflagging	unceasing
Unfledged	young and inexperienced
Unfrock	to deprive (a monk, priest, minister, etc.) of ecclesiastical rank, authority, and function
Ungainly	lacking grace in movement or posture
Unimpeachable	free of guilt; not subject to blame
Unkempt	not properly maintained or cared for
Unprecedented	having no precedent
Unremitting	not slackening or abating; incessant
Unsavoury	morally offensive
Unseemly	not in keeping with accepted standards of what is right or proper in polite society
Unstinting	very generous
Unsullied	free from blemishes
Untenable	incapable of being defended or justified

Untoward	contrary to your interests or welfare
Unwieldy	difficult to use or handle or manage because of size or weight or shape
Unwitting	not aware or knowing
Upbraid	express criticism towards
Upshot	the final issue, the conclusion, or the result
Urbane	sophisticated; polished; refined in manner
Usurp	seize and take control without authority and possibly with force
Usury	the act of lending money at an exorbitant rate of interest
Utilitarian	having a useful function
Utopia	an imaginary place considered to be perfect or ideal

V

Vacillate	be undecided about something
Vacuous	devoid of matter
Vagary	an unpredictable or erratic action, occurrence, course, or instance
Vainglorious	feeling self-important
Valediction	the act of saying farewell
Vanguard	the leading position in any movement or field
Vantage	the quality of having a superior or more favourable position
Vapid	lacking significance or liveliness or spirit or taste
Variegated	having a variety of colours

Venal	capable of being corrupted
Vendetta	any prolonged and bitter feud, rivalry, contention
Venerate	regard with feelings of respect and reverence
Veracity	conformity to truth or fact; accuracy
Verbatim	using exactly the same words
Verbose	using or containing too many words
Verisimilitude	the appearance of truth; the quality of seeming to be true
Vertiginous	having or causing a whirling sensation; liable to falling
Vestige	an indication that something has been present
Vex	to irritate; annoy; provoke
Viable	capable of being done
Vicarious	suffered or done by one person as a substitute for another
Vicissitude	a change or variation occurring in the course of something
Vie	compete for something
Vigilant	carefully observant or attentive
Vignette	a brief literary description
Vilify	spread negative information about
Virtuoso	having or revealing supreme mastery or skill
Virulent	infectious; having the ability to cause disease
Viscuous	thick
Vitreous	relating to or resembling or derived from or containing glass
Vitriol	abusive or venomous language
Vituperative	marked by harshly abusive criticism
Vociferous	conspicuously and offensively loud

Volition	the act of making a choice
Voluble	marked by a ready flow of speech
Voluminous	large in number or quantity
Voracious	devouring or craving food in great quantities
Vulnerable	capable of being wounded or hurt

W

Waft	be driven or carried along, as by the air
Wag	move from side to side
Waive	forego; dispense with
Wallow	an indolent or clumsy rolling about; delight greatly in
Wanderlust	very strong or irresistible impulse to travel
Wane	a gradual decline (in size, strength, power, or number)
Wastrel	someone who dissipates resources self-indulgently
Waver	the act of moving back and forth
Welter	be immersed in; a confused multitude of things
Wheedle	influence or urge by gentle urging, caressing, or flattering
Whet	make keen or more acute; stimulate
Whimsical	determined by chance or impulse or whim rather than by necessity or reason
Whittle	cut small bits or pare shavings from
Wilful	done by design; intentional

Wily	marked by skill in deception
Winnow	blow away or off with a current of air
Winsome	charming in a childlike or naive way
Wizened	lean and wrinkled by shrinkage as from age or illness
Wont	an established custom
Wraith	a visible spirit
Wreck	a serious accident; smash or break forcefully
Writ	a legal document issued by a court or judicial officer
Wry	humorously sarcastic or mocking

X

Xenophobia	a fear of foreigners or strangers
Xenophylic	an attraction to foreign peoples, cultures, or customs
Xylophone	a musical instrument
Xerothermic	characterised by heat and dryness

Y

Yearn	have a desire for something
Yoke	a connection usually between cows on a farm
Yore	time long past
Yeoman	farmer who owns and works his land
Yield	bear, produce or provide
Yokel	simple-minded country person; bumpkin

Z

Zany	ludicrous, foolish
Zealot	a fervent and even militant proponent of something
Zenith	highest point; apex
Zephyr	a slight wind
Zest	great enjoyment or excitement; gusto
Zoology	study of animals

List of Deceptive Words

Deceptive words include two categories of words – ones which have more than one meaning, such as *tender* and *steep* and ones which sound like a particular word but mean something totally different, such as *noisome* and *officious.* We'll cover the more frequently tested/confused of these in the list in this chapter. We'll also be covering words which are frequently confused with each other such as *complacent* and *complaisant.*

1. **Appropriate** – The commonly known meaning is suitable for a particular purpose. However, it also means to take without permission or consent or to steal as in *the CEO appropriated a part of the company's reserves for himself.*

2. **Arresting** – Apart from the literal act of the police arresting someone, this also means to capture one's attention or imagination or to be captivated.

3. **Artless** – Sounds like a negative word meaning somebody who lacks art but is actually a positive word which means simple or free from deceit and cunning.

4. **August** – Apart from the month, this word is often construed to mean auspicious. However it actually means grand or majestic as in *an August performance of a classic play.*

5. **Colour** – Biased, skewed, partial

6. **Disabuse** – Sounds like a negative word because of 'abuse' but is actually a positive word meaning to free a person from deception or error.

7. **Dispatch** – Apart from the act of sending or shipping something, this also means to hasten or to be quick.

8. **Disquiet** – This has no connection with quiet or loudness; it actually means anxious.

9. **Essay** – Apart from a literary writing, this is also a verb that means to attempt or to perform as in *an actor essaying the role of King George.*

10. **Exact** – Can also mean demanding or requiring strict adherence to rules as in *an exacting task.*

11. **Exhaustive** – Most students know of one meaning which is tiring as in *an exhaustive task.* However exhaustive also means all encompassing or comprehensive as in *an exhaustive list of resources.*

12. **Flag** – This also means a fall in energy levels or enthusiasm as in *the public's interest in the movie is flagging.*

13. **Flip** – Disrespectful or sarcastic with casual disregard for authority.

14. **Fractious** – No connection with fraction, this actually means unruly or disobedient as in *a fractious crowd.*

15. **Frustrate** – to defeat, nullify, thwart

16. **Green** – Amateur or immature; beginner

17. **Husband** – This is also used as a verb meaning to use frugally or to conserve.

18. **Intimate** – While most people think of it as very close as in *intimate relations between two people,* this also means to inform as in *intimate someone of your arrival time.*

19. **Libertine -** Comes from liberty but usually has a negative connotation meaning unrestrained or immoral.

20. **Milk** – To exploit thoroughly

21. **Noisome** – Has no connection with noise, in fact means offensive or disgusting, usually odour.

22. **Obtuse** – lacking intellect; insensitive

23. **Officious** – Has no connection with official; means dominating, aggressive, or interfering.

24. **Pan** – To criticize severely as in *the movie was panned by the critics.*

25. **Pedestrian** – Common, prosaic, or ordinary

26. **Pluck** – Courage or bravery

27. **Ponderous** – Has no connection with ponder; means boring, dull, or tedious.

28. **Prompt** – The commonly known meaning is timely or punctual. However it also means to encourage as in *the teacher prompting the student for an answer* or to assist.

29. **Proscribe** – Often confused with prescribe, this is in fact the opposite and means to banish, denounce, or exile.

30. **Qualify** – Apart from the common usage, this also means to limit or restrict as in *to qualify an offer for a job.*

31. **Rail** – This is also used as a verb meaning to criticize, condemn, or mock

32. **Rank** – Emanating a foul smell as in *the hut ranks of cow dung*

33. **Redoubtable** – Does not mean doubtful; rather it is a positive word meaning majestic or impressive as in *a redoubtable work of art.*

34. **Restive** – This is the opposite of rest i.e. anxious or restless

35. **Sap** – To remove energy, vitality, or strength

36. **Sere** – Often confused with seer, which means a sage, sere actually means dry or withered as in *sere land.*

37. **Signal** – This also means significant or outstanding as in *a signal achievement.*

38. **Skirt** – The verb form of this word means to avoid or to go around as in *the senator skirted the issue of corruption*

39. **Slight** – This also means to ignore or to look down upon

40. **Sophistry** – Has no connection with sophisticated; it is in fact a negative word meaning a false or a deceptive argument.

41. **Specious** – Often confused with 'spacious', specious means pleasing to the eye but deceptive

42. **Steep** – Apart from an incline, this also means to soak in a liquid

43. **Stock** – of the common or ordinary type as in *stock engine of a car* as against a modified one.

44. **Wag** – Apart from the wagging of a dog's tail, this also means amusing or humorous.

Words which are frequently confused with one another:

1. **Complaisant** - Obliging; agreeable or gracious; compliant:

   Complacent – Self satisfied, unbothered

2. **Apathy** - Indifference

   Antipathy - Dislike

3. **Adapt** – Adjust according to the environment

   Adept – Skilled or proficient

4. **Allude** – To refer indirectly

   Elude – To escape detection or capture

5. **Appraise** – To determine the worth or monetary value of something

   Apprise – To make aware or inform

6. **Ascent** – Upward movement

   Assent – Agreement; approval

   Accent – The manner of speaking

7. **Commensurate** – Corresponding to or in proportion to

   Commiserate – To express sympathy or pity

8. **Decry** – To denounce or criticize

   Descry – To perceive or detect

9. **Meddlesome** – Interfering in other people's matters

   Mettlesome – Courageous

10. **Odious** – Offensive; hateful; detestable

    Odorous – Emanating a foul odour

11. **Temerity** – Audacity; boldness

    Timorous – Fearful; shy; timid

12. **Crave** – To long for; to pine or yearn for

    Craven – Cowardly; pusillanimous

13. **Horde** – A large group

    Hoard – To accumulate or stock

14. **Complement** – Something that accompanies or makes perfect

    Compliment – Expression of praise or approval

15. **Principal** – Chief; first in rank; foremost

    Principle - Values

16. **Repel** – To drive back or to resist

    Repeal – To revoke or withdraw

Concluding Notes:

Through this book we have endeavoured to provide you with all the Verbal concepts and questions tested on the GRE in one place. This book has been written in a lucid, easy to understand style; in fact we have made a conscious effort to avoid diagrams and jargon as much as possible and focus on understanding the meaning of sentences and passages instead.

While we have tried to ensure that the book is completely free of errors, in case you do spot one please post it on the GRE Verbal Grail thread on the Forums section of our website. Also in case there are some concepts/questions that you could not understand from the book or that you would like to discuss with us, please post the same on our forums and we'll respond to you within 48 hours.

We also welcome any other feedback that you may have on how we can make the next edition of this book even better; do mail us the same on feedback@aristotleprep.com

We wish you all the best for your preparation.

The GRE Verbal Grail Editorial Team

Made in the USA
San Bernardino, CA
26 March 2015